GEOGRAPHY IN EDUCATION

GEOGRAPHY
IN
EDUCATION

Norman J. Graves

Reader in Education,
University of London Institute
of Education

HEINEMANN EDUCATIONAL BOOKS

Heinemann Educational Books Ltd

LONDON EDINBURGH MELBOURNE AUCKLAND TORONTO
KINGSTON HONG KONG SINGAPORE KUALA LUMPUR
IBADAN NAIROBI JOHANNESBURG
LUSAKA NEW DELHI

ISBN 0 435 35310 1 (Cased)
ISBN 0 435 35311 X (Paper)

Published by
Heinemann Educational Books Ltd
48 Charles Street, London W1X 8AH

Set in Linotype Times
Printed in Great Britain by
Richard Clay (The Chaucer Press) Ltd, Bungay, Suffolk

Contents

Introduction

This book came to be written as a result of the courses developed at the University of London Institute of Education for the P.G.C.E., B.Ed., Diploma in Education and M.A. within the field of geographical education. Although geographical education in Europe and North America has roots which go back deep into the past century, it is only since the late 1960s that an attempt has been made to develop an integrated approach in which the various disciplines which throw light on the problems of education have been extensively used to illuminate practice in the teaching and learning of geography. This book is an attempt to practise a multi-disciplinary approach and is in line with my contention that any 'real life' problem requires such an approach. In many such situations, it is possible for teams of specialists to get together and make a joint attack on the problem. In teaching, the nearest approach to this is the team teaching technique. But the teacher is still much of the time left on his own with the job of getting his students to learn something worthwhile, in a manner which will be effective and efficient. In this task the geography teacher needs to be aware that within his own subject there are philosophical problems of deciding what is worth teaching and there are psychological considerations of various kinds when he has to decide what to teach and how to teach it. There are also problems of a sociological origin in getting children to learn, though these are not specific to geography and have not been considered to any great extent in this book.

In writing this book, I have benefited considerably from the discussions I have had with my colleagues at the University of London Institute of Education and at the Schools Council. I have also had much stimulation from the students in the M.A. seminar and from individual research students. I should like particularly to mention Don Biddle who deepened my appreciation of curriculum theory and opened my eyes to the ferment of ideas on geographical education currently developing in Australia, and Michael Naish and Frances Slater who read the manuscript and made valuable suggestions. As chairman of the International Geographical Union's Commission on Geography in Education (1972-76) renamed Geographical Education (1976-86), I have been favoured with many international contacts which have not only made me aware of information not easily available in the United Kingdom, but also of the differing value positions held in different parts of the world. In spite of my gratitude to friends and colleagues for the help they have given, the views and imperfections of this work are essentially my own.

Lastly I should like to thank Mrs Nola Owers who, in spite of a busy life as secretary to two departments, wife and mother, has managed to type a manuscript that was not always a model of clarity.

December 1974

CHAPTER ONE

The Field of Geography in Education

The almost exponential growth of the 'education industry' since the beginning of the twentieth century poses numerous questions, not only for those engaged in the process of educating new generations, but also for those concerned with the allocation of resources. An education system is inevitably part of the social and economic environment in which societies evolve. The process of formal education itself helps to create the intellectual environment with which young (and some not so young) minds interact and thus, to some extent, influences the quality of the mental life of societies. But people's ideas, perceptions and attitudes are not limited in effect to the inner intellectual life, to the interplay of argument. In the present context and particularly in industrial societies, ideas lead to action and action involves altering the environment in some way or other. History provides plenty of examples of the paramount influence of ideas on the quality of the environment. It is possible that the medieval disputation as to the sex of angels had little practical effect in society at large, though the creators of ecclesiastical paintings were involved. But that an entrepreneur was justified in seeking maximum short-term profits from a venture, be it in farming or in industry, or that social as opposed to private costs were not recognized until recently are both ideas which have proved potent in altering the environment, be this in the semi-arid areas of the U.S.A. or in the old industrial towns of the United Kingdom.

The interconnection between education and environment is a complex one. It is not the purpose of this book to unravel all the various strands (a daunting task) but to examine one aspect of education which has always maintained close ties with the environment, namely geographical education. The aim of this chapter is to introduce the problems which will be examined in depth in subsequent chapters. Geography as a subject has been concerned with the environment within which human beings live, ever since the Greeks named it as 'a description of the earth'. What this rather loose definition was able to encompass has varied considerably throughout historical times. It will be part of our task to examine briefly the way in which ideas about what is the proper field of geography have evolved. It will be possible to argue that the division between regional and thematic (or systematic) geography has ancient roots; that a philosopher such as Immanuel Kant saw geography as one of the fundamental divisions of knowledge whilst a more recent worker in epistemology avers that geography is in no way a part of the basic foundation of knowledge, but rather a superstructure built upon other more fundamental bricks. It will be shown that those writing geography have erred between taking the Greek definition literally (describing an area in great detail though perhaps to no great purpose), and writing what Varenius called 'general geography', that is attempting to find general 'laws' which would describe and explain the relationships between man and his physical environment or even between man and his total environment. The polarization of such divergent views of geography has been manifest in the decades following 1950 and forms part of the continuing debate within geography, though fortunately others have joined in the debate: mainly physical scientists, social scientists and philosophers. We owe a considerable debt to these, since they have widened the discourse from what might have remained a sterile internal dialogue of no great consequence to the progress of knowledge.

The discussions on the nature as well as the content of geography manifest in the writings of professional or practising geographers are one strand in the web of geographical education. Quite another is a study of what has been taught as geography in the primary and secondary schools of Western Europe and North America. While it is to be expected that there should be some relation between what professional geographers are thinking and what goes on in schools, the closeness of this relationship is not always evident. This may be due to poor communication or it may be that teachers in school see geography as having a role to play which is fundamentally different from the role which it may have in universities or in research or in planning. Teachers may view geography as a means to an end rather than an end in itself. But in order to come to some conclusion on this issue, it will be necessary to examine the evidence which we have on the evolution of school geography, to see whether, for example, school and university geography are now coming closer together or drifting further apart.

Such evidence, however, needs to be reviewed in the light of certain criteria. What is the basis on which teachers may set themselves certain objectives in educating through geography? If teaching the ideas or principles of geography is not the end of geographical education, what then are the alternative aims of such an education? What aspects of geography contribute to these ultimate aims and which do not? In other words one is asking the question: 'What is worthwhile teaching in geography and how do we know this?' This is a long way from the formulation of such simple objectives as 'the recognition of a plateau from a contour map' or being able to handle meaningfully the concept of 'the field of influence of a town'. In examining objectives of various kinds, some light will be focused on the distinction between long-term and short-term objectives as well as on whether such objectives are extrinsic or intrinsic to the educational process. A further question which also needs discussion concerns the curricular arrangements within which these objectives are set. Is it necessary for the achievement of such objectives that geography should be taught as a separate subject? Could these objectives be better achieved by not arranging a curriculum or part of a curriculum along traditional subject lines? If so, what should these curriculum arrangements be? Is it possible to put forward rational arguments for incorporating geographical objectives within some integrated studies curriculum? Or, to go one stage back in the reasoning, is it possible to set forth any objectives of general validity, given the wide variations in individual perceptions and motivations?

Assuming for the present that such questions could be resolved, one is still left with the problems relating to the learning of geography. What do we really know about the way children or adults learn the ideas, skills and attitudes which may be taught in geography courses? The honest answer to this must be: 'very little'. For example, there is the ever present 'chicken and egg' puzzle of the relationship between perceptualization and conceptualization. What children can make of a landscape depends on their perception of that landscape, what they actually see in the fields, on the hills, in the valleys, and so on. Their very involvement in the landscape enables them to acquire accurate concepts of such features as scarps, valleys, plateaux, nucleated settlement, etc. But similarly, it may be argued that what they perceive is dependent on those concepts which they already possess; perceptualization is not an automatic process of registering a series of mental images like a camera, rather is it a selective process whereby the existing mental 'equipment' enables the learner to structure what his eyes are scanning. The extent of perceptualization is limited by the conceptual framework at the learner's disposal. To return to our example, a young boy or girl standing on a ridge with a view of an escarpment in the distance, will only perceive it as a hill or a ridge unless he already has an accurate mental image of a class of physical features called 'escarpment'. There is, therefore, a continual interplay between learner's perceptions and their concepts. These problems are compounded by various factors relating to one or other of these two aspects. Much learning activity occurs in the classroom where the observation which goes on is at second hand, that is, it is maps, pictures, diagrams, and print which are being observed and not the landscape. Such documents bring their own spate of difficulties. One need only look at the tangle of visual messages contained on a topographical map to be aware that young learners may find it difficult to make sense of the overlapping symbols there portrayed. Here the things being perceived seem to confuse rather than clarify. Until he has grasped the language of the map, the learner is unable to make sense of his perceptions. The same is true of other languages, for example, many adult learners find contemporary research papers in geography difficult to understand because they have not grasped the mathematical language which many such papers use.

Similarly concept formation is an intricate process partly dependent on the nature, length and quality of a learner's experience. The longer one's experience in the world, the more appropriate its nature, the greater is the likelihood of one understanding such concepts as 'central business district' or 'motorway network'. But no amount of experience will enable a learner to grasp the concept of 'location quotient' excepting that experience which consists of teaching him to handle that concept in such a way that its definition becomes clear.

Some learning of geographical concepts can take place almost incidentally during the course of experience. But other concepts one can only learn through being placed in a situation in which there is a conscious intention to learn. In both cases the quality of the experience is important in determining the extent of the learning.

A pupil whose experience never transcends the inner city area in which he was born is likely to find it difficult to make sense of a rural environment overseas. A pupil, however, who has travelled with his parents to different areas of his country or of the European continent, will find it much easier to acquire concepts which relate to different environments. Superimposed on this experience of different environments, comes the linguistic experience of the learner. In other words, if the learner is encouraged to talk about his experiences, to reveal in words what he perceives, to discuss some of his misconceptions, to explore verbally the implications of certain concepts, then he is likely to make rapid progress in acquiring not only a vocabulary, but also a body of concepts represented by this vocabulary, useful in codifying further experiences and therefore in acquiring further concepts.

But what after all is a geographical concept? We have assumed that these concepts are self-evident, but are they? Is there one class of concepts or, as has been hinted at already, are there several? Are these classes of concept of the same order of difficulty when it comes to learning them, or do they form a well-defined hierarchy in which progress in geography can only be achieved by a process of acquiring low-order classes of concepts and gradually working up to high-order concepts? Is it possible so to structure the learner's experience that he acquires concepts in such an order?

Attaining such intellectual tools as concepts is not, however, achieved in a sterilized value-free environment. Learners acquire attitudes as well as skills and concepts. Some attitudes may be irrelevant to the learning process in geographical education, but others may be potent in enhancing or limiting this process. Thus, a learner who acquires an open-minded attitude to enquiry, who comes to believe that no question ever has a definitive final answer, who becomes aware that any argument must respect the evidence available, has acquired attitudes which will serve him well in furthering his intellectual education. A pupil who becomes impatient of doubt, who always wants to resolve an argument without respecting the evidence, who is easily emotively swayed in favour of a particular solution, is one who may find it difficult to make progress intellectually. But how are those attitudes acquired and from where are they acquired? Similarly one may enquire about the nature of pupils' attitudes to foreign peoples and to the environment. How far do they feel a responsibility towards their local environment? Do they feel moved to take action when something threatens the quality of that environment or do they remain apathetic? Are these attitudes acquired in school geography lessons or do such attitudes stem from the ethos of the society in which they live?

Finally, is it possible to evaluate curriculum development and measure progress in the learning of geography? Can we with conviction point to someone and affirm that he has achieved a certain level of geographical understanding? Have we the means whereby we can test children's comprehension of certain geographical ideas and their ability to apply them in novel situations? If we have, how far may such testing encourage geographers to become convergent thinkers and thereby limit the creative spark associated with divergent thinking?

These and many other questions will be discussed in the chapters which follow. It would be as well to accept at the outset that none will be answered in an authoritative final form.

CHAPTER TWO

Geography in the Perspective of Time

From the Greeks to Humboldt and Ritter
Though it is difficult to ascribe a precise beginning to the study of geography, we do know that it was the Greeks who gave the subject its name. Geography (γεωγραθια) or literally 'writing about the earth' was an occupation favoured among the scholars of the ancient world. Given the small extent of the world known to the ancient Egyptians, Babylonians and Greeks, it is not surprising that they should have been curious about what lay beyond, and that they based their knowledge on what could be inferred from a study of the known world. Many fanciful descriptions of what surrounded the inhabited world, or of what supported the sky or of how the stars were suspended were produced by the ancient Egyptians. Homer (c. 850 BC) used some of this folklore about distant lands in his epic poem *Odyssey* and because the ordinary Greek derived his knowledge of the 'œcumene' or habitable world from this source, Homer was dubbed the father of geography. But accurate recording of the 'œcumene' probably began with Herodotus (c. 485-425 BC) who travelled widely in what is now called the Middle East, in order to understand the setting of the historical events which he subsequently wrote about. His books indicate that he had a fairly accurate knowledge of the ancient world from India to the Strait of Gibraltar and from the Sudan to the steppes of the present day Ukraine.

Throughout the classical period, discussion, observation and speculation about the earth as the home of man continued, with various scholars setting down their ideas in books, some of which survived to be scrutinized during the Renaissance. One of the most notable feats of the period was Erathosthenes' (c. 230 BC) calculation, in the Nile Valley, of the circumference of the earth. It proved remarkably accurate. This very calculation was based on the assumed spherical shape of the earth, which scholars like Aristotle had proved to their satisfaction as long ago as the fourth century BC. Hipparchus (c. 160-125 BC), basically interested in astronomy, was able as a by-product of his observations of the sun, moon and stars, to devise a meridional division of the earth into climate zones. He hazarded the prediction that some zones would be too hot and some too cold for man to inhabit.

Much of what we know about the geography and geographers of classical times is derived from the writings of Ptolemy of Alexandria (c. AD 90-168) who accepted Hipparchus' ideas. A copy of his great work *Guide to Geography* was brought from Byzantium (modern Istanbul, formerly Constantinople) to Florence at the very beginning of the fifteenth century. The manuscript was in eight books and contained a map of the world and twenty-four regional maps. The work was translated into Latin in 1409. During the next two hundred years a number of editions were pub-lished in Europe under such headings as 'Geographia' or 'Cosmo-graphia'. It is probable that the work reached Europe altered from its original form by Byzantine scholars as there are some contradic-tions between the text and the maps and between different parts of the text. This was not known at the time and Ptolemy's books were acclaimed as great works of Greek science. There is little doubt that they influenced people's conception of the world and probably encouraged Columbus to believe that he could reach Asia by sailing westwards, since Ptolemy's map shows a great eastward extension of Asia.

Ptolemy's world was a non-rotating sphere at the centre of a universe which included sun, moon, stars and planets themselves orbiting round the earth. He used lines of latitudes and longitudes to cover the sphere by a grid and a conical projection to represent part of the curved surface of the world on his map. He gave the latitudes and longitudes of some 8,000 places, though inaccurately as we now know, partly because there were few accurate astronomical calculations of latitude and longitude and he was forced to rely on travellers' reports, and partly because in translating angular measurements into physical distances, he made an error in the length of the unit he used, an understandable error given the many different units used by pre-vious astronomers and geometers (Luberman 1961).

Strabo (c. 64 BC—AD 21?), wrote in Greek a *Geographica* which although he lived before Ptolemy, did not become known until the early sixteenth century, that is after Ptolemy's work had been available for over a century. Strabo's work, which was in seventeen books, was mainly concerned with describing various parts of the known world, partly from his first-hand experience as a traveller. He claims to have travelled from Armenia in the east to the shores of the Tyrrhenian Sea in the west and from the Black Sea in the north to Ethiopia in the south, though this is not always evident from what he wrote. Some areas through which he passed, such as the Peloponnese, are dealt with in a very summary fashion. The importance of Strabo's work lies in his representing the regional descriptive side of Greek geography whilst Ptolemy's was mainly concerned with the mathematical aspects of the world sphere (Dickinson and Howarth 1933).

Strabo settled in Rome in AD 14 and is probably the last of the Greek geographers of antiquity. The centuries which followed were barren of new developments in geography, though many Latin writers such as Pliny (AD 23-79), travelled widely in the service of Rome and added factual knowledge of various areas to the general store of geographical facts. The break up of the Roman Empire and the spread of Christianity as a religion indirectly led to a stultification in the growth of geographical and other knowledge. First, travel became much more restricted during the so-called 'Dark Ages' so that the exchange of ideas became more difficult. Second, the gradual ossification of the teaching of Jesus of Nazareth into a dogma backed by the resources of the Catholic church made the adventure of ideas less welcome than it had been in the heyday of the Greek city states. Further, though Arab scholars wrote extensively on regions of the known world, for example: Ibn Hawqal, Mas'udi and Idrisi (Sharaf 1964), their works were not translated into Latin (or any other Western vernacular) during the Middle Ages, that is roughly from the fall of Rome in the fifth century AD to the capture of Constantinople by the Turks in 1453. The most important publication of this period was that of the *Travels of Marco Polo*, a Venetian who went overland to China in 1272. This book was not, however, conceived as a 'geography' of Asia, but simply as a record of travels, though not all that the book records was observed personally by Marco Polo (Crone 1964).

The Renaissance, conventionally dated as beginning with the fall of Constantinople in 1453, was also the period of sea travel and geographical discovery. The increase in astronomical observations and the greater accuracy of instruments made charts more reliable, and the increasing boldness of seafarers made it possible to fill in the coastal features on maps and charts. This is the period of the discoveries of Columbus (1492-1498), of Cabot (1497-1498), of Vasco da Gama (1497-1499), of Magellan's circumnavigation of the world (1519-1523). A compilation of what was known about the world at that time was made by Sebastian Münster (1489-1552) in his *Cosmographia Universalis* which was published in 1544. Pride of place in this work goes to Germany where he lived and he describes its various areas in some detail. But he also made inferences about changes in the earth's crust through the effects of flooding by the sea and of the work of rivers, such inferences being made as a result of his knowledge of the Rhine and of Holland (Dickinson 1969).

The early distinction made by some Greeks between regional description or chorography and general statements about the whole of the earth, or general geography (what might now be called systematic geography), continued during this period and was made particularly clear by Bernhard Varenius (1622-1650) in a book originally published in Latin in 1650 called *Geographia Generalis*. Varenius, like Münster, was of German origin, but had settled in Amsterdam after taking a medical degree at the University of Leiden. Such was the catholicity of his interest that he became a geographer and wrote a book on Japan as well as his *Geographia Generalis*. The quality of the *Geographia Generalis* was such that Sir Isaac Newton edited two Latin versions which were printed in 1672 and 1681 so that they might be used by Cambridge University students. Two English translations were subsequently made, one dating from 1693 based on Newton's edition, and one dating from 1736 based on an edition by Jurin, who like Newton was also educated at Trinity College, Cambridge. Further editions in English appeared in 1736 and 1765. Thus for over half a century, Varenius' *Geographia Generalis* became the standard work used by English students. It is clear that Varenius was conscious of the subject boundary problem in geography. In the 1765 edition may be found the following definition:

> Geography is that part of mixed mathematics, which explains the state of the earth, and of its parts, depending on quantity, viz. its figure, place, magnitude and motion, with the celestial appearances, etc. By some it is taken in too limited a sense, for a bare description of several countries; and by others too extensively, who along with such a description would have their political constitution.

He also explained that there was a distinction between general or universal geography and special or particular geography. The first type of geography was concerned with the characteristics of the earth about which generalizations could be made irrespective of political units. The second was concerned with describing particular countries under a twofold heading: chorography which dealt with large areas, and topography which dealt with much smaller tracts of land. Varenius was acutely conscious that descriptive regional geography was more generally taught than general geography. He felt that such geography scarcely merited to be considered a science since it was essentially factual. It was necessary, he argued, for geography to possess a body of laws generally applicable which could be used to explain the phenomena met in regional studies. Thus, in his view, special or regional geography would be a form of applied geography. Although it is possible to see to some extent the manifestation of his ideas in his book on Japan, he died too young to be able to devote much time to writing special geography (Baker 1955). Indeed, given his short life, it is surprising that he is considered to have had such a prominent place among the theoreticians of geography.

Although Varenius clearly had an influence on the thinking of geographers who came after him, it is doubtful whether this influence extended beyond learned circles. Most books of a geographical nature which were published in the eighteenth century seemed to ignore his basic thesis. For example, if the 1785 edition of *Salmon's Geographical and Astronomical Grammar* is examined one finds a varied compendium of information about various countries in which incursions into the history, religion and morals of the inhabitants are linked to assessments of national character which would pain those who today labour to improve international understanding. The following extract makes this point clear. It is about Ireland, and under the sub-heading 'Population, Manners and Amusements' one can read:

The inhabitants of Ireland are supposed to be about 2 millions. On examining their ancient records, they are found, at the most brilliant period, to advance to an imperfect civilization and to exhibit the most striking proofs of the vices and virtues of humanity. The descendants of the old Irish, who inhabit the interior and Western parts of the kingdom, are generally represented as ignorant, and blundering; impatient to injury, and implacable in their resentments: yet quick of apprehension, courteous to strangers, and patient of labour. The greatest part of them are *priest-led* Papists, and live in huts or cabbins, built of clay and straw, with a partition in the middle, which separates the cows, horses, and poultry, from the family.

But it is to be hoped, that the numerous English Protestant working schools, lately established in Ireland, and the repeal of the several obnoxious acts, will contribute to rescue these credulous people from the slavery of priests and the errors of Popery.

The Irish who inhabit Dublin, Waterford, and Cork, are supposed to be descendants of the English, are more liberal in their ideas of religions, and contribute to the improvements of arts, sciences, and commerce. They nearly resemble the English, in their language, dress, manners, and customs.

To be fair, *Salmon's Geographical Grammar* is divided into 'General geography' and 'Particular geography', but there is no evidence that the general principles of 'General geography' illuminate the 'Particular geography'.

Throughout the seventeenth and eighteenth centuries factual knowledge of the world increased considerably; this is manifest in the 1785 (13th) edition of *Salmon's Geographical Grammar* which contains some seventy-eight pages of 'New Discoveries' towards the end of the book. The seventeenth century saw the penetration of the North American continent by French and British settlers and explorers; the Russians were exploring Siberia, and the Dutch the East Indies, New Guinea and part of New Zealand. It was in the eighteenth century that the true extent of Australia and New Zealand became clear after the voyages of Cook. Thus writers in the nineteenth century had a much greater store of knowledge to draw on than had Varenius and their work shows greater sophistication. But before coming to these it is necessary to consider a writer who made his mark principally in philosophy and yet is also considered a geographer: Immanuel Kant (1724-1804).

Kant's claim to be a geographer comes from the fact that from 1756 he gave a series of lectures on physical geography at the University of Königsberg, these being eventually published in 1802. He lectured for more than forty years on geography as well as philosophy, and appeared to have been keenly interested in geography though it must be admitted that he considered that reading works on geography was a relaxation from philosophy. He was an 'armchair geographer' in the sense that he never travelled far from Königsberg, his lecture notes being derived mainly from earlier and contemporary works and travel books, such as Varenius' *Geographia Generalis*, Buffon's *Histoire Naturelle* and Linnaeus' *Systema Naturae*, as well as from papers and journals of various academic and scientific societies. The interest which Kant has generated among geographers derives not so much from the geography he wrote but from what he wrote about the nature of geographical knowledge. This is understandable given that Kant's main preoccupation was philosophy rather than geography. The source of Kant's views on the nature of geographical knowledge may be found in his introduction to his published *Physische Geographie* lectures (May 1970). It should be understood that Kant's concept of physical geography was wide and certainly not limited to what we now call geomorphology and climatology.

Perhaps the best way of understanding Kant's view of geography is to be aware of the philosophical issues over which he pondered. Like many philosophers he was interested in the basis of, or grounds for, knowledge, and in the way knowledge could be classified. This epistemological curiosity was particularly relevant at the time because of the apparent difficulty of admitting that knowledge could be acquired from two sources: from experience (empirical knowledge), and from reasoning. The success of Newton and others in being able to predict the behaviour of material things by the application of mathematical laws, seemed to suggest to some that knowledge could be discovered essentially by a process of reasoning. Descartes in France and Leibnitz in Germany were partisans of knowledge through reasoning, and tended to play down the role of experience. To some extent Kant, in his *Critique of Pure Reason*, was attempting to reconcile these two methods of acquiring knowledge. His argument is that knowledge derives from sense perceptions but that these are necessarily interpreted by man's conceptual framework which is itself the product of reasoning about sense experience. Thus the real world exists, but our knowledge of it is limited by what is knowable to the mind and what is knowable must depend in part on experience. In spite of this, Kant lay great stress on the distinction between 'a priori' (knowledge through pure reason) and empirical knowledge in most of his writings. To him geography was part of empirical knowledge since it was a 'science' derived from the experiences of men. It was more than 'common knowledge' (what we would call general factual knowledge) because it was systematized, and classificatory, and because it was circumscribed, being concerned with the surface of the earth and not other aspects of reality. However, if geography was an empirical science, how did it differ from other such sciences; for example, from physics or from history which Kant also thought of as empirical science?

Kant's answer tended to imply that such exact sciences as physics had a greater body of theoretical or 'a priori' concepts, principles and laws associated with them, often mathematically expressed. Geography was a less exact form of knowledge, but because it covered a wide field, was particularly suitable as an introduction (a propaedeutic) to more theoretical sciences. The problem of distinguishing geography from history led Kant to state categorically that geography was a description of 'nature' as it is at the present, whereas history described changes in 'nature' over time. He was of course conscious that such a simple distinction created its own problems. If history was the history of nature, in other words of changes in the various 'geographies' of the past, what was the study of changes in men's ideas and relationships to one another? He solved that particular problem by classifying such a study as part of anthropology, though what Kant called anthropology is probably more akin to what we would now call social psychology and history.

To sum up, Kant contributed little that was new geographical knowledge, either in terms of facts or in theories. But he did contribute substantially to the debate on the nature of geographical knowledge. He saw geography as one of the basic forms of empirical knowledge dealing with the phenomena of the earth's surface. It was therefore a useful introductory classificatory study in the process of education, which would be deepened later by the study of more specialized and theoretical subjects like physics. He saw it as being essentially concerned with nature. His views on the relationship between man and his environment were never expanded sufficiently for us to be clear about them (Tatham 1951).

While Kant was lecturing at Königsberg, two other Germans were studying and preparing themselves for their professional lives, which in different ways were to have an important influence on the development of geography. They were Alexander von Humboldt (1769-1859), and Karl Ritter (1779-1859). Both are claimed by French and German geographers to be the founders of modern geography on the grounds that their work was seminal and influenced later generations of geographers in both countries, though the contribution of each is markedly different from that of the other. Humboldt was essentially a practising scientist with wide interests. Ritter, though not completely 'chairbound', was more of a compiler of and thinker about empirical data than an active researcher in the field. It is reported, according to letters he wrote during a journey in northern Italy, that he showed far more interest in the notables he was likely to meet at the next stage than in the landscape around him (Kramer 1959).

Humboldt early evinced an interest in botany which never left him. When he went to the University of Gottingen in 1788 he was attracted by the study of geology and even published brief papers on the igneous rocks of the Rhineland in 1789. He followed his studies at Gottingen (after a short spell in Hamburg) by joining the School of Mines in Freiburg in Saxony where he learned more about geology and something about the practicalities of mining. He then obtained a post with the Prussian State of Franconia's Department of Mines which gave him the opportunity of travelling extensively in southern Germany. His desire to travel and find out more about the world had been stimulated earlier by his meeting Georg Forster, who had, with his father Johann Forster, travelled round the world with James Cook. It was not long before Humboldt was able to realize his wish to travel farther afield. His mother died in 1797 and left him a substantial fortune which enabled him to indulge in what was to be his life's work, without at first needing to earn a living. He used his fortune to finance his expeditions to Latin America and the subsequent publication of his findings, so much so, that in later life he became dependent upon the income from a post he held as chamberlain to the King of Prussia (Kellner 1963).

Humboldt travelled in South and Central America from 1799 to 1804; he explored the Orinoco and established that the Casiquiare channel did in fact link the Amazon and Orinoco basins; he went up the Magdalena Valley (Colombia), climbed up the Andean cordillera, visited Quito and went down to the coastal areas of Peru. He went by sea to Acapulco and travelled overland in Mexico examining the mining of silver and other metals. He returned to Europe via the United States where he briefly met President Jefferson in Washington. He had travelled more than 40,000 miles in all sorts of conditions and often in great hardship. It is perhaps apposite to mention that he crossed humid tropical disease-ridden areas at a time when there existed no protection through vaccination against yellow fever or any other tropical disease. His travels were therefore accomplished in conditions which would have daunted a lesser man, yet he was not content merely to travel, he also carried out many scientific observations which he carefully recorded and stored for eventual publication and interpretation. His activities included the determination of the latitude and longitude of many places in Latin America, the surveying of various river channels, the collection and classification of many plants, the determination of the altitude of various places in the Andes. This led him to suggest a relationship between altitude and vegetation. He also collected geological specimens in the Andes, recorded the position and shapes of the volcanoes of the area, measured the temperature of the Humboldt current (named after him) and so on. Perhaps some idea of his activities in Latin America can be gleaned from the following brief quotation from a letter he wrote in what is now Venezuela.

> The oppressive and almost unbearable heat did not prevent me from observing the solar eclipse of the 28th of October. On the same day I took altitudes of the sun with Bird's quadrant; I give the results below, and I should be glad if you will kindly look them through and correct them.... In making these observations, my face was so severely burnt that I was obliged to keep my bed for two days and apply medicinal remedies. The reflection from the white limestone is distressing to the eyes and liable to injure the sight. The metal of an instrument exposed to the power of the sun's rays is heated to a temperature of 124°F.
>
> (Bruhns 1872)

When finally he returned to Europe, Humboldt settled in Paris where he lived for most of the next twenty-three years, collating and preparing the publication of his scientific observations. Paris was a particularly fertile environment in the intellectual sense at that time. Humboldt was able to discuss his observations and science in general with such men as Gay-Lussac the physicist and chemist, Laplace the astronomer, Lamarck and Cuvier the biologists, to mention but the most famous. From 1827 to the end of his life he lived in Berlin where he worked as the King of Prussia's chamberlain, but also found time to travel and to write what was to be for him the crowning achievement of his scientific work, namely the book *Kosmos* which appeared in four volumes from 1845 to 1859, a fifth volume appearing in 1862 after his death and collated from notes he had drafted.

Humboldt, like many other men of science at that time, was not a specialist and never thought of limiting his activities to one scientific field. His contributions to knowledge range from what we would now call botany, through physics and chemistry to astronomy and geology. He discovered many new facts and suggested a number of new concepts, for example that of isotherms. What, then, makes him one of the founders of modern geography? First, in all his scientific work he was clearly interested in the differences which were manifest in different parts of the earth's surface, for example, differences in vegetation.

Secondly, he worked with meticulous care and attempted to maintain a high degree of accuracy in all his measurements; in other words he represents the quantitative scientific approach which is one of the hallmarks of modern geography. Thirdly, he attempted to see relationships between the phenomena he was studying, 'to bring out the ways in which the great variety of observable phenomena of the landscape are associated and interconnected with each other at different places' (Dickinson 1969). One might sum up by saying that he was basically a scientist with an interest in areal differentiation and spatial interaction, to use current terminology.

One can ask a further question about Humboldt; given Kant's contemporary interest in the nature of geographical knowledge, was Humboldt aware of Kant's views and did he pronounce on this topic explicitly? The evidence is not clear. Humboldt's brother, Wilhelm von Humboldt, is reputed to have been much taken by Kant's philosophy, and to have read the whole of Kant's works. There is no reason to believe, however, that Wilhelm influenced Alexander in this matter. Neither is it clear that Humboldt was very interested in a debate on epistemology. On the one hand there is some evidence that Humboldt agreed with Kant's general view of the position of geography in the structure of knowledge; this is derived from Humboldt's lectures at the University of Berlin in 1827-8 and from his *Kosmos* which contains statements bearing a striking resemblance to those in Kant's introduction to his *Physical Geography*. On the other hand, also in his *Kosmos*, one finds criticisms of Kant, though these tend to be criticisms of the 'geography' rather than of the philosophy of Kant (May 1970). Basically, Humboldt was not very concerned with philosophy; he was much more concerned with empirical research and his statement in *Kosmos* that there exists unity in nature must be seen more as a view that reality is inevitably a synthesis rather than any fundamental proposition about the nature of geography.

Karl Ritter, however, was interested in the 'nature of geography' and wrote a number of tracts on the nature and methods of geography, but, as Tatham (1951) points out, their content and clarity are such as to make it difficult to pronounce with conviction on Ritter's view of geography. A few words on Ritter's background will help us to see him in perspective.

He studied philosophy, mathematics, history and natural science at the University of Halle. After his initial studies he became tutor to the family of a Frankfurt banker and in 1813 accompanied one of the elder sons to the University of Gottingen. It was while he was at Gottingen that he published in 1817 the first volume of *Erdkunde* which was about Africa, a continent about which little was known at the time. The book was very well received, and as a result he was offered a post as professor of geography at the University of Berlin, which he took up in 1820 and at which he remained until his death. Ritter first met Humboldt in 1807 soon after Ritter had published two volumes on Europe (1804 and 1807), but when Humboldt settled in Berlin in 1827, the two became friends and both acknowledged having benefited from each other's ideas. The first edition of *Erdkunde* was replaced subsequently by new volumes which he continued to write throughout his professional career. At his death, some nineteen volumes had been published, but world coverage was incomplete, since the volumes only covered Africa and Asia. Europe, which was the area he knew best at first hand, was not included. One detail interesting to educationists: Ritter's original interest in geography is said to have been awakened by the teaching which he had at school which was based on Rousseau's and Pestalozzi's principles, such as, for example, that direct contact with nature on country walks was more likely to lead to fruitful observation and learning than mere second-hand learning from books (Sinnhuber 1959). If this is true then it is a lesson that Ritter did not follow up to any extent in his later professional life. It is reported than when taxed on his lack of first-hand knowledge of Palestine and Sinai about which he wrote fourteen volumes, he replied, 'What new information could I derive from a visit to Palestine? I know every corner of it' (Freeman 1961). The idea that his mental images of Palestine could have been improved by a direct experience of the area seems not to have found favour with him. This is in accord with what Kramer (1959) states about his attitude to travel which was mentioned earlier.

There is no doubt that Ritter was a man of wide scholarship. His writings show a mastery not only of the physical geography of the countries he writes about, but also of their history, politics and ethnology. How far by modern standards could they be judged works of geography? First, it is argued by Dickinson (1969) that 'Ritter conceived of geography as an empirical science rather than one based on deductions from rational principles or from *a priori* theories.' This is undoubtedly so, granted we remember that he handled second-hand information and that he seldom tried to work out the laws governing the relationship between the empirical facts. Secondly, Ritter was concerned to describe areas which he considered to be unique because of the peculiar areal associations which could be found there. In this he was a precursor of the regional geography of Vidal de la Blache. Thirdly, he saw that geography would have to go beyond description and would need to explain the inter-relationship existing within an area. Again here we have something similar to what Vidal de la Blache was to call 'une description explicative des paysages'. Thus one could argue that if Humboldt was a founder of the 'modern' scientific strand of mainly systematic geography, Ritter was the founder of the 'modern' regional strand of geography. It is also clear that Ritter was aware of certain philosophical problems about the nature of geography which he was unable to resolve. For example, recognizing that geography obtained its data from many different sources, he felt that what gave the subject its unity was its concentration on the earth as the home of man; yet at the same time he realized that some aspects of physical geography could be studied although the relationships so derived (e.g. the relationship between wind and sand dune movement) were totally independent of man.

Lastly, it may be said that Ritter and Humboldt were probably characteristic of their time in the sense that they were born in the century which saw a great opening of the mind to scientific thought, where argument based on authority was being rejected in favour of argument based on sense impressions. They were almost bound to favour the collection of data and to pay somewhat less attention to the ways in which this data could be analysed and interpreted. Further, the examples given by such men as Diderot in France or earlier Chambers in Britain in producing encyclopedias plus the fact that geography purported to describe the earth, led Humboldt and Ritter to produce works of a monumental nature where breadth of coverage was one of the dominant characteristics. It is perhaps symptomatic that neither succeeded in completing his great work before his death.

It has been said that Ritter's writings in geography showed the influence of his teleological point of view, namely the idea that what happened on earth was fashioned by and for some divine purpose. Whilst it is true that this represented his deep religious conviction, it is doubtful whether this conviction substantially affected what he wrote on geography (Dickinson 1969). In other words, to describe an area of the world and analyse the interacting elements within it is one thing, to state that what is being described is a manifestation of God's will is another; the latter statement does not *ipso facto* invalidate the analysis in the former.

The growth of environmental determinism

The next link in the story of the development of geography lies in the publication, in 1859, of the *Origin of the Species by Means of Natural Selection* by Charles Robert Darwin (1809-1882). Not that Darwin ever claimed to be a geographer. His main interest was botany, but his theory of evolution gradually gained acceptance in the nineteenth century and proved an inspiration to many geographers, who saw in Darwin's ideas on natural selection the possibility of a general theory of man-land relationships: namely that as organisms needed to adapt to their environment in order to survive, so man needed to adopt modes of living which were consonant with the environment in which he lived, that is, that man's life on earth was to a large extent moulded by the kind of physical environment in which he lived. Geography could then become the study of the way man responded to his physical milieu and, by an extension of its function, geography might predict the way in which man ought to respond to a new environment. The subject could therefore acquire the status of an applied science and one which could be useful to the colonizers of the period.

Strangely it was not in the writings of British but in those of German and American geographers that one can see most clearly the influence of this interpretation of Darwin's ideas. The crudity of the interpretation seem to increase as time goes by. Friedrich Ratzel (1844-1904) who became professor of geography at Leipzig in 1886 had had an earlier training in biology during which he had come into contact with Darwin's theory of evolution. He became interested in the migration of animal species and also, after travels in Europe and North and Central America, in human migrations. In the first volume of a two-volume work called *Anthropogeographie* (1882 and 1891) he examines the ways in which human beings have grouped themselves on the earth's surface, the influence of the physical environment and of migrations on these distributions, and the effects produced by the physical environment on individuals and societies, such as the effect of climate on natural character. Dickinson (1969) and Wanklyn (1961) are at pains to point out that nowhere in Ratzel's work can one find a point of view which could attract the label of 'environmental determinism'. Ratzel was simply pointing out that human beings as individuals or as members of societies have to submit to certain pressures from the physical environment, and modify their behaviour accordingly. He extended his ideas in his *Politische Geographie* first published in 1897, in which he likened the state to an organism which tends to grow and multiply, which exists in a given area, but as it grows tries to expand and ultimately finds constraints imposed by physical conditions or by the existence of similar neighbouring organisms. From this was born the concept of 'lebensraum', by which Ratzel meant the geographical area within which organisms develop. He saw that states tended to augment or decrease their 'lebensraum' according to the forces acting on the state organism. In this sense the concept was politically neutral, but it was taken up by the Nazis in the nineteen-thirties to imply that the German nation had a right to an almost limitless 'lebensraum' as the 'master race'.

It was perhaps inevitable that as geography came to be seen as the study of the interaction of man and his environment, some simplification of this thesis should occur until geography came to be regarded as the study of the way the *physical* environment *controls* the life of man. Frederic Leplay (1806-1882) who can be thought of as an early French sociologist, was convinced that the physical environment determined the type of work done and this in turn determined the forms of social organizations, hence his famous formula—place: work: family. Henri de Tourville (1843-1903) and Edmond Demolins (1852-1907), who were Leplay's disciples, spread the gospel of simple environmental determinism. For example, according to Demolins, the steppe is eminently suited to the horse, the horse is used by man to develop the pastoralism which is natural to the steppe; it is used to develop mobility, to maintain contacts between groups and therefore to maintain cultural unity. This very existence of the steppe was alleged to have created a whole way of life.

Ellen Churchill Semple (1863-1932), an American who had studied under Ratzel in Leipzig and was fired by his ideas, expounded her interpretations of these in several books addressed to an English-speaking public. In *Influences of Geographic Environment* (1911) we get some taste of her thinking from the following passage: 'The evidence of history shows us that there is such a thing as a desert born genius for religion. . . .' She goes on to explain

The dry, pure air stimulates the faculties of the desert-dweller, but the featureless [sic] monotonous surroundings furnish them with little to work upon. The mind finding scant material for logical deduction, falls back upon contemplation.

It is possible to find many examples of a similar nature in which human attributes are directly ascribed to a physical environmental influence, as for example when she argues that no great art or poetry can emanate from the Alpine area because 'its majestic sublimity paralyses the mind'.

Ellsworth Huntington (1876-1947), also an American, wrote in a similar vein, though in his books he tends to apply his theories either to peoples living closer to nature than those of Western Europe, or to the explanation of the rise and fall of civilizations. His journeys to Central Asia from 1903 to 1907 led to the publications of *The Pulse of Asia* (1907) in which he ascribed the differing qualities (as he perceived them) of the Kirghiz mountain people and those of the Chantos plainsmen to their natural environment. In a later book, *Civilization and Climate* (1915) he proposes the thesis that civilizations prosper and decay in response to changes in climate. He points to the case histories of the Middle Eastern civilizations, to those of Central Asia and to the Maya civilization in modern Mexico, though he ascribes the decline of these civilizations to increasing aridity in the Middle East and to increasing humidity and higher temperatures in the Yucatan peninsula.

There is little doubt that climatic changes have had an influence on the general character of life in certain areas, if only to modify the kind of agriculture that might be practised. Nevertheless it is difficult to aver that climatic change is the principal causal factor in the rise and fall of civilizations. It was, however, a tempting thesis and Huntington could not resist indicating what he thought might be the optimum conditions for the maintenance of an industrial civilization such as that of Western Europe and North America. It will come as no surprise that he thought that for physical health temperatures should range from 55°F to 70°F (12·8°C to 21·2°C), that they should be a little lower for mental health, that they should be variable rather than constant; that relative humidity should be around 80% (*World Power and Evolution*, 1920); in other words he was describing the sort of conditions which might be experienced in a West European spring and summer. It would seem a classic case of the *post hoc ergo propter hoc* argument.

However naïve environmental determinism may appear today, it must be remembered that it was taken quite seriously by many teachers and by some of the public at that time, particularly as the social sciences of psychology and sociology were in a state of infancy, so that the more subtle relationships between the various elements in a given society and its physical environment had not been disentangled. It is as well to clarify two points at this stage. First, geographers who held the view that the physical environment to some extent controlled the way of life of people living in that environment should be called 'environmental determinists' and not just 'determinists' since philosophically anyone believing in a cause and effect relationship is a determinist (Martin 1951). Secondly, that although the inspiration for the environmental determinist strand in geography probably came from Darwin's theory of evolution, most geographers who espoused this view misunderstood one of Darwin's most important points, namely the influence of chance in the process of evolution (Stoddart 1966).

The process whereby organisms adjusted to the exigencies of their environment tended to be seen as a simple cause and effect relationship. Darwin, on the other hand made quite another point, namely that the organisms which survived in a changed environment did so not because they somehow adapted to these new conditions, but because *chance* mutations in the physical make up of some organisms made these capable of surviving. These new characteristics of the organisms were then inherited by the succeeding generations. Thus the mechanism of evolution under natural conditions is seen to involve a large element of chance, or to put it in other words, evolution is an illustration of a *stochastic* process. Further the time scale over which this process operates is enormous in comparison with the time scale over which human societies have evolved. Nevertheless, it may be argued that even if societies are viewed as organisms evolving in a physical milieu, the changes occurring in these societies probably owe as much to chance as to their conscious attempts to adapt to the environment. One need only think of the way the British economy has evolved since 1945 to be aware that the conscious attempt to revitalize the North East region and Clydeside has met with setbacks due to factors beyond the British Government's immediate control, that is, chance factors of foreign origin. Indeed, even in the Soviet Union it is not possible to plan for every eventuality, so that events do not necessarily conform to plans. This recognition of the influence of chance in human affairs is not, of course, a plea for a fatalistic outlook; in fact concern over the quality of the environment which is currently being expressed, is indicative of a belief that man can act in such a way as to promote ecological harmony rather than cascading catastrophe. But this in no way ignores that in the nature of things many events are chance events.

The Franco-British view

While Ratzel was teaching and writing in Germany, Vidal de la Blache (1845-1918) was developing his own brand of geography in France and Halford John Mackinder (1861-1947) was promoting the cause of a 'new' geography in Great Britain. Both Vidal de la Blache and Mackinder had numerous disciples so that their ideas were disseminated in both countries for many years after their active professional lives were over. They were responsible for creating what were in effect the first university departments of geography in France and Britain. Their names are coupled together not because they were coevals, not because of any strong identity of views, but because their view and practice of geography contrasted with that of the 'environmental determinist'. Vidal de la Blache was a patient researcher into detail, who, gifted with a fine turn of phrase, could describe a cultural landscape and tease out the inter-relationships which existed in an area between its human and physical features. His work involved both field and library investigations and resulted in such masterpieces of descriptive and explanatory writing as *Tableau de la Géographie de la France* (1903) and *La France de l'Est* (1917). His tendency was to examine '*reality*' in its complexity and to note how the pattern of inter-relationships might differ from area to area. In modern parlance, he was much more concerned with the idiographic, or particular character of a place, than with the nomothetic, or with generalizations which could be made about any set of relations. He expressed his ideas about geography by a phrase that was to remain the hallmark of his approach: '... ce que la géographie, en échange du secours qu'elle recoit des autres sciences, peut apporter au trésor commun, c'est l'aptitude à ne pas morceler ce que la nature rassemble, à comprendre la correspondance et la corrélation des faits, soit dans le milieu terrêstre qui les enveloppe tous, soit dans les milieux régionaux où ils se localisent' (Vidal de la Blache 1913), which may be liberally translated as '... what geography can contribute to the common store of knowledge in exchange for what it receives from other disciplines, is the capacity for not disintegrating what nature brings together, for understanding the connections and correlations between phenomena, either in the global framework which encompasses them or in the regional environments where they are localized.' To use yet another expression which was to become almost a cliché, geography's essential contribution to knowledge as a whole was its 'synthetic' viewpoint. As we shall see later, some epistemological problems arise when one attempts to delimit a discipline by such a criterion; but it is broadly true that most geographers seemed to be satisfied with Vidal de la Blache's explanation of the distinctive character of geography, and indeed almost sixty years after it was first propounded, his view is still acceptable to many geographers (Fisher 1970). Only in regional geography do many geographers see anything distinctive about geography.

As Wrigley (1970) points out, Vidal de la Blache could demonstrate the intimate interaction between man and his local environment only in a society which was still largely agrarian where inter-regional trade and industrial development were in their infancy. Thus Vidal de la Blache is happier dealing with pre-industrial societies than with modern economies, and his works have a strong historical flavour. They appealed to those who found the 'environmental determinists' somewhat difficult to stomach. Vidal de la Blache made no claims that the physical environment in any way controlled the way people lived in a given area. He merely pointed out that there was often a connection between man and his environment, with influences being felt in both directions. The historian, Lucien Febvre, used the word 'possibilism' to describe Vidal de la Blache's views on the relationship between man and his environment. 'Possibilism' was the view that any physical environment offered a number of possibilities for development or for living, but that what in fact evolved was as much a factor of man's culture as of his environment. The physical environment in no way dictated how man must live in a given area (Febvre 1922).

Vidal de la Blache had a strong following in France, in Great Britain and in the U.S.A. In France, this was not surprising, for after acquiring a doctorate in 1872 he taught for five years at the University of Nancy, and, much more important, in 1877 he was appointed to the Ecole Normale Supérieure in Paris where he stayed for twenty-one years. It was there that he was able to mould an élite of young prospective *lycée* teachers who were to spread the gospel of geography throughout France. Among his pupils were such well known geographers as Jean Brunhes, Camena D'Almeida, Albert Demangeon, Lucien Gallois, Emmanuel de Martonne, Maurice Zimmerman, Raoul

Blanchard and Henri Baulig. Not only was he able to attract many students to geography who might otherwise have read another subject, but he was able to convince many that his particular brand of geography was the true one. Few French geographers moved away from Vidal de la Blache's conception, apart from those who took up physical geography as a speciality and even those, like de Martonne, remained faithful to Vidal's views on human regional geography. Only in the nineteen-sixties was there much evidence of a marked rethinking in France of the basic viewpoint of geographers (Pinchemel 1965; Claval 1969). Though some had been moving in new directions at an earlier date, there are few publications which manifest this. In Great Britain, most geographers of the inter-war and early post-war years would probably have seen themselves as broadly in sympathy with Vidal de la Blache's basic tenets. Certainly teachers in secondary schools felt that their main objective was to show pupils how people lived in various parts of the world and how their lives related in some way to their environment. In the U.S.A., the influence of Vidal de la Blache was less, though important figures like Isaiah Bowman and Carl Sauer owed something to him for their approach to geography.

Halford John Mackinder was much more a man of action than Vidal de la Blache, though he also made signal contributions to academic geography. Unlike Vidal de la Blache who graduated in classics and then turned to history and geography, Mackinder read natural science at Oxford, then took a further degree in history, later still studied law and was called to the Bar. He had always been interested in geology since his school-days; this, plus his developing interest in history and his awareness that geography in France and Germany was more than a catalogue of facts, led him to a new conception of geography, which he proceeded to disseminate during his travels as a university extension lecturer (Cantor 1960). It was as a result of these lectures that he was invited to address the Royal Geographical Society in January 1887 (Gilbert 1972). The paper which he read, 'The scope and methods of geography', made out a case for a 'man-land' conception of geography which he defined as 'the science whose main function is to trace the interaction of man in society and so much of his environment as varies locally' (Mackinder 1887). As one reads the paper today one is conscious that words have evolved in meaning. For example, the word environment is not defined by Mackinder but from the context it seems clear that he meant the *physical* environment. Mackinder illustrated his conception of geography by giving a description of south-eastern

England, in which he first examined the physical landscape as a product of geological evolution and secondly the settlement pattern in terms of the gradual peopling of the area during which process there was an adaptation to and a modification of, the physical landscape. He was, thus, very close to the position of the French geographers, though he did not stress regionalism to the extent that they did. His book *Britain and the British Seas*, first published in 1902, also manifests the same general view and though it contains descriptions of various parts of Britain, these are not depicted in the minutiae of detail that were contained in the French regional monographs. It painted a picture of Britain at the turn of the nineteenth century that was bold and evocative.

Perhaps to many geographers the best known part of Mackinder's paper on 'The scope and methods of geography' is the section in which he expounds his views on the educational purpose of geography. 'It is the duty of the geographer,' he wrote, 'to build one bridge over an abyss which in the opinion of many is upsetting the equilibrium of our culture. Lop off either limb of geography and you maim it in its noblest part.' This might be seen as an early anticipation of C. P. Snow's Cambridge lecture of 1959 on *The Two Cultures* (Snow 1959). Mackinder seemed to be arguing that scientists and scholars in the humanities were no longer talking the same language but that geography, because of its 'synthetic' nature, could help to restore the dialogue. The argument is not very explicit, but it would seem that Mackinder believed that those studying geography, because they must learn to think as physical scientists (when studying physical geography) and as men of letters (when studying human geography), would never become culturally stunted by being narrow specialists. It is not clear whether he intended everyone to study geography or whether an élite would suffice. The argument would today seem a little naïve to be taken very seriously, but it was one which weighed with such geographers as Wooldridge and East (1951).

Like Vidal de la Blache, Mackinder was responsible for initiating the teaching of geography at a university institution and was therefore a seminal influence in British geography. At Oxford he launched what eventually became a department of geography. Starting first by lecturing in physical and political geography he gradually attracted an appreciative audience owing to his masterly exposition of whatever subject he taught. He was more successful with political geography which he dovetailed to fit in with the history courses at Oxford, whereas the physical geography was an isolated course which in no sense integrated with the then existing degree structure.

While lecturing at Oxford, Mackinder continued to campaign for an extension of the teaching of geography in Great Britain. He became aware that if geography was to prosper in schools, then many more teachers with a geographical training would be required. He tried unsuccessfully to get the Royal Geographical Society to sponsor a 'London School of Geography', but after further discussions the Royal Geographical Society offered to help in the creation of a School of Geography at Oxford. After negotiations with Oxford University, the school was opened in January 1900, with Mackinder as its director. He obtained the services of A. J. Herbertson and two other dons and the 'School' began teaching for what was to be the first university qualification in geography in England, namely the Oxford Diploma in Geography, the first examination for which was held in 1901. Only four candidates sat for this examination, though numbers increased over the years and by 1914 there were 41 candidates. Mackinder also organized summer schools in geography which were mainly attended by school-teachers wishing to improve their knowledge. In 1914 about 200 teachers attended such schools. Many British geographers of repute began their careers in geography at one of these summer schools, for example Unstead and Roxby, later to become professors of geography at London and Liverpool Universities respectively.

As a man of action Mackinder must be seen not simply as an academic but as a promoter, someone able through his dynamic qualities to get an organization set up and working. It is symptomatic that while he was lecturing at Oxford, he also became in 1892 Principal of Reading College (later to become Reading University College in 1902), he helped to found the Geographical Association in 1893, he began lecturing on geography at the London School of Economics in 1895 and was appointed its director in 1903. He did not resign his appointment at Oxford until 1905, by which time the School of Geography was well established and continued to thrive under Herbertson's direction.

Andrew John Herbertson's (1865-1915) impact on British geography was certainly no less than Mackinder's though of a different character. It is probable that his influence on *what* was taught in British schools was enormous and has since been unsurpassed. This comes from his major contribution to academic geography, the division of the world

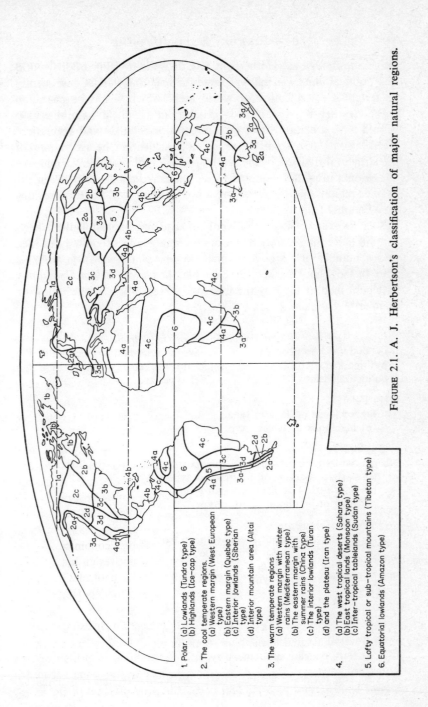

1. Polar. (a) Lowlands (Tundra type)
         (b) Highlands (Ice-cap type)

2. The cool temperate regions.
      (a) Western margin (West European type)
      (b) Eastern margin (Quebec type)
      (c) Interior lowlands (Siberian type)
      (d) Interior mountain area (Altai type)

3. The warm temperate regions
      (a) Western margin with winter rains (Mediterranean type)
      (b) The eastern margin with summer rains (China type)
      (c) The interior lowlands (Turan type)
      (d) and the plateau (Iran type)

4. (a) The west tropical deserts (Sahara type)
   (b) East tropical lands (Monsoon type)
   (c) Inter-tropical tablelands (Sudan type)

5. Lofty tropical or sub-tropical mountains (Tibetan type)

6. Equatorial lowlands (Amazon type)

FIGURE 2.1. A. J. Herbertson's classification of major natural regions.

into natural regions. Herbertson felt that the division of the world into political units was inappropriate for scientific work. Consequently he sought a classification of world areas which would be based on natural rather than man-made criteria, in which 'a natural region should have a certain unity of configuration, climate and vegetation' (Herbertson 1905). To arrive at such a classification, he used a map of the structural division of the world, one of temperature belts and one of seasonal rainfall, attempted to see the correspondence between the various regions and then drew up a final map of world natural regions (*See* Figure 2.1).

Such an exercise was undoubtedly of academic interest. But Herbertson did more than merely throw out an idea. He incorporated this idea into a number of textbooks which he wrote in association with his wife for the school market. For example, the *Oxford Senior Geography* first published in 1910 by the Clarendon Press opens in the following manner (*See* Figure 2.1):

The natural regions of the world

In studying the geography of the World it is better to consider the well-marked natural regions which do not change rather than the political divisions which do. The chief types are:

(1) Polar
    (a) lowlands or Tundra type;
    (b) highlands or Ice-cap type.

(2) Cool Temperate
    (a) western margin, or West European type;
    (b) eastern margin, or Laurentian type;
    (c) interior lowland, or Siberian type;
    (d) interior highland, or Altai type.

(3) Warm Temperate
    (a) western margin, or Mediterranean type;
    (b) eastern margin, or China type;
    (c) interior lowland, or Turan type;
    (d) plateau or Iran type.

(4) The Hot Lands
    (a) western desert, or Sahara type;
    (b) summer rain, or Monsoon and Sudan types;
    (c) wet equatorial lowland, or Amazon type;
    (d) lofty plateau, or Bolivian type.

(N.B. This textbook classification of the natural regions is a simplified version of the classification used in Figure 2.1.)

Herbertson's textbooks on geography were immensely successful. Over 1·4 million copies were sold by 1950 (Gilbert 1965) and at least one book originally published in 1899, *Man and His Work* was still in print in the late nineteen-sixties. It may readily be understood that Herbertson's natural regions soon became the basic framework within which geography was taught in the schools of Britain. Indeed he was widely imitated by other textbook writers like Archer, C. B. Thurston, Suggate, Stembridge and Stamp, the latter's output of textbooks subsequently far surpassing Herbertson's. Stamp acknowledged his debt to Herbertson's concept of natural regions, and admitted that he had so grown up with this concept that it had seemed normal to adopt it (Stamp 1957). Herbertson's basic approach was also recommended in the Board of Education's *Handbook of Suggestions for Teachers* issued in 1915. Similarly, H. C. Barnard's *Principles and Practice of Geography Teaching*, published in 1933, advocated a basically Herbertsonian approach (Barnard 1933).

What then was Herbertson's method as manifest in his school textbooks? First, as already indicated, his treatment of the world tended to be within the framework of his natural regions. This in itself, it could be argued, was simply one classification of world areas, no better perhaps but certainly no worse than any other. Yet one pedagogically worrying aspect of this classification was that at school level it tended to be handed down to pupils as though it were a kind of geographical gospel, to be absorbed but not questioned. The really interesting question, namely how does one arrive at such a classification, was never discussed. Further, a natural region on the scale postulated by Herbertson was a generalization having little meaning for younger pupils.

Secondly, the global treatment by 'natural regions' tended to argue from the physical background to the human response. Thus though there was never any crude environmental determinism in Herbertson's view of geography, as may be seen in his paper 'Regional environment, heredity and consciousness' (Herbertson 1915), yet there existed a subtle suggestion in his textbooks, that man's life and work were shaped by the physical environment in which he lived. Generations of school children came to think of regions of food gatherers, of regions of hunters, of regions of nomads and oasis dwellers, of regions of vine, olive and wheat cultivators, of regions of seal hunters and so on. This legacy is still with us to a certain extent in spite of the enormous economic changes which since 1900 have made such simple categorization inappropriate. The regional approach became entrenched, in one form or another, in school geography.

Evolution and revolution in the twentieth century

During the eighteenth century, geography began to be taught in certain institutions of higher learning, though the substance of what was taught varied immensely in quality. During the nineteenth century, there was a further extension of geography teaching, particularly in universities where German was the language of instruction, and there emerged some substantial works of geography, such as those by Humboldt and Ritter which were a real advance on the gazetteer-type geographies of the previous centuries. By the end of the nineteenth century, geography was a firmly established discipline in Germany and France and it was developing rapidly in the U.S.A. and Britain. Ideas on geography were evolving and to some extent crystallizing around the concept of 'man-land' relationships, though the extent to which 'land' was stated to influence 'man' varied according to whether geographers took a more or less environmentally deterministic viewpoint or one characterized as 'possibilism'. German and some American geographers tended to favour a somewhat more deterministic stance than French and British geographers who were inclined to the 'possibilist' view.

From 1900 onwards, it is possible to see a gradual consolidation both of the position of geography in education at all levels and of the 'possibilist' point of view. In the United Kingdom, the number of geography departments in universities increased during the inter-war and post-1945 years, and geography became a popular subject among university students. Similar changes occurred in Europe and North America, though in the U.S.A. the relative growth of geography was probably not as great as elsewhere. In the U.S.A., W. M. Davis (1850-1934) was a giant figure among geographers who gave a particular direction to the study of geomorphology through his advocacy of the 'cycle of erosion' theory of landscape evolution. He was in part responsible for the growth and development of a systematic branch of geography during a period which was mostly characterized by a concentration on regional geography. Certainly in France and Britain, the major publications of the inter-war years were in the field of regional description; books such as the *Géographie Universelle* (volumes appeared at various dates between the wars) which was a kind of latter-day *Erdekunde*, and A. G. Ogilvie's *Great Britain: Essays in Regional Geography* (1928) were typical of the period. There was a painstaking accumulation of detail about the regions described; the relief, geology and structure were followed by the climate, then the soils and agriculture, with industry, settlement and communications ending the description. How far each author attempted to bring out the 'personality' of each region depended to a large extent on the literary skill of the author. Some were more successful than others. De Martonne's *The Geographical Regions of France* (1933) compared favourably with Ormsby's *France* (1931) which was painfully detailed.

The situation of research workers in geography was to some extent ambivalent. Many, having acquired a basic understanding of geology, climatology and some history, proceeded to compile regional monographs of medium or small-scale areas. Some gave broad systematic sketches of a political area along largely thematic lines. Stamp and Beaver's *British Isles* first published in 1933 is a work of this nature. Others carried out thematic regional surveys, as in the case of Stamp's *Land Utilization Survey of Great Britain and Northern Ireland*, in which the main purpose was to obtain a picture of land use as it existed in the nineteen-thirties based on the categories then devised. Explanations of land use patterns were offered in terms of historical, economic and physical factors. Some became interested in particular problems relating to geomorphology or climatology or economic geography, and research papers began to be published in fields where the traditional views of geography as a 'synthesis' of other knowledge was clearly not operative. Of course, some tried to bridge the gap by attempting both research along thematic lines and traditional regional description. Many French geographers, like Henri Baulig on the Massif Central, worked on problems in geomorphology and described in detail the 'geography' of the areas they worked in. Inevitably the pressure to specialize and tackle a limited field of enquiry led to more and more research workers concentrating on thematic aspects of geography. Thus were born what Henderson (1968) has called the 'adjectival forms of geography': agricultural geography, urban geography, social geography, settlement geography and so on. By the nineteen-sixties most research papers published were in the thematic aspects of geography.

Parallel to this trend towards specialization, there developed a tendency to use quantitative techniques of analysis. This development occurred first in North America and Sweden during the late nineteen-forties and nineteen-fifties and spread to Great Britain in the nineteen-sixties. It may be plausibly argued that such developments were an inevitable concomitant of the specialist studies then developing. The explanation of phenomena, whether in geomorphology or in economic geography, required a body of theory to be developed and such theory might be expressed in mathematical terms or tested through the use of statistical techniques such as use of correlation coefficients or the chi square test (Burton 1963). Thus geography was, in effect, joining the mainstream of scientific work which was going on in the physical and social sciences. It could be argued that geography was in fact *rejoining* a stream of scientific enquiry which she had abandoned when espousing the doctrine of 'possibilism'. To some extent, the 'environmental determinists' had a theory which they thought purported to explain human activities in certain areas. They were mistaken in that their theory was too crude and failed in too many cases. But the 'possibilists' had no theory at all. The ambivalence which characterized geographical research for many years was a consequence not only of the differing interests between 'region describers' and 'nomothetic theorists', but also between those who saw geography as an 'arts subject' akin to literature and those who saw it as a science. This raises the problem of the criteria used for defining a subject which we shall come to in Chapter 4.

Trends in the United Kingdom
Although the trend towards a more scientific geography was evident in the research work of some geographers before the 1939-45 war and in the immediate post-war period, it was not until the nineteen-sixties, that this trend began to be very noticeable. The rapid acceleration of the output of books and research papers in the new scientific style may be traced to the fact that a number of young British geographers spent some time studying in the geography departments of some North American universities. A cross-fertilization of ideas occurred which led to an increasing flow of information across the Atlantic. Geographers at Cambridge, Nottingham and Bristol universities were active in propagating new ideas, so that these universities became diffusion centres. This was manifest, for example, in the launching of a series of conferences at Madingley Hall near Cambridge attended by many teachers of geography from secondary schools and colleges of educa-

tion. The fruits of the first two conferences were published in *Frontiers in Geographical Teaching* (Chorley and Haggett 1965, revised 1970) a book which proved to have considerable influence on most geographers and not only on school-teachers, since it was the first British book which expounded clearly the polarization of views on the future development of geographical scholarship and teaching. Since 1965, some far-reaching changes have occurred in the courses in geography run by British universities and to a lesser extent in the kind of geography taught in schools. It may be useful to end this chapter by indicating in summary form what differences in emphasis are clearly attributable to the 'new' scientific geography.

First it is necessary to be clear that progress in knowledge occurs through various forms of research and that what is stated here refers to changes in substantive geography rather than to the teaching of geography. Indeed, at any level, whether at university or at school, what is taught nearly always lags behind what is currently known about a topic. Secondly, any such summary tends to depict the characteristics of the so-called 'new geography' as being very distinct from the 'old geography', whereas in reality there is much more of a continuum. Bearing these 'caveats' in mind, let us now proceed to enumerate these characteristics.

Perhaps the most important change which has occurred is the realization that any progress in understanding the phenomena studied by geographers involves the conscious use of scientific method and the development of a body of theory to explain such phenomena. From this starting point all else follows. For, if a theory is to be developed, then some understanding of the nature of theory and of the process of theory building was required. Hence the work of Harvey who in his volume *Explanation in Geography* (1969) reviews the whole field of explanation and points out the distinction between scientific and normative theory and shows that geographers inevitably use both, but should in no way confuse them, since normative theory is not testable empirically. Now, one way in which theory is gradually developed, is to put up tentative simplified 'models' of reality which help the research worker both to clarify his own mind and to point the way to other perhaps more complex models. Hence the acceleration in the output of models to be used in geography as evidenced by the publication of Chorley and Haggett's *Models in Geography* (1967). Models may be of various kinds. An iconic model such as a relief (hardware) model is a scaled down (or up) version of aspects of reality;

an analogue model is one in which the phenomenon is described in terms of an analogous but different process, for example as when the extent of the interaction between two towns is explained in terms of a modified form of Newton's gravitational law; a symbolic model is one in which the relationships to be explained in the phenomena are represented by such symbols as mathematical symbols. As mathematics has become the 'language of science', it is therefore not surprising that there has been in geography an increase in the use of mathematical symbols to denote geographical relationships. Often symbols are but a shorthand way of expressing a relationship which would take longer in words, as when one expresses the well-known relationship that the field of influence of a town (A) is dependent on or a function of (f) the number of its services (S), in the form $A \propto f(S)$. If the relationship is a complicated one, then the symbolism is more elaborate and those who are not familiar with the language of mathematics cannot understand what is being said. A further development of this is that if a geographical relationship can be expressed in the form of a mathematical equation, then often the symbols may be replaced by numerically expressed quantities. This is very useful since the relationship so expressed may be verified empirically. Thus, if one expresses the load of a given river in terms of the relationship

$$L = kV^3$$

where $L =$ Load in tonnes

k is a constant depending on the characteristics of the river

$V =$ Velocity in kilometres per hour

then by taking measurements of load and velocity one can verify whether this relationship is empirically true. If it is true then it enables us to predict what the load of a river may be at different velocities.

In the development of theory, however, it is not always possible to jump straight into a relationship which can be expressed mathematically and verified directly. Thus the quantitative aspects of geography are often not related to a simple mathematical relationship, but to the need to treat data statistically because what is being tested is not a deterministic relationship, but a probablistic one. For example, one may suspect that in a flood plain consisting of gravel and silty alluvium, there may be arable land on the gravel and pasture on the silty alluvium. However, this is not a relationship which will either always hold true or never hold true. Sometimes it will be so and at other times not so. The job of a statistical test is to determine whether it is likely that such a relationship holds true on a sufficient number of occasions to make it highly probable that the correspondence between gravel and arable is not just a matter of chance. Once such a correspondence has been established as highly probable, one can go on to formulate a possible explanation. Unfortunately, submitting data to statistical tests is a long and laborious process unless one can use a computer, and it is therefore one aspect of the quantitative revolution in geography which many have found difficult to accept. Further, the statistical procedures also use the language of mathematics which leads to further difficulties.

One type of model which has been widely adopted by geographers to help in the explanation of phenomena is the 'system'. A system may be defined as a whole consisting of elements which interact. A river basin can be described as a system in which the elements are the precipitation, the river channels, the run off, the evaporation, the infiltration, and so on. Systems may be defined as (i) *isolated* (e.g. the universe) in which there is no input of energy or matter and no output, (ii) *closed* in which there is input and output of energy but not of matter as in the case of the atmosphere system, and (iii) *open* in which there is both an input and output of energy matter. Most systems are

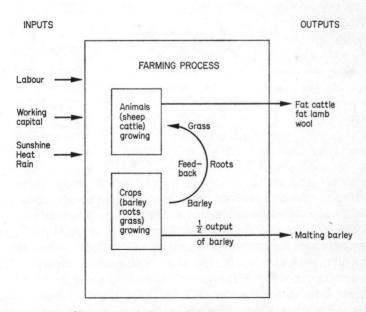

FIGURE 2.2. A fat stock farm as a system.

open systems. Essentially a system is a means of analysing the relationships existing within a unit of study. For example, in any given area of the earth's surface, it is possible to analyse the agricultural system or the industrial system and show the interaction between the various elements, be these farms and markets or factories and power stations. Most systems may be expressed in the forms of diagrams which are like flow charts (Figure 2.2). The use of systems by geographers is probably best exemplified by Chorley and Kennedy's *Physical Geography: a Systems Approach* (1971).

It is possible to sum up the changes which have occurred in the methodology of geography by drawing a 'geographic theory' diagram which attempts to show the ramifications and interconnections of such geographic theory (Figure 2.3).

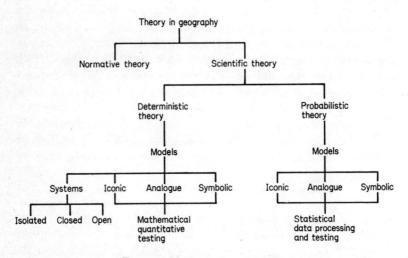

FIGURE 2.3. Theory in geography.

Having examined the kind of methodology that researchers in geography now use, let us briefly look at the problems which they tend to tackle. It seems that the common element of those problems is that they have a spatial component. This is well illustrated in, among others, Morrill's work (1970) *The Spatial Organization of Society*, Abler, Adams and Gould's (1971) *Spatial Organization: a Geographer's View of the World* and Haggett's (1972, 1975) *Geography, a Modern Synthesis*. Essentially geographers are saying that spatial regularities are evident over most of the world; *spatial patterns* tend to repeat themselves and it is part of the geographer's role to explain these. Spatial patterns are familiar phenomena and may of course be studied in physics, botany, chemistry and so on. Geographers tend to be concerned with spatial patterns which are manifest as a result of human activity at the local, regional, national and global scales. For example the patterns manifest by the land use around a farm represent the local scale; the spatial interaction between a town and its field of influence represents the regional scale; the distribution of towns in a country represents the national scale and the pattern of world trade in iron ore represents the global scale. The explanation of these patterns involves the geographer in an analysis of the *processes* which are responsible for the patterns. An example of such processes is the diffusion processes which have been studied by Hagerstrand in Sweden. Thus the extent to which farmers adopt a particular technological innovation forms a pattern which is explicable at any one time by the process of diffusion of the idea and its adoption or rejection by the farming community. Again farmers' reaction to a particular hazard like floods or drought is dependent on their perception of this hazard. That is, geographers in explaining a particular land use pattern are led to explore within the process leading to that pattern, not just the influence of the actual incidence of floods and droughts but their perceived incidence by farmers. This line of enquiry has led to a series of enquiries which are generally known as perception studies. These studies help to make clear the decision-making processes. It was pointed out by Kirk (1963) that what mattered in understanding spatial patterns was what he called the behavioural environment, that is the phenomenal (or objective) environment as perceived by man.

There are clearly many spatial patterns and processes which could be studied by geographers. Is there any trend which indicates the kinds of patterns studied in the last twenty years? Perhaps to affirm that a definite trend may be seen is to court a rebuttal, but it seems to me that geographers are more and more concerned with matters which affect society as a whole—that is they are concerned with patterns which have some social relevance and about which they can make certain recommendations (Harvey 1973, Berry 1973). For example there are a number of geographers who are working on what may be broadly termed matters of environmental concern—whether this be the diffusion of pollution or the mapping of the quality of the urban environment. These concerns are also related to those of town planning, or of more limited planning like the planning of school catchment areas. In a word, a good many geographers like Professor House of Oxford University are working more in 'applied geography' than in 'pure geography'.

If these tendencies are to be maintained, a problem is posed as to the position within geography of what has traditionally been called physical geography consisting of geomorphology, climatology and biogeography. It would seem that, though research in these fields will inevitably continue, they will be increasingly looked upon as ancillary to the mainstream of geography. Thus geographers will need to indicate clearly to which 'paradigm' of geography they wish to subscribe (*See* Chapter 10). Some may wish to adhere to a view of geography which can be called the 'ecosystem' paradigm which permits the continued integration of physical and human geography within a systems framework. Others may wish to make a clean break with tradition and subscribe to the 'spatial organization' paradigm of geography which views geography as being concerned with the patterns of man's activities and not (at least at the research level) with explaining patterns of natural landscape and patterns of climate. Yet others may be happy to adopt an eclectic attitude and accept a pluralistic situation.

CHAPTER THREE

Geography as a School Subject

Introduction

It is proposed in this chapter to examine the growth and development of geography in schools with special reference to its position in the schools of the United Kingdom. However, opportunity will be taken to make comparisons with the teaching of geography in France and North America where these seem fruitful. Inevitably, given the late development of geography as an academic discipline and the relative recency of universal education, much of the evidence is about a (historically) modern period. However, some documentary evidence exists about geography teaching of an earlier period and we shall begin by reviewing this.

Early geography teaching

Schools, in the sense of formal institutions in which children and adolescents are taught certain ideas and skills, have existed since Greek and Roman times in Western Europe. Indeed, much of the jargon of education stems from some of the early words used to describe these schools and their curricula. For example, the use of 'chair' to describe the post of professor comes from the 'high chair' (cathedra) occupied by the teacher which dominated the stools on which his pupils sat. Similarly, when pupils were literate in the sense of being able to read and write, they went on to a 'grammar school' where they made a formal study of the Latin language and its literature and from there to a 'rhetor', who might or might not be in a separate school, where they studied rhetoric or the art of oratory. During the Middle Ages in Europe, there were a number of grammar schools inherited from the Roman period, in which many of the leaders of the church had been educated. Inevitably, given the importance of theology as a mode of explanation and of the Scriptures as documents for study, there were conflicts about the curriculum of these schools. Eventually there emerged the basic curriculum of the seven liberal arts which were: the trivium, consisting of grammar, rhetoric and dialectic; and the quadrivium, consisting of arithmetic, geometry, music and astronomy. The study of Latin grammar was to enable a better understanding of holy texts to be gained and, to a large extent, this study dominated the curriculum. Music was required for church services, rhetoric for declamation and arithmetic for minor calculations. Geometry and astronomy were often neglected. Geography as such is not mentioned. Given the main objective of education at that time, namely to turn out priests and to a lesser extent officials, this is not surprising.

Towards the close of the Middle Ages, the increase in international and overseas trade, the gradual development of a middle class of merchants and the growing nationalism of language groups in Europe, led to a change in attitude towards education and the curriculum. As the influence of the Renaissance in scholarship spread, so the narrowness of the traditional curriculum tended to be seen as a barrier to further learning, and there developed a disposition to include new 'subjects' and new ideas. Often the introduction of these new ideas occurs rather through the influence of private tutors who taught the sons of the nobility or of the merchant class, than through the traditional grammar school, which was bound to the old curriculum through its association with the church. But in time the curriculum of the grammar school began to change, though in many cases one must wait until the eighteenth and nineteenth centuries before this change is very evident.

Suggestions that geography or some form of geographical study should be included in the school curriculum began to be made in the sixteenth and seventeenth centuries. These were made by scholars and others when expounding their views on education. Erasmus saw geography as useful for the understanding of history, so did Sir Thomas Elyot in his book *The Governour*. This was effectively a plea that much ancient history could not be completely comprehended without the scholar having an atlas by his side and knowing something of the regions where the events described were happening. Komensky or Comenius (1592-1670), to use the more common Latin form of his name, was keen that geography should be an introduction to what we might call today environmental study. He wanted young children to learn about their immediate environment through direct contact with it, as well as acquire knowledge of a less direct kind about the rotundity of the earth, its divisions, the oceans, seas, and their movements.

There is no evidence that these counsels were ever widely put into practice. Watson (1909) who made a study of the growth of modern subjects in English schools, found it difficult to trace a single reference to the teaching of geography, though apparently at Westminster School members of certain forms were instructed after supper (in summer only) in the finding of places on 'mappes'. Winchester College is said to have possessed a 'Mappa Mundi' in the mid-seventeenth century, though what it was used for is not stated. The present writer, when carrying out a survey on the teaching of the geography of Asia in 1967 was told by Winchester College authorities that geography was not taught there, a state of affairs which was rectified in 1975. Much of the evidence suggests that whatever geography was taught by private tutors or learnt individually through the books which were undoubtedly being published in the sixteenth and seventeenth centuries, the public and grammar schools did little or nothing to teach the subject. It is only in the eighteenth century that one begins to see some form of geography being taught in a number of schools; those which seem to stand out in England were the dissenting academies.

Geography and the dissenting academies

Until well into the eighteenth century, many new grammar schools were being founded, but these (often created by men who had risen from small beginnings to eminence and who wanted to perform an act of charity) were tied by their statutes of foundation, modelled on previous statutes, to the traditional curriculum. Further, these grammar schools were Catholic in religion and after the Reformation, Anglican. Consequently, the children of non-conformists, whose numbers had increased considerably during the seventeenth century, and who were strongly represented among the middle classes, were unable to find suitable schooling. Non-conformists, therefore, established (often under great difficulties in the days of the Restoration) schools of their own known collectively as the dissenting academies. These schools were much more open to new and 'practical' knowledge than were the grammar schools. Subjects like modern languages, history, geography and science were included in the curriculum. The level to which these subjects were taught was often higher than that of the universities.

The natural sciences were the subjects most developed by these academies and it would be wrong to suggest that geography was an important part of the curriculum. For example, in the early period of the academies' existence (1662-1691), in no more than three out of seventeen known academies is specific reference made to geography. The number of academies which taught geography rose during the eighteenth century; from 1691 to 1750 at least seven out of thirty-five taught geography, and from 1750 to 1800 the number was eleven out of twenty-three. The literature on the history of education of this period contains many references to the teaching of geography at these academies, though it is a little difficult to establish precisely what the nature of this teaching was. Clearly there seemed to be a considerable reliance on manuals of geography like *Gordon's Geography* and Dionysius' *Perigesis* (a translation of the original Greek), the latter having been in use for some considerable time among private tutors and in some grammar schools. It would appear that not until the second half of the eighteenth century, did some deliberate teaching of geography take place in such academies as the Warrington Academy where Joseph Priestley taught. Although some of the teachers did much to stimulate interest in travel and in the character of areas overseas, it would seem that the main contribution to geography teaching that the academies made was in the field of mathematical geography, that is, in teaching how latitude and longitude were derived, what the nature of such special latitudes as the Tropics and Arctic and Antarctic circles were, what a great circle was, and so on (Robinson 1951). This is understandable since the renovation of knowledge associated with the 'enlightenment' of the eighteenth century was stimulated by the development of scientific and mathematical knowledge. Unfortunately perhaps for geography in schools, the dissenting academies were closed in the nineteenth century as they were suspected of favouring revolutionary ideas. The possible development of scientific geography was, therefore, stunted.

Geography in school, 1800-1880
The position of geography in schools at the beginning of the nineteenth century was hardly an enviable one. In most schools it was not taught, and in those schools where it was taught, it amounted to little more

than a list of facts and figures to be committed to the memory. The position was exactly the same whether one considers the *elementary* schools or the *secondary* schools, (though these terms were not often used at that time) and whether one considers our neighbours in Europe or ourselves. The difference between England and Wales and, for example, France, was that in the latter country the education system, including both primary and secondary schools, was centrally controlled and the Ministry of Public Instruction did in fact prescribe the curriculum, and geography was part of it, whereas in England there was no such compulsion. However, the compulsion to teach geography in France seems not to have been enforced vigorously, for an inspection of the Lycée Louis le Grand in 1840 revealed no trace of geography teaching (Dupont de Ferrier 1922). The inspectors added the comment, 'We know this to be true of many other schools'.

It may seem strange that the state should prescribe the teaching of a subject that secondary-school teachers were apparently either unwilling or ill-equipped to teach. It would seem to have been generally accepted among officials concerned with the curriculum that no man could be called educated, if he had no knowledge of the position of various countries, of their colonies, of their chief towns, of their products, of their customs and so on. A similar attitude could be discerned in England and in the United States at the time. There the publication of a textbook written by the Reverend Jedidiah Morse in 1784 and re-issued in several editions during the first half of the nineteenth century, made possible the teaching of geography in the schools and colleges of the Union. Morse summarizes, in the preface to the 1789 edition, his views on the value of geography in education which probably represent an attitude generally held at that time.

> To discharge the duties of public office with honor and applause, the history, policy, commerce, productions, particular advantages, and interests of the several states ought to be thoroughly understood.... There is no science better adapted to the capacities of youth and more apt to captivate their attention than geography. (Morse 1789)

Of course such geography need not in itself be as captivating as Jedidiah Morse would have us believe. In fact as late as 1865 a French Ministry of Public Instruction circular to secondary school teachers bluntly states, 'Geography is a nomenclature with which it is necessary to burden the memory, and which, like all nomenclatures is quickly forgotten. Hence we make the pupils learn it twice; first in the lower

school in an elementary way, then in the upper school in more detail'
(Ministère de l'Instruction Publique 1865). Consequently in schools
where this inventory of factual information was taught, it was usual
to sugar the pill by using manuals which included doggerel verse. For
example, the dreaded capes and bays of England were made more
palatable by such verse as:

> Again taking ship, South by East if you steer,
> Both Chichester Shoals and the Selsey you'll clear,
> Here keep off the coast, lest by chance you get shocks,
> And steering for Shoreham, avoid Bognor Rocks.

(Bisset 1805)

A generally used technique was the catechism as in the following
example taken from a French text:

DÉPARTEMENT DE SEINE ET MARNE

Demande Ce département est-il fertile?
Réponse Oui, il est fertile en grains, vins et fourrages.
D Quel est le chef-lieu de préfecture?
R Melun sur la Seine. C'est la patrie de Jacques Amyot.
D Quels sont les chefs-lieux de sous-préfecture?
R Coulommiers, ville connue par ses fromages;
Meaux sur la Marne. Le choeur de l'église Cathédrale
passe pour un chef d'oeuvre.
Fontainebleau, avec un beau château et une vaste forêt;
et Provins qui fabrique des conserves de roses et de violettes.
D Quelles sont les autres villes?
R Nemours, patrie du mathématicien Bezout,
Lagny, Nangis, La Ferté-Gaucher, et la Ferté-sous-Jouarre.

(Letellier 1812)

There were many ingenious and naïve devices all used to the end of
making pupils learn the administrative divisions of France. Allévy
used:

(1) like-sounding words in a sentence placed above the facts to be
learned as in:

Avec *sa voix*   il fait un *chant*
Savoie   chef lieu Chambéry

(2) nonsense syllables which it was hoped would help the memory to
recall the equivalent facts:

al ------ gap ------- bri ------ em

Hautes-*Alpes*, chef-lieu: *Gap*

Sous-préfectures: *Briançon, Embrun*

(Allévy 1851)

The picture is not one of unrelieved gloom. In the U.S.A. and in England, textbooks began to be illustrated with maps, diagrams, and sketches, and by 1860 American books even contained reproductions of photographs. The intellectual content of some texts began to rise. In France this was evidenced by the publication of Cortambert's *Eléments de Géographie Physique* (1849) which was destined for secondary schools and was essentially a study of what we should now call systematic geography. It included a study of the earth as a planet, the relief of the earth and the causes of changes in this relief, hydrography, climatology, mineralogy, biogeography and what Cortambert called anthropo-geography, which was a description of human races and their distribution over the earth's surface. In the U.S.A. also physical geography books began to appear in the eighteen-fifties, but probably the best known was Guyot's *Physical Geography* (1873) which was 'hailed as a milestone in the teaching of high school geography' (Mayo 1965). It is probably significant that these pioneering works were to a large extent concerned with the physical aspects of geography, the only part of geography which could in any sense claim to be scientific at that time. In England the trend towards physical geography may be judged by the publication in English of Alexander von Humboldt's *Kosmos* as *Aspects of Nature* in 1847, and by Mary Somerville's *Physical Geography* in 1848. Mary Somerville was a scholar who became interested in geography and published several works of a geographical nature which proved popular. Her *Physical Geography* went into seven editions and considerably influenced contemporary teachers (Baker 1948).

The elementary schools of England began to take up geography in large numbers. The various religious bodies responsible for organizing elementary education in England set up Normal Schools (Training Colleges) and in some, geography became a popular subject. The National Society's Normal School, St John's College (later to form the College of St Mark and St John), had a lecturer in geography, W. Hughes, who proved an enthusiastic campaigner for geographical education. Not only did he turn out several generations of teachers capable of teaching geography, but he also wrote textbooks on geography and pamphlets on geographical education. Thus gradually geography became established as an accepted subject of elementary education. This process was aided by the 'Code' (a set of regulations setting up standards for elementary school instruction) first published in 1858, which laid down requirements for training pupil teachers in geography. Encouragement was given to the training colleges to teach geography when in 1851 a grant of ten shillings per student taking geography was allocated to them for the purchase of books, maps, globes and other equipment. However, it should be remembered that in spite of this growth of geography teaching, the quality of what was taught improved but slowly, and most of the manuals in use by teachers and pupils still attracted the opprobrium of the more enlightened educators. The historian J. R. Green, wrote in 1880, 'No drearier task can be set for the worst criminals than that of studying a set of geographical text-books such as the children in our schools are doomed to use.' The emphasis on memorizing factual information was still very prevalent as may be judged by the following extract from a circular to Her Majesty's Inspectors in England and Wales.

> To obtain the mark of 'good' for geography the scholars in the upper division should be required to have prepared three maps, one of which, selected by the inspector, should be drawn from memory on the day of the inspection.
> (Circular 228, 6 August, 1883, which remained in force until 1898)
> (Hart 1957)

This tradition did not die in the nineteenth century. I can still remember some of the geography lessons I had as a primary-school child in France in the early 1930s in which I had to learn the main rivers of France and their right and left bank tributaries in order from source to mouth!

A break-through in the conception of school geography (1880-1900)
In the nineteenth century ideas spread but slowly. The process of diffusion was dependent partly on oral and partly on written communication. There were no mass media in the modern sense of the term. Consequently, though examples existed of texts whose conception of geography was more in line with disciplined enquiry than with that of a gazetteer, these were read by but a few teachers, most of whom would not have had the means of purchasing many books.

What combination of circumstances then led to a blossoming of geographical education in the late nineteenth century? Perhaps the most clear-cut case is that of France. The defeat of 1871 in the Franco-Russian war had proved a considerable psychological shock to a nation which under Louis-Napoléon seemed to be re-emerging as a great power. The blame was laid in part on the educational system in general and in particular on the abysmal state of geography teaching. There came to light several cases of officers being incompetent in map reading and lacking in geographical knowledge on the field of battle. As a historian of French education put it, 'Our general staff had made gross geographical errors and misread their maps; we needed to learn geography' (Weill 1921). So the then Minister of Education, Jules Simon, commissioned Emile Levasseur and Auguste Himly to undertake an investigation of, and draw up a report on, the teaching of history and geography in France. Both subjects were to be considered since they were normally taught by the same teacher. The choice of investigators was an obvious one. Emile Levasseur had taught in various 'lycées' until 1872 when he was appointed to the Collège de France; not only was he considered an eminent scholar, but he had always had a great interest in the teaching of geography in French secondary schools, had helped to draft syllabuses and written several textbooks. Auguste Himly was chosen, no doubt, because of his official position. He was then at the Sorbonne and the only university professor of geography in France. Both investigators visited some eighty 'lycées' and 'collèges' and drew up a report (Levasseur and Himly 1871) which makes the usual references to the neglect of the subject in secondary schools, to the absence of geography specialists and to the utter futility of much of what was taught. They diagnosed the malady to be largely due to the absence of appropriately trained geography specialists because the universities (Facultés des Lettres) did not teach geography. This view was supported by Richard Cortambert (son of Eugène Cortambert) who, at the first International Geographical Congress at Antwerp in 1871, maintained that no progress in geographical education would be made until a body of geography specialists had been trained and sent to do their missionary work in the secondary schools of France (Congrès 1871).

Acting with commendable speed the Minister of Education set up a commission to draw up new syllabuses in geography for secondary schools, and these were duly published in 1872. The commission insisted however, that it was more important to have good teachers than a good syllabus. It is difficult to be certain, but circumstantial evidence points to Emile Levasseur as the one who engineered the development of geography teaching in the last quarter of the century in French secondary schools. First he had a clear idea of what he believed geography to be as a subject. His paradigm for geography was what we would now call a 'man in his environment' study. Secondly, he extolled its educational value as a discipline of mind rather than as a body of factual information. Thirdly, he campaigned for its better teaching and strongly recommended that geography as a subject should be strengthened at the prestigious Ecole Normale Supérieure where many of France's élite secondary school teachers were trained (Levasseur 1872). Indeed, it is possible that he was directly responsible for the eventual transfer of Vidal de la Blache from the chair of geography at Nancy to the Ecole Normale Supérieure in 1877, for only after that date were a large number of able and enthusiastic geography teachers trained. From that time onwards, geography developed rapidly in the French secondary school system and achieved a position of considerable prestige on the curriculum. The position had so far changed by 1905, that 200 teachers of history and geography petitioned successfully for the introduction of geography to the 'classes de philosophie et de mathématiques' (equivalent to the upper sixth form) which until then had had no geography teaching (Annales de Géographie, 1905).

In both England and the U.S.A., the absence of geography as a discipline in higher education was also blamed for its lowly state in schools. In England the Royal Geographical Society appointed John Scott Keltie to carry out an investigation similar to that undertaken in France by Levasseur and Himly. In his report (1886) Keltie reiterated the familiar tale of woe and made clear that until a body of geography specialists were trained, there could be but little progress. The Royal Geographical Society was successful in 1887 in getting the University of Oxford to establish a readership in geography, which led to the development of geography courses elsewhere and to a flowering of geographical education in some of the public and in the state grammar schools after the establishment of the latter in 1902. Again as in France, the availability of a great teacher, Halford John Mackinder, to occupy the post was probably conclusive in deciding the Oxford University authorities to set up this readership.

In the U.S.A. William Morris Davis was also pointing a finger in the same direction. He had arrived at Harvard in 1878 as an instructor in geology and by 1885 was, as assistant professor of physical geography, proselytizing students to accept an evolutionary view of geography or physiography. But he was conscious that until geography was generally taught at the higher education level it would make little impact in schools. 'There can be no question that the neglect of geography as a subject for mature study has had and still has an injurious effect upon the condition of geography in the schools' (Davis 1902). The situation in the U.S.A. was, however, different from that in England and France. Geography was a popular subject in the high schools by the end of the nineteenth century, but it lacked academic rigour and was generally taught as an elective course for part of a school year. Consequently the National Education Association, a body concerned with the study of education which had set up a 'Committee of Ten' to report on the secondary school curriculum in 1892, decided to look into the situation of geography. The committee which examined geographical studies included W. M. Davis, and perhaps not unnaturally, the recommendations made concerned physical geography rather than geography as a whole. These were that physical geography should be taught in the late grammar school and early high school and that physiography should be taught in the later high school years, physiography being a more advanced form of geomorphology, though it was also to include oceanography. There seemed to be an attempt, first to raise the status of physical geography to the same level as that held by Latin and mathematics, and secondly to include in physical geography elements of botany, zoology and meteorology.

The Committee of Ten of the National Education Association's report in 1894 was considered to be authoritative and many of its recommendations were put into practice. As a result, the teaching of physical geography reached its peak in the decade following the publication of the report. One of the most important factors reinforcing this was the acceptance of physical geography as a college admission subject by the College Entrance Examination Board, a body which examined for entry to America's most sought after universities (Rosen 1957). This meant that physical geography could be considered on a par with other subjects with respect to university entrance. In England, on the other hand, when J. S. Keltie had enquired of the headmasters of 'public schools' why geography was not taught, many replied with the down to earth observation that the study of geography would not get their students into universities.

The change which occurred in school geography towards the end of the nineteenth century can be attributed to a combination of circumstances. There was an organized 'geographical lobby' in the form of the Royal Geographical Society in England, or in the form of small pressure groups which were influential in government circles in France.

But in both England and France, the growing consciousness of the existence of a colonial empire and of the growth in overseas trade, predisposed the community as a whole to believe that geographical education could be of practical value in terms of the knowledge and map reading skills it conveyed. At the same time in both countries, though earlier in France than in England, the conception of geography as a study of the relationship between man and his physical environment was becoming generally accepted and as a result of pressure from the 'lobbies', was being developed in the universities. Thus gradually the basis for the sound development of geographical education in the schools was being established, and by the outbreak of the first world war, geography was a growing part of the curriculum of secondary schools in both countries. Associations of secondary school teachers of geography had also been formed, the Geographical Association in 1893 and the 'Société des professeurs d'histoire et de géographie de l'enseignement secondaire public' in 1910. In the U.S.A., the situation was somewhat different in that the conception of physical geography which held sway in the early years of the twentieth century was a Kantian one (*see* Chapter 2), namely that physical geography could provide an introduction to the physical and biological sciences. This was to have consequences which made the subsequent history of geographical education in the U.S.A. very different from that in France and England.

The consolidation of geographical education in schools (1900-1965)
The growth of geography teaching in the twentieth century in the schools of England and Wales was little short of spectacular. Once the basic shortage of geography specialists had been overcome, the obstacles which remained to be surmounted were of lesser moment. And undoubtedly the shortage began to disappear. After Oxford had given the lead, various other universities followed suit. It began to be possible to read for degrees in geography at Liverpool University in 1917, at London in 1919 and subsequently other universities or university colleges fell into line. Until the outbreak of the second world war, the growth in the output of geography graduates was steady but not large, and supply still fell short of demand (I.A.A.M. 1939). With the expansion of the universities after 1945, not only were many new geography departments created, but existing ones expanded so that the number of honours graduates in geography turned out each year

rose from about 700 in the mid 1950s to about 1300 in the late 1960s. Only a few new universities like Kent and Warwick had no departments of geography. Thus while not all graduates in geography went into teaching, the supply of potential teachers of geography increased considerably during the period under consideration. The supply of such graduates also increased as polytechnics began to develop departments of geography reading for London University external degrees and C.N.A.A. degrees.

Further, with the setting up of local education authority secondary schools following the Education Act of 1902, the universities began to develop their departments of education as 'training departments' for graduates intending to teach. Since secondary school teachers were in general specialists, appointments began to be made to lectureships in *methods* of teaching various subjects, among which were lecturers in geography method. Hence geographical education was often being developed by two university departments, the geography department and the education department. Some of the lecturers in geography method began to be very influential in schools through their advocacy of particular teaching procedures or strategies, or of particular aspects of geography. Thus R. L. Archer (Professor of Education at University College, Bangor) wrote with two colleagues a textbook on *The Teaching of Geography in Elementary Schools* (1910) in which he sought to put over the thesis that geography should be taught in the spirit indicated by the works of Mackinder and Herbertson, as a man-environment study. In 1926 James Fairgrieve, then at the London Day Training College (later the University of London Institute of Education) produced his celebrated *Geography in School* which was to be the bible of many young geography graduates about to embark on a career in secondary schools.

Fairgrieve's work probably best illustrates the kind of geographical education which was in the ascendency in the inter-war years and in the twenty years following the second world war. He was a mathematics graduate who became interested in geography and began teaching it in schools in Scotland and later in London. In 1912 he was appointed to the London Day Training College to provide courses in geography method for aspiring secondary school teachers. He began from the standpoint that geography's function was to study man in his environment, but he was very concerned with the way in which this idea was put over to children and adolescents. He firmly believed in what we would now call the inductive method, that is in starting from the particular fact or facts and attempting to get pupils to see any trends or tendencies and work out any generalizations. He felt that to use a deductive method was not only to get away from the *'reality'* of geography but that it was also pedagogically inefficient since children found this difficult and uncongenial. This initial stance led to a good many features which are characteristic of geography in schools during that period. First, since the noting or observation of 'reality' was the first step, there developed a considerable vogue for field work in geography. This was not new, since Geikie in his book on the teaching of geography had advocated it in 1887, but it began to be taken up by a number of enthusiastic teachers in the years before World War II, either as local geography or as more distant school journeys. Many schools collaborated in the first British Land Use Survey organized in the inter-war years by L. D. Stamp. The vogue for field work reached a climax in the 1960s when some Certificate of Secondary Education examining boards made it a quasi-compulsory element in the geography course. Secondly, since 'reality' could not always be observed at first hand, it had to be observed vicariously. It was, therefore, necessary to provide pupils and teachers with pictures, slides, films and other audio-visual aids to learning. Fairgrieve himself pioneered the use of the silent film in the teaching of geography and the publication of sets of 'geographical pictures'. Thirdly, in order that information about other areas of the world should appear to be meaningful to children and adolescents, it was important to provide sample or case studies of farms, factories, villages or even of communications, with a good measure of human interest (Robeson and Long 1956). Again, Fairgrieve led the way by writing a series of books called *Real Geography* in collaboration with Ernest Young. This case study technique became so well established that only a small proportion of teachers of geography did not use it in the 1960s, and several books of such case studies became available for classroom use (e.g. the *Study Geography* series, by Bell, Dybeck and Rushby, 1967). Fourthly, since the 'reality' to be studied was rooted in 'real' areas on the earth's surface, the unit of study was the region. This seemed to accord well with the use of Herbertson's natural regions, the existence of which in school textbooks we have already noted in Chapter 2, and with the prevalent occupation with regional geography of many university teachers of geography in the inter-war years. Thus typically, the boy or girl learning geography in that period would be following a regional syllabus, the teacher would emphasize the human geography of the areas studied by using audio-visual aids and sample studies, whilst the physical aspects of landscape and climate would be treated incidentally as they arose in the regions covered by the syllabus. Although no official enquiry was undertaken to find out what was the situation of geography teaching in schools in England and Wales during the period under consideration, two sample surveys carried out in 1960 and 1967 seemed to indicate that the picture given above was substantially true in the nineteen-sixties (Hogan 1962, Graves 1968) and that, as the study of man-land relationships, geography was probably more widely and better taught than at any other time in the history of its existence as a subject in the school curriculum. There were, inevitably, many schools where geography teaching was still a 'burden on the memory rather than a light in the mind'.

There were, however, two related but divergent tendencies which appeared in the period after World War II. The first was the social studies movement. To understand this movement it is necessary for us to return to our consideration of the situation of geography teaching in the U.S.A. We saw that at the beginning of the twentieth century, under the influence of W. M. Davis, geography as taught in the high school became essentially physical geography as an introduction to science. But such courses competed with the general science courses put on by physicists, chemists and biologists, and ultimately the science courses proved more attractive to the students. Gradually physical geography began to disappear from the secondary school curriculum though courses in commercial geography remained popular. By the 1930s only a few schools still ran courses in physical geography and by the 1940s the subject was no longer acceptable to the College Entrance Examinations Board. Parallel with this decline in physical geography, was a growth in social studies as a subject in American high schools. This was very much in line with the development of a curriculum relevant to the needs of young Americans and not necessarily based on traditional scholarly subjects (Wesley 1942). The human aspect of geography tended to become absorbed into such social studies courses so that geography as an independent subject all but disappeared from the American high school scene (James 1969). Now the American high school was a comprehensive or non-selective school, and to some extent afforded a model for the English post-World War II secondary modern and comprehensive school. Further, the then current ethos of secondary education for all in England, was to emphasize education for democracy and citizenship, to stress the importance of fitting the child to the society in which he was to work. Hence the attempt to develop a species of social studies for the non-selective schools of England and Wales by combining history, geography and civics. It is difficult to be certain of how extensive the movement towards social studies was in the 1940s and 1950s since no survey was made to ascertain this. Williams (1963) states that in the early 1960's it was still alive. But it is clear that geographers in England did not take kindly to it, just as professional geographers in the U.S.A. refused to cooperate in the 1920s with social scientists in developing a geographical component to the social studies courses (James 1969). Both the Royal Geographical Society and the Geographical Association were hostile to social studies. The R.G.S. published a pamphlet (1950) defending the position of geography in the curriculum and the G.A. published an article in *Geography* showing that American experience in social studies was not a happy one for geography (Scarfe 1950).

The second tendency was possibly initiated by S. W. Wooldridge, professor of geography at King's College, London, who wrote an article called 'On taking the Ge out of geography' (Wooldridge 1949) which was an attack on social studies and on the limited teaching of physical geography in secondary schools.

As I was teaching in schools during the period which followed Wooldridge's article, I was very conscious of the impact which his ideas made on many teachers of geography, particularly as he was very active in the Geographical Association. Wooldridge argued that geography was about place, not about man, that physical factors were as important as non-physical ones in shaping human activities, and that since children grew up in a physical as well as a cultural landscape, they were entitled to learn about the former as well as the latter. He felt that the neglect of physical geography was in part due to the innate difficulties of some of its concepts, to the attempt by many teachers to cover the world regionally in five years, which left little time for physical geography, but particularly to the influence of those in university departments of education and in the training colleges who advocated that the teaching of physical geography should be incidental to the teaching of regional geography. He further averred that he conceived of geography as being bound by 'the concentric circles of neighbourhood, home region, country and world', suggesting that school geography might well be considered at these four scales. It is significant that, some three years later, the

Geographical Association produced a pamphlet entitled *Geography in Secondary Schools* (Briault and Shave 1952) in which a concentric type of syllabus was advocated on the lines adumbrated by Wooldridge.

Whatever the rights and wrongs of teaching social studies in secondary schools, there is little doubt that the movement made little headway in the climate of opinion current in the 1950s and 1960s. Most geographers and historians (Burston 1962) tended to be against such teaching and had no wish to lose their identity as subject specialists.

As was pointed out earlier, the expansion of British universities made possible the staffing of geography and history departments in the secondary schools, so that the integration of departments was unnecessary for staffing purposes. Further, as experiments in social studies tended to be made in secondary modern schools and with the 'less able' classes, it had little chance of becoming a prestige subject in the English education system (Cannon 1964). The pressure from vocal sociology graduates to introduce some aspects of sociology in schools was not yet very strong and economics and constitutional law and practice (British Constitution) were usually taught as sixth-form courses only. The consequence was that geography teaching continued in the Fairgrievian tradition with two modifications. The first was that the secondary grammar and other 'academic' schools began to pay more attention to geomorphology as an aspect of physical geography (Marchant 1964), particularly in the sixth form. This led an American critic to feel that there was in English syllabuses an over-emphasis on physical geography (Rogers 1968). The second was that in many of the then developing secondary comprehensive schools, experiments were being carried out with non-regional syllabuses, especially with the concentric type syllabus. By 1964, the year when the 20th International Geographical Congress was held in London, geography in English and Welsh schools seemed in a healthy state. Nearly all pupils studied the subject in the first three years of the secondary schools, and a majority carried on studying it in the fourth and fifth years. Of all pupils who sat for the O level examination (c. 16-year old level) approximately twenty per cent of all candidates took geography as a subject. Considering that these are single-subject examinations and that there is no compulsory grouping of subjects, the position was a very satisfactory one. Further, a new examination, the Certificate of Secondary Education, was to be launched in 1965 to cater for a proportion of the pupils who did not sit for the O level examination. Again the regional boards set up to administer this examination included geography as one of the subjects to be offered. Compared with the situation in U.S. schools, geography was flourishing in Britain.

The crisis in geographical education in Britain (1965 onwards)

The apparent serenity of the geographical education scene was to be shattered by changes which were occurring within academic geography, within educational theory and within the structure of the education system. It is perhaps an exaggeration to use the word crisis to describe the situation which ensued, but it is intended to convey the idea that those involved were not sure of where they were going, that a certain amount of confusion existed about the philosophy and objectives of geographical education and that no clear consensus emerged in the years immediately following 1965. The catalytic agents which provoked the crisis were, as we saw towards the end of Chapter 2, a number of young university teachers of geography who had sojourned for some time in the American university departments of geography and had been fired by the developments in geographic knowledge which broke loose from the more traditional view of geography as the explanatory description of landscapes. They communicated these ideas through teachers' courses and conferences and through the publication of *Frontiers in Geographical Teaching* in 1965. Many who taught in the selective grammar and public schools had for some time been aware that much of school geography, exciting though it might be for the younger pupils, proved less challenging intellectually for the older students. Indeed, one of the reasons why the teaching of geomorphology developed in secondary schools was precisely because it was deemed to offer more thought-provoking content than human geography. These teachers then began to espouse the cause of the 'conceptual revolution' in geography and advocated the greater use of quantitative techniques, models and other attributes of the new geography. The first schools to be significantly affected were the public schools since the Oxford and Cambridge examining board which catered for them modified its A level geography syllabus in order to bring it into line with what was considered to be appropriate content; namely systematic aspects of geography with a growing emphasis on human geography and in particular urban analysis, and on techniques of investigation including such quantitative tools as the coefficients of correlation, the chi-square test, and the nearest neighbour statistic.

The overwhelming majority of teachers of geography found it difficult at first to accept the view put forward by the innovators. Many did not grasp the significance of the changes proposed, others felt that such changes were appropriate to university geography but inappropriate at the school level. Yet others argued that the emphasis on theoretical geography would nullify the attempts which they had made to teach the so-called 'real geography', whilst a vocal number averred that geography had always drawn its school recruits in the sixth form from those on the arts rather than on the science side, and that if the subject became too scientific, this would put off most potential customers. Gradually over the years, attitudes began to change. It is probably true that today a large number of teachers of geography accept the need for a body of theory to underpin human geography and are prepared to introduce the teaching of such theory in the upper age groups of the secondary school. Similarly, it is probably true that the innovators are now less insistent than they once were on the teaching of statistical techniques, since many of these are unduly laborious unless desk calculators or a computer terminal are available. The example set by the units of study produced by the American High School Geography Project (Graves 1968) helped to convince teachers that the new geography had something to offer. Although the project was designed for conditions in the United States, it suggested various fundamental changes in approach which could be tried in the United Kingdom, such as the greater use of hypothetical cases and simulation techniques to highlight the issues involved in, say, a decision about the location of a manufacturing plant. The insistence in the past that only real cases be considered, often so complicated the problem as to make it too difficult to deal with honestly at the secondary school level. The use of a hypothetical case makes it easier for students to grasp the principles involved (Naish 1974).

The second change which was to affect geographical education was the growth in education theory, particularly in so far as it concerned curriculum development. Again from the U.S.A. there developed a body of normative theory, that is, theory about what the school curriculum should be and how it ought to be structured. This will be dealt with in some detail in Chapter 6, but suffice it to say here that the work of Tyler (1949), and Taba (1962) had some impact and resulted in new thinking about the curriculum which was to influence experiment and practice in England. In particular, projects financed first by the Nuffield Foundation and then by the Schools Council were launched to give the teaching of some school subjects a new look as in Nuffield Science and the Schools Council Project, Geography for the Young School Leaver, and also projects to promote curriculum integration such as the Integrated Studies Project based on Keele University. It was the latter type of project which caused a good deal of confusion among teachers in general and teachers of geography in particular. It had long been appreciated that in the study of a 'real-life' problem, for example, the building of a bridge across an arm of a harbour, a multi-disciplinary approach was required since no one subject was capable of providing answers to all the questions posed. But how a curriculum could be conceived and articulated on the basis of such topics or problems had not been effectively demonstrated. Attempts were, therefore, made by some teachers to integrate geography with other subjects, while others held back not knowing precisely where such experiments would lead. The Goldsmiths' College Curriculum Laboratory launched a hybrid system known as the four-fold curriculum in which some straight subject teaching was to be combined with inter-disciplinary enquiry (James 1968), though the extent to which its ideas were taken up was limited. The traditional subject curriculum was also being disturbed through the attempts of some social scientists to claim a place for some aspects of sociology, anthropology, and psychology on the time-table. Consequently geography as a subject was in danger of being squeezed out of the curriculum through the development of integrated studies on the one hand and social science on the other.

The third change was that of the reorganization of secondary education. Although several local education authorities were, in the nineteen-fifties, reorganizing their secondary schools along comprehensive lines, it was not until the Labour Government produced in 1965 its famous circular 10/65 indicating that it was national policy to develop secondary comprehensive education, that various local authorities began producing appropriate plans. Gradually plans were put into effect and secondary education in many areas was transformed from a selective to a non-selective system. Since few education authorities were in a position to build a complete set of brand-new schools, various mergers between grammar and secondary modern schools took place often using two separate buildings. Many problems resulted: in administration, in controlling large bodies of adolescents, in welding together differing traditions, in getting teachers who had only taught the most able children to deal with the full range of ability. These problems were so pressing that priority was given to solving them and teachers concentrated on what seemed difficult social situations rather than on developing the teaching of particular curriculum subjects. Conditions were, therefore, not ideal for pursuing intellectual innovation within the geography curriculum, though some teachers attempted it. To many it seemed clear, nevertheless, that the traditional curriculum could not remain unaltered, indeed, that no curriculum or syllabus could stand still for any length of time. The social and intellectual climate was too dynamic to permit of an ossified curriculum. The problem was: how to dynamize the curriculum?

CHAPTER FOUR

Geography in the Structure of Knowledge

Introduction

The aim of this chapter is certainly not to give a definitive answer to the oft-posed question 'What is geography?', but to attempt to clarify some of the issues involved in attempting to answer it. As long as man has thought and expressed his thinking in language, he has tried to classify his experience of the world into various types of knowledge. The labels that have been used have varied from civilization to civilization and according to the main preoccupations of the people concerned. The Eskimo was much preoccupied with making a living in an environment that for most of the year was cold and ice- or snow-covered. It is not surprising that his knowledge and language reflected his concern to survive in such an environment. The Kalahari Bushman's knowledge was of a different kind and so was his language. The civilizations of the Middle East and of the Mediterranean, as we saw in Chapter 2, acquired a knowledge of their environment which led not only to the development of concepts relating to concrete objects and actions, but also to ideas of an abstract kind, such as those concerned with mathematical relationships, with morality or ethics, and with politics. The Greeks, as we have seen, were responsible for coining the word *geography*. The words mathematics, ethics, politics, geography, suggest that for practical purposes we accept that knowledge can be classified into various categories which are meaningful to most people. But these words do not tell us on what basis such a classification is made, whether the same criteria are used for all sub-divisions of knowledge or whether different criteria apply to different sorts of groupings of knowledge. Indeed, the debate about the nature of geography has often been about the sort of criteria used for defining its knowledge content. We need to start, therefore, by examining more closely what we mean by knowledge and how we can classify it.

Knowledge and its classification

It would be pretentious in a book of this kind to tackle in depth problems which have puzzled philosophers for centuries. Nevertheless since we are concerned with knowledge, we cannot escape from some consideration of the nature of knowledge and of our grounds for believing that we have knowledge of ourselves and of our environment. Indeed, we found ourselves to some extent involved in the debate about epistemology when we considered Kant's view of knowledge (Chapter 2).

The word epistemology was suggested by J. F. Ferrier, a Scottish philosopher, in 1854 and has gained general acceptance among English-speaking philosophers as an alternative to the phrase 'theory of knowledge'. However, the sort of questions posed by epistemological enquiry long preceded any label given to it since men have always asked fundamental questions concerning the nature of and grounds for knowledge. The kind of questions asked were whether knowledge was something which existed externally to man, but which man apprehended gradually through the exercise of his mental powers; whether knowledge on the contrary was merely a creation of human minds; whether such a creation was simply based on man's use of his reason or whether it was based on his perception of an external reality, that is, based on experience of the external environment; whether it was a combination of man's view of experience and of the transformation of this experience by his rationality.

Such questions were inevitably further provoked by the development of knowledge and by the tendency for knowledge to become differentiated into what are now generally called, rather loosely, subjects. At first, all those who sought knowledge, whatever its form, were called philosophers, a connotation analogous to that of scholar or 'savant' at the present time. Hence philosophy covered all knowledge. Gradually the noun 'philosophy' began to be given an adjective, so that scholars studied moral philosophy or natural philosophy (science), or even mental philosophy (psychology). This was a recognition that the accumulating store of knowledge could not simply be placed under one heading, but seemed capable of subdivision. Subdivisions which had a great influence on epistemological thinking were those which were manifest in the development of mathematics, for example, in Newton's differential and integral calculus, in the growth of physical science, in the expansion of biological knowledge, in the inception of the social sciences in the form of economics and sociology. The apparently close relationship between mathematics and the 'laws' of physics led to the debate between the empiricists and those who favoured pure reason as the basis for all knowledge. But these arguments about fundamental ways of knowing did not in themselves resolve the problem of how subjects within the totality of knowledge came to be differentiated, unless it could be argued that some were based on one way of knowing, e.g. mathematics through reason only, and others on a different way of knowing, e.g. chemistry through experience and experiment. However, it is now generally accepted by philosophers, that such a fundamental difference does not exist, that all knowledge is partly empirical and partly derived from reasoning about experience.

Philosophers interested in epistemology have, however, concentrated their attention on the nature of particular subjects. They have attempted to prise out what is essentially distinctive about a subject; what, for example, is peculiar about the way knowledge is acquired, that is about its methodology, or about the nature of the concepts used in the subject. Examples of such work may be found in Braithwaite's *Scientific Explanation* (1960), in Collingwood's *The Idea of History* (1946), in Brown's *Explanation in Social Science* (1963). It is perhaps as well to point out that not all who write on aspects of epistemology are necessarily professional philosophers. Or if they have become *de facto* philosophers, they may have started as scientists or historians or economists and developed a deep interest in what are generally called the methodological problems of their subject. Thus in geography, Hartshorne (1939, 1959) and Harvey (1969) have turned their attention to such problems, though a large number of geographers have written more or less briefly on the nature of geography from Ritter to L. D. Stamp, in fact there was a time when almost every inaugural address by a new professor of geography consisted of his own, often highly idiosyncratic, view of what geography was really about.

The question which we are seeking to answer, namely, is there a fundamental way in which knowledge may be classified, might be resolved if we examine what has been said by the so-called 'philosophers' of science, of history, of the social sciences, or of geography. Unfortunately, such an examination may show that such enquiries were not all made with the same purposes in mind and what has been revealed is disparate both within the disciplines and between them. Thus, some see history as the study of the factors leading to a unique event or situation (Oakeshott 1933), whilst others see in history the operation of certain covering laws and broad tendencies, as in the more obvious case of Toynbee, or in the evidence provided by the publication of the periodical *History and Theory*. In other words, some historians would argue that historical explanation does not in any way resemble scientific explanation, whilst others maintain that there is very little difference between them. W. H. Burston brings these differences out in his book *Principles of History Teaching* (1963). Similar disagreement exists about the difference between those who see social science as being basically the same structurally as physical science and those who aver that there is a gulf between them which is unbridgeable.

The implication of this seems to be that if we are searching for criteria to distinguish various subjects from one another by seeking clear-cut distinctions about the modes of explanation enunciated by the philosophers of the subjects concerned, then we shall be disappointed and perhaps muddled. The real problem is that in attempting to classify knowledge we have not specified the purpose for which we are going to use the classification. Thus it may well be that access to knowledge by an educational institution is best served by one type of classification, whilst the epistemologist with his concern for fundamentals is best served by a different classification. The suggestion is that knowledge need not necessarily be organized in the same semi-permanent boxes. It is already clear that in practical life knowledge is allocated to classifications which are different from those used in school. Thus what belongs to physics in school may be classed as civil engineering or electrical engineering in the workaday world. What is biology in school may form part of agricultural knowledge in the farming world. What may be taught under geography at school may form part of navigational knowledge for a seaman.

Clearly, what we are concerned with is the classification of knowledge within the context of education, or with what sociologists have called 'educational knowledge' (Bernstein 1971). In this context, we can observe that knowledge has been divided into such categories as mathematics, English, physical science, biological science, history, geography, art and craft, technical drawing, physical education, home economics, and so on. Such a subdivision of knowledge, within the state system of education, is largely a reflection of what society, through its political authority, thought it was desirable that children and adolescents should learn, either for practical reasons (e.g. making good housewives) or for cultural reasons (e.g. a cultured person should have an appreciation of art). Now in so doing, teachers and education authorities have accepted some 'subjects' as they have been developed by scholars at a higher level (e.g. physics), and some which are essentially a collection of precepts and practices which are means of developing certain skills or habits in pupils (e.g. home economics). Although the merits of including this or that subject in the curriculum has often been hotly debated, this has been on the basis of the contribution of the subject to the pupil's general education, rather than on the question of whether such a subject had a rightful place in a fundamental structure of knowledge. Thus even if we look at the classification of subjects within the context of the school, it is difficult to argue that any purpose-built classification exists, except perhaps in the case of arts and crafts, physical education, home economics, which were subjects clearly devised to serve the purpose of the school.

Sociological perspectives

Recently some sociologists have focused their attention on knowledge and particularly on 'educational knowledge'. If I understand them correctly, they reiterate the point already made by philosophers that knowledge cannot be considered as having an existence of its own, but that it simply represents a creation of the human mind. To take an obvious example, lines of longitude and latitude do not exist as such but men have agreed to accept the mental concept of a graticule as useful and convenient to human purposes. In other words the nature and classification of knowledge is problematical. They further argue that no knowledge is independent of the social forces which created it, so that whether this type or that type of knowledge developed, is determined by the values placed on such knowledge by groups holding power in a society. In early nineteenth-century England, for example, the landed aristocracy, if it valued knowledge at all, tended to value knowledge of the dead languages and their associated literature. In the late nineteenth century power had somewhat shifted to those who were in charge of industry and commerce and the knowledge valued tended to be that required for the higher positions in management and the professions. Such a view of the relationship between power and valued knowledge also implies a view of the relative status of various types of knowledge. Thus the valued knowledge required by those in power and their associates is seen as high status knowledge, whilst other knowledge which might be of use to clerks and manual workers is seen as low status knowledge. Thus, while access to various types of knowledge is nominally available to all, high status knowledge is only available to those who are able to attend those institutions which purvey it and access to such institutions is restricted (Young 1971).

Another aspect of the sociology of knowledge is the idea that the development of specialized knowledge (i.e. subjects, or disciplines) creates a group of practitioners with vested interests in such knowledge. Consequently these will create a certain mystique around this knowledge and attempt to isolate it from other aspects of knowledge. A curriculum composed of subjects of this sort will tend to be relatively rigid or 'closed' in the sense that subjects will tend to be isolated one from the other. This collection-type curriculum (Bernstein 1971) is contrasted with the more 'open' or 'integrated' type of curriculum in which the boundaries between subjects are less firmly drawn.

What is the relevance of this to geographical education? First it is clear that geography has moved from being a low status subject taught only in elementary schools, to a higher status subject taught in secondary and higher education, though it has not yet achieved the prestige of mathematics or natural science. How this can be explained in terms of the power structure of society is more problematical. It might be argued that the rise of geography may be associated with the influence of the merchant and military classes in society, especially the latter whose influence in the Royal Geographical Society in England was strong. Secondly, although geography as a subject is equally accessible to low and high status pupils (with some exceptions), it is probably true that the kind of geography taught in low status schools is very different from that taught in some of the prestige schools. Social forces acting on the educational system do not ensure equality of opportunity to study modern intellectually stimulating geography to all pupils. Thirdly the extent to which geography may be taught in an integrated curriculum or in a collection type of curriculum will depend on the status of the school or class within the school: the higher the status the more likely is geography to be taught as a separate subject.

Such an analysis of the way curricula are differentiated in schools is undoubtedly illuminating but it does not answer the normative question as to the criteria which ought to be used to plan curricula. If, however, the thesis that 'educational knowledge' is determined by the power structure of society is accepted, then it may be interesting to speculate what the changing social relations in a country may do to the geography curriculum in the future. Will the increasing democratization of social relations and education lead to a more open curriculum in which students may have the greater power of deciding whether or not they will incorporate geographical knowledge in their studies?

Planning curricula is part of a sociological process but one in which there is some degree of freedom to act. Even if mathematics, physical science, history and geography are classifications of knowledge brought about by a particular kind of society, they are organizations of knowledge which have existed for a long time and which have been taken up by schools. What is it that has resulted in these areas of knowledge being classified as separate subjects?

A fundamental structure of knowledge?

To such a question there appears to be a series of commonsense answers. Mathematics is concerned with quantifiable relationships, history is concerned with describing and explaining past events, physical science is the description and explanation of certain material phenomena, geography describes and explains the character of areas on the earth's surface, and so on. Such a commonsense view requires elaboration, particularly as some teachers and educationists have argued that fundamental differences between 'subjects' do not really exist and that therefore the school curriculum should be integrated, that is, learning should go on not in lessons clearly devoted to one subject or another, but in 'integrated studies' which allow pupils to learn whatever they can from the topics put before them. Any division of knowledge is held to be basically artificial (Naish 1972).

Phenix (1964) in the U.S.A. has argued that education is a process whereby people acquire understandings or 'meanings' and that these may be designated into six groups which he calls 'symbolics, empirics, aesthetics, synnoetics, ethics and synoptics'. '*Symbolics*' is a realm of meaning on which most others depend, since it comprises the understanding of symbols used in ordinary language, in mathematics and in gestures and rituals. These symbols are arbitrary but socially accepted and sanctioned. In some cases the symbols have currency only in some linguistic areas, such as the English language, in others the symbols are internationally understood as in mathematics. *'Empirics'* is the term used to describe the physical, biological and social sciences, since these all rely on scientific method and accept certain rules for the verification of the meanings which they propound. *'Aesthetics'* is concerned with the meanings to be found in contemplation of the arts and music. *'Synnoetics'*, a term derived by Phenix from Greek roots, denotes a kind of knowledge of objects and persons, arrived at through personal experience, but of an intuitive, rather than a rational nature. *'Ethics'* denotes moral meanings, in which what is important is the development of the idea of what ought to be done in personal conduct. *'Synoptics'* comprises those fields of knowledge which according to Phenix combine or integrate other meanings, for example, philosophy, religion and history. Phenix places geography in 'empirics' though he believes it also has strong integrative tendencies. In the United Kingdom, Hirst (1965), who was concerned with the fundamental basis of a liberal education, has argued fairly convincingly that knowledge may be subdivided into fundamental 'forms' independently of the ultimate use to which this knowledge is put. In other words, whatever divisions of knowledge may be practically useful in everyday life, there exists a division of knowledge which is inherent in what we call knowledge. The argument runs as follows. Our minds have over the millennia perceived our experiences in particular ways. In so far as we have been able to communicate with one another through language and other symbolic means, we represent this experience by concepts which have agreed meanings. Thus we call our main source of energy the sun, our most abundant liquid water; we refer to certain sound impressions as music, we denote certain movements of fluids as convection currents, and so on. This is a system of public, generally agreed meanings different from private meanings or impressions peculiar to one individual and not generally shared or understood. Now, the argument runs, our conceptual formulation of our experiences has evolved along lines which have become progressively differentiated. That is, certain experiences have led us to formulate concepts which belong to an inter-related group, fundamentally distinct from another such group of concepts. For example, the ideas of mass, volume and density or specific gravity are inter-related concepts in a subject we generally call physics, as are the interconnected ideas of potential difference (measured in volts), current (measured in amperes) and resistance or impedance (measured in ohms). These concepts, it is argued, have no relationship with, say, the concepts of economic rent, marginal utility, or social costs used in economics, or with those of goodness, right and wrong, as used in ethics.

The concepts within each 'form of knowledge' are not only related to one another by what has been called the logical grammar of that form of knowledge, but the propositions relating the concepts to one another have tests for truth which are characteristic of that form of knowledge. In mathematics, the tests for truth are those that insist that any conclusion to a proposition must be shown to be logically consistent in a step-by-step analysis with the axioms agreed upon. It is not sufficient to feel intuitively that a solution to a problem is 'correct'. In physical science the tests for truth lie in the experimental verification of a hypothesis. Here a logical demonstration of a truth will not normally be acceptable until it has been demonstrated experimentally to be so. Thus, though Hertz had predicted the existence of radio waves, his formulation remained an unverified hypothesis until such a time as radio waves were detected experimentally. In other forms of knowledge, the characteristic tests for truth are not so simply stated by Hirst and many have doubted that they differ fundamentally from those for mathematics and science. In fact, one critic has suggested that there is only one universal test for truth, namely whether a proposition is verifiable logically or through experience. However, it is true that specialists in the realms of aesthetics and theology might claim tests for truths in their subjects which go beyond logic and beyond the sort of sensual experience referred to earlier. It might, of course, be argued, that the word 'truth' takes a different meaning in the latter context.

Hirst's contention that knowledge has a fundamental structure has forced him to specify the components of this structure and to match these with what may be found in the reality of the education 'industry'. Inevitably since his argument is that forms of knowledge have evolved over time, the list of such forms must be open-ended with respect to the future. Even his present list has changed somewhat over the recent past. In 1965 (Hirst) it consisted of physical science, mathematics, history, aesthetics, ethics, theology, and the human sciences. Later in 1970 (Hirst and Peters) it consisted of mathematics, physical science, interpersonal knowledge, ethics, aesthetics, theology and philosophy.

It is perhaps not surprising that a subject like history is one that Hirst hesitates over, given the disagreement among historians as to what is fundamental about historical explanation. When it comes to geography, however, Hirst consistently omits it from the list of 'forms of knowledge', in the same way as he omits such subjects as engineering, architecture, medicine. The basis for this omission is that these subjects do not have concepts of their own or characteristic tests for truth peculiar to themselves, but are in one sense parasitic in that they borrow concepts from the forms of knowledge and use the appropriate tests for truth. For example, geography, it is argued, has no concepts which were created within geography and relate to one another in a logical grammar. The concepts used in geography are all borrowed from geology, meteorology, economics, psychology and so on. A test for truth in geomorphology is different from a test for truth in political geography. Therefore, unlike Kant who saw geography as one of the fundamental subdivisions of knowledge, Hirst sees it as a compendium made up of much more fundamental forms of knowledge. For subjects like geography, education, architecture and medicine, Hirst uses the term 'fields of knowledge'. They are seen to be specially contrived assemblages of knowledge to deal with particular sets of problems in human experience: education with the problems of rearing, training and teaching mainly the younger members of society; architecture with the problems of building design and construction; medicine with the problem of the care of the human body. But what of geography? Could it be a field whose special concern is the problem of spatial organization?

Geography as a field of knowledge
If one accepts the fundamental structure of knowledge postulated by Hirst, then one can admit that geography as a present body of knowledge fits a 'field' more than a 'form' of knowledge. Indeed, the examination of a number of contributions to geography, whether as substantive works or as research articles, will tend to reveal the multi-form nature of the ideas used (Graves and Moore 1972). There are, however, a number of difficulties about accepting Hirst's ideas on 'forms of knowledge'. In the first place, we have seen that different tests for truth are more difficult to specify when we consider such forms as social science, history and aesthetics, than when we consider mathematics and physical science. In the second place, it is seldom true that a form of knowledge is so

pure that its concepts are unique to that form. Some concepts are of such a high level of generality that they are applicable to several forms of knowledge; for example, the concept of 'node' finds an application in mathematics, in physics, in social science, in biological science and of course in the field of geography. Thirdly, mathematical concepts or operations so pervade other forms of knowledge that it is difficult to maintain that the concepts concerned are in a sense 'pure'. For example, most concepts in physics which go beyond simple observational statements tend to be defined in terms of relationships of a mathematical nature. Density is mass divided by volume. Force is the product of mass and acceleration. Is the concept of an isotherm, invented by Humboldt in the early nineteenth century, a purely mathematical concept? The idea of measuring the elasticity of demand in economics by means of a relationship of the nature $\dfrac{y}{x} \cdot \dfrac{dx}{dy}$ is another case in point. Hirst argues that in such cases mathematics plays a purely ancillary role. Yet without the mathematics, many concepts would be very difficult to define with any degree of precision. The language of mathematics appears to be essential to the formulation of concepts and relationships in a number of forms or fields of knowledge.

The limitations of Hirst's conception of the structure of knowledge do not, however, resolve the problem of geography's position within it. If the structure of knowledge is not as clear-cut as Hirst seems to suggest, then overlapping between various forms and fields can be accepted without difficulty, and in this sense geography is the arch example of an overlapping subject. Geomorphology overlaps into geology, climatology into meteorology, human geography into economics, politics, sociology and history. The question often asked is 'Is there any aspect of geography which could not be studied under any of the overlapping disciplines?' The honest answer to this is: no, and this would also be true of many other fields of knowledge such as medicine, and education. But, it may be countered, these fields are clearly centred on such foci as the human body or schooling. On what is geography centred?

It is important to distinguish here between what geographers actually do and what some say they ought to do. Geographers have never lacked advice about what they ought to be doing or what geography ought to be. It is tempting to make the analogy with a political party which is constantly being told by its devotees what the party line ought to be if the party is not to be split into factions. There seemed to be a fear among some geographers that excessive specialization would tear the fabric of geography apart. This is analogous to a situation in which scientists were bemoaning the fact that natural philosophy has now been dismembered into physics, chemistry, physical chemistry, bio-chemistry, botany and zoology. What we must do first is to look at what geographers actually do and then decide whether what they do needs changing.

If one examines the output of geographers in the past ten years, it is possible to divide this output into four classes. First, there are those works which are essentially concerned with geomorphology or climatology, and may be thought to belong to the physical science form of knowledge as defined by Hirst. Examples of such works would include C. A. King's *Techniques in Geomorphology* (1966) and T. J. Chandler's *The Climate of London* (1965). Secondly, there are those works which deal with the spatial aspects of society's organization in the contemporary world, like P. Haggett's *Locational Analysis in Human Geography* (1966), B. T. Robson's *Urban Analysis* (1969) and to take an American example, M. E. Eliot Hurst's *A Geography of Economic Behavior* (1972). These may be classed among the social sciences, since they are basically using scientific method on social data. Thirdly, there are those works whose affinity is closest to history, which are concerned with elucidating the spatial organizations of former societies. Such works are best represented by H. C. Darby's *Domesday Geography Series* or by W. G. East's *An Historical Geography of Europe* (1935). Fourthly, there are those works which under various titles describe a country or area or continent. They are basically information-giving texts about a particular area of the earth's surface. The information they give usually consists of descriptions of physical features, climatic conditions and the agriculture, industry and communications of the area concerned. Such works may be represented by Wreford Watson's *North America* (1963) and Jean Mitchell's *Great Britain: Geographical Essays* (1962). Sometimes a distinction is made between those works which deal with an area region by region and those which deal with the area by topics. But the fundamental purpose is the same, to inform about an area. It is difficult to ascribe this type of geography to any given form of knowledge since the content may include ideas from several forms of knowledge. Geography of this sort has generally been called regional geography.

Given those four subdivisions of geographical endeavour, which correspond to some extent with what William D. Pattison (1964) calls the four traditions of geography (an earth-science tradition, a spatial tradition, a man-land tradition and an area studies tradition), one may ask again whether the field of geography centres around any particular focus? It would seem that the objectives of geomorphological study and of climatology are clear but distinct from the rest of geography. The *results* of such a study may be useful to the human geographer and planner, but the subjects themselves are quasi-independent. Man's activity and its results are not the object of study. It would be dishonest to pretend otherwise. On the other hand, historical geography, analytical human geography and regional geography are all concerned with the spatial arrangements of man's occupation of the earth and the regularities which may be manifest and sometimes predicted. Consequently this common thread gives some grounds for including these within the field of geography. Thus geography would seem to be emerging as a study whose special concerns are the patterns which man's occupation of the earth has imposed in the form of agricultural and industrial development, settlement and communications upon the surface of the planet. This could be called the 'spatial organization' paradigm of geography (*see* Chapter 10). This was put in another way by Simons (1969) who argued that geography's special concern is to study mappable problems, though clearly such a way of defining geography would *not* exclude geomorphology and climatology. It is important to understand that this view of geography's main concern in no way implies what kinds of methods would be used to study the phenomena revealed by the patterns. Geography is but one way in which certain aspects of knowledge may be delimited. In the language of logic and mathematics, it is a set comprising the intersection of elements from several other but different sets. If Hirst's forms of knowledge are one way in which knowledge may be divided into sets, then geography merely abstracts elements from some of these sets to form its own set which intersects with the forms of knowledge set (Figure 4.1). Thus how knowledge is classified depends on the criteria used and the purposes for which the classification is required.

An empirical investigation of the recent writings of selected geographers by Cox (1975) has shown that over three quarters of the substantive content is concerned with the concepts of location, distribution, areal association and variation, and spatial interaction.

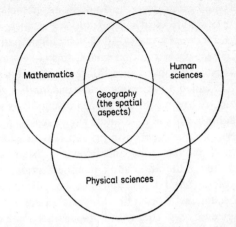

FIGURE 4.1. Geography in relation to Hirst's forms of knowledge.

Geography and the disciplines of knowledge approach

Another approach to the classification of knowledge has some relevance to our purpose in this chapter. It is that suggested by King and Brownell (1966) in their book *The Curriculum and the Disciplines of Knowledge.*

King and Brownell start from the premise that schools and colleges are basically institutions whose objectives are or should be the intellectual development of the student body. As such, schools are concerned with giving students an encounter with what King and Brownell call the *disciplines of knowledge.* Like Phenix and Hirst, they affirm that knowledge is not 'one' but pluralistic, and consists of several disciplines of knowledge each adding meaning to the experience of total reality as perceived by human beings. How do they then define a discipline of knowledge?

Interestingly, they start by arguing that a discipline is a community of persons. This is to emphasize that the discipline derives from the workings of human minds communicating with one another in the search to give meaning to an aspect of experience. A discipline is therefore an expression of the human imagination since progress is achieved partly through the intuitive creative leaps of the mind. It is also a domain in the sense that attention is focused by the community on certain phenomena or processes or institutions—but no organizing principle determines what these should be. Indeed, if one thinks in terms of history and geography, the domains are notoriously wide and overlap, though there are clearly areas into which these disciplines do not penetrate, for example, the world of sub-atomic particles. A discipline also has a history or tradition even if this is now more honoured in the breach than in its observance. More important, a discipline has what Schwab has called a *syntactical* and a *substantive* structure. By a syntactical structure are meant the modes of enquiry used within the discipline though not unique to it, and by the substantive structure are meant the interlocking concepts and principles which form part of the language of the discipline. King and Brownell also view a discipline as having a heritage of literature and a communications network manifest in the professional bodies, journals, and meetings run by the community of scholars. A discipline also has an emotive appeal to its adherents—they enjoy working within it—at least some of the time.

It is clear that King and Brownell's view of the disciplines of knowledge, while setting out criteria for distinguishing a discipline, is not so restrictive as that suggested by Hirst in his 'forms' of knowledge. There is no problem about including geography since geography has a community of scholars, a syntactical structure and substantive structure, a heritage of literature and so on. Consequently geography can be considered, given King and Brownell's initial premise, as a discipline of knowledge that students may benefit from encountering. This is the case for including geography in the curriculum made perceptively by David Shortle in his thesis *Geography and the disciplines of knowledge approach to the curriculum* (1974).

Summary

Building a curriculum is a complex process which will be considered in Chapters 5 and 6. But in so far as a curriculum is a means of passing knowledge on from one generation to the next, the question often posed is: 'What kind of knowledge should be included in the curriculum?' This inevitably leads to a consideration of what knowledge is and how it can be analysed and classified. We have seen that there are no generally agreed criteria for classifying knowledge for curriculum building purposes, though attempts have been made by Hirst and King and Brownell among others.

According to Hirst geography is a 'field of knowledge', according to King and Brownell it is a 'discipline of knowledge'. I am inclined to feel that King and Brownell's somewhat less restrictive classification of knowledge makes possible the consideration of geography as a 'discipline of knowledge'. It is possible, that as geographic theory develops, as human geography becomes more and more differentiated from physical geography, as the spatial organization or ecosystem paradigms of geography gain general acceptance, so will geography become a branch of social science. In this sense its position will be analogous to that of anthropology and sociology. Its success as a social science will depend on the extent to which its findings are sought by other workers in that general field. We shall return briefly to this theme in Chapter 10.

CHAPTER FIVE

Aims and Objectives in Geographical Education

Introduction

This chapter is concerned with the clarification of the nature of educational aims and objectives and their relevance to geographical education. It begins by examining educational objectives in general, particularly looking into the question of extrinsic and intrinsic aims in education. Some attempt is made to see how far the claims which have been made for the value of geographical education are justified. An analysis is then made of the way in which the objectives of geographical education may be classified and this points to certain normative aspects of geographical education which were mooted in the last chapter.

Aims in education

Inevitably teachers, parents and pupils often ask questions about the purposes of education or at least about the purpose of the sort of education with which they have come into contact. These are often questions which covertly imply that the education received seemed in some way defective according to some unspecified criteria for assessing its worth. Or, if the questions do not imply this, they suggest that the questioner was not clear as to the objectives sought by those who were educating him. Often, the critics of educational systems contrast the lessons to be learned from 'life' with those to be learned inside a classroom, implying the superiority of the one against the other. Similarly, a geography teacher may well ask how far what he is teaching contributes to the 'general education' of his pupils or students, indicating thereby that he sees his activities as a step in the process of turning out an educated person. All these questions make a number of assumptions about education and aims which are seldom explicitly stated. It is, therefore, appropriate first to clear the ground by making explicit the concepts used in such a discussion.

There is, of course, no generally agreed *technical* definition of the term education. Consequently when the word education is used, different people tend to have slightly or sometimes widely different mental images of this word. Compare the mental image of a girl whose secondary education was obtained in a select girls' independent school with that of a girl who spent her adolescent years in a downtown state comprehensive school. Both will be thinking in terms of the schooling which they received and the differing experiences to which they were subjected, which they may or may not have enjoyed. Is there, therefore, any broad agreement about the concept of education which would enable us to discuss it rationally?

I propose to use the concept of education as outlined by R. S. Peters (1963, 1966). According to Peters, education cannot be easily described as a particular activity, rather it is a term encompassing a group of often quite disparate activities—involving teachers and learners—such as those of learning a skill, a method of experimenting, a way of thinking, an appreciation of art or poetry, and so on. In other words, education is a process of getting someone to learn something. However, further implied in the concept is that what is being learned is worthwhile. This is acceptable enough, though difficulty arises in stating precisely what is worthwhile. This is bound to involve the realms of values and indeed teachers are probably very conscious that most disagreements in educational discussion often stem from varying views as to what is worth teaching and learning. Thus, reverting briefly to the field of geography, one may argue that getting children to learn about the production of cocoa in Ghana is factual information of little general value, whereas teaching them map-reading skills or graphicacy will be much more valuable (Balchin 1970). Peters characterizes worthwhile activities as those which: (1) are concerned with the pursuit of theoretical knowledge, a pursuit which is never ending since knowledge is changing all the time; (2) are morally unobjectionable, that is they do not offend against what would be a generally acceptable code of behaviour in a modern society, for example, teaching someone to defraud the Inland Revenue would not be education; (3) are not trivial, that is they are *not* concerned with matters of no great significance to the individual or to society in which he lives; for example, teaching someone to play tiddly-winks would hardly rank as a worthwhile activity; (4) are essentially disinterested in the sense that they are not directed to some ulterior extrinsic end. That is to say worthwhile activities are their own self justification and do not need to be looked upon as serving an ulterior purpose. Clearly there are different possible interpretations of the values implicit in the above descriptions. For example, some might find that income tax 'fiddling' is a morally justifiable occupation; some might consider the teaching of golf a trivial activity whereas others would not. Indeed John P. White (1973) in his book *Towards a Compulsory Curriculum* argues that no such absolute distinctions can be made between worthwhile and non-worthwhile pursuits. However, if we can accept for the time being that the process of education may be described as an initiation into worthwhile activities, we can then proceed to the problem of aims in education.

The statement made earlier that worthwhile activities need no ulterior purpose is important since it underpins Peters' argument that education cannot be directed to extrinsic ends. At first, such an argument seems contrary to much of one's own experience, and certainly contrary to much of the intercourse which goes on between teacher and pupil. When pupils question the value of learning this or that body of knowledge, a justification is often given in terms of the necessity of obtaining qualifications which will lead on to certain jobs which will provide the wherewithal for a living and possibly for material comfort. Undoubtedly the many pupils in developing countries who sit for examinations do so because of the expectation of a non-manual occupation with a reasonable income if they pass. In the United Kingdom, there exists empirical evidence that young school leavers see the objectives of schools as being largely *instrumental*, that is directed to extrinsic goals, such as those of obtaining a good job, those of being able to cope with the demands of adult life and so on (Schools Council 1968).

To conceive of education as having extrinsic ends is, according to Peters, to neglect the criteria which are inbuilt into the concept of education. Since education involves the pursuit of activities which are defined as worthwhile, it is useless asking what education is for. Such a question can only lead to a description of the activity. Or putting it another way, the objectives of education are intrinsic to the process of education. Thus the person who sees education as a means to a professional career, is misusing the term education, since he is presumably mainly concerned with the training required to qualify him for that career and training by itself is not education. Similarly, a school which merely made sure that its pupils were so trained that they easily found jobs as electricians, nurses, cooks, engineers, policemen, and so on, would have failed to educate them. It is important to note that education need not exclude vocational training, but that vocational training by itself is not a sufficiently broad activity to be called education. One can only point out that many who are involved in the 'education industry' do not subscribe in practice to this concept of education, but behave as though schools had essentially instrumental roles in society.

To sum up: education *per se* is a process designed to produce a person who having been initiated into a number of worthwhile activities is willing to continue with some of these on his own. Such a person has acquired a breadth of understanding or cognitive perspective, so that his outlook on life has been transformed by his education. The process of education has no aims extrinsic to itself but schools which educate may also perform other functions for society, and in this sense follow activities which have extrinsic ends. In other words, not all that goes on in schools is education (Peters 1966, 1973)! As long as we bear this caveat in mind, we shall avoid confusion in dealing with the aims and objectives of geographical education.

Geography and the aims of education

The subjects of the curriculum are ostensibly part of the educational process. If one of the characteristics of an educated man is that he should have been initiated into wide cognitive perspectives, then one way of doing this is to introduce him to the various forms and fields of knowledge which have been developed by human intellectual endeavour. To have been educated involves knowing something of the languages of mathematics, of science, of aesthetics; it involves being acquainted with historical thinking, with social and political issues, with geographical perspectives, with philosophical discourse, and so on. While this may be readily conceded in theoretical terms, curriculum designers (such as head teachers or principals) have often been reluctant in the past to open the doors to new subjects, so that the natural sciences, modern history and geography and more recently the social sciences, had great difficulty in obtaining a place on the school timetable. In striving for the inclusion of geography in the curriculum and its maintenance, geographers and other subject specialists have often been led to making extravagant claims for their subject's contribution to education, which may now seem a little difficult to substantiate.

It is important to bear in mind that the aims of geography as a school subject have always been influenced by the prevailing 'philosophy' of education, by the prevailing economic climate and by the prevailing paradigm of geography. The word paradigm is here used to mean the idea of geography held by geographers such as geography as the study of man-land relationships. Sometimes these influences reinforced one another, sometimes they were opposed (Underwood 1971). The decision to include geography in the secondary schools of France was to a large extent the product of the belief that an educated man should be acquainted with all branches of knowledge and therefore could not remain ignorant of the various continents and regions of the earth. The concept of students acquiring 'une culture générale' is still an important one in France, and has led to a generally much broader curriculum being in force than in English schools, particularly in the equivalent to the sixth-form stage (16-18 years). On the other hand, in Britain during the nineteenth century, attempts were made to justify the role of geography in education in terms of its utility for commerce and industry. Since Britain had a pre-eminently industrial and commercial economy with huge overseas markets, it was deemed important that those who were to work in industry and commerce should know something of the origins of raw materials and the destinations of finished products. Such a view led inevitably to the development of commercial geography epitomized in Chisholm's *Commercial Geography* (Chisholm 1889). This attitude was also expressed in works on geographical education of a later vintage. Fairgrieve (1926), who saw the functions of education as those of helping people 'to earn a living' and helping people 'to live', felt that geography teaching contributed to the first as well as to the second of these functions. 'It would seem self-evident,' he wrote, 'that, with the widespread business interests of the inhabitants of Britain, some knowledge of other lands would be desirable.' Similarly, in the emergent post-colonial nation states, geography may be taught partly to reinforce the concept of the nation.

The strictly economic or political and therefore instrumental view of the aims of geography in education was not held by many or for any length of time. Such a view was very difficult to sustain, for a different body of 'geographical' facts would have been relevant to different occupations and, in the twentieth century, many of the facts learnt at school would, to a large extent, be out of date by the time the student started earning a living. Indeed, any justification of geography on the basis of the factual information that the subject might contain, whether it be to develop a 'culture générale' or a knowledgeable citizen of the world, is one likely to run into difficulties for the same reasons. Consequently one finds that attempts were being made to develop aims of geography teaching which were less dependent on the particular factual information which might be taught. For example, when Archibald Geikie (1887) wrote on the teaching of geography, he stressed the value of the subject for developing children's powers of observation and of reasoning. He was less concerned with the particular factual content taught than with the mental processes developed. In particular he felt that geography could help children to understand the scientific method of acquiring knowledge. Geography was clearly not the only subject which could help to develop such an understanding, but it must be remembered that at the time Geikie was writing the teaching of science was little developed. In France a set of 'instructions' for geography teachers (Ministère de l'Instruction Publique 1890) made these same points as Geikie, but also saw geography as contributing to the student's moral development. The argument was broadly that geography demonstrates that the world owes no one a living, that success in obtaining the fruits of nature and in harnessing natural energy stems from hard work and man's intelligent adaptation of nature. In other words, geography is seen to contribute to the development of the solid virtues dear to some of our puritan and Victorian ancestors. There is an elaboration of this argument which would probably find favour today. It is that the study of geography teaches us to be tolerant of other peoples through our understanding of the struggles of others, of their ways of life, of their beliefs and of their perceptions of their natural and man-made environments. This argument is also linked to another which has been taken up by many protagonists of geographical education, namely that a knowledge of geography makes it easier to make balanced judgements about national and world problems. Fairgrieve's (1926) faith in geography as a school subject was expressed in the following terms: 'The function of geography is to train future citizens to imagine accurately the conditions of the great world stage and so help them to think sanely about political and social problems in the world around.' This statement became the leitmotiv of many generations of geography teachers in Britain and elsewhere. In the inter-war period and in the 1940s and 1950s, it provided a valuable focus for the activities of geography teachers, since teaching can only too easily degenerate into the routine passing on of information.

In considering these general aims of geography teaching reference must be made to one mentioned in Chapter 2 and first promulgated by Mackinder, namely that geography as a subject helps to bridge the gap between the natural sciences and the humanities. It is a view of the teaching process which is currently fashionable among curriculum designers, who are urging teachers to pull down the subject barriers, whatever these may be. The fear that students will turn into narrow-minded scientists or scientifically ignorant men of letters, reappears from time to time among certain educators, though the evidence on which this fear is based is far from certain. However, whatever the merits of the case, there is no doubt that for many years a claim was made for geography to have a strong place in the curriculum on the grounds that it had an integrating role and demonstrated the relationships between diverse disciplines in the study of a given area. Since the then prevailing paradigm for geography was the 'areal differentiation' or regional synthesis paradigm, this fitted well into such a justification for geographical education. It was never made clear by Mackinder why this gap-bridging function of geography could not equally well be performed by insisting that any curriculum should consist of sciences and the humanities rather than one or the other. Was it because students could still learn physics and history and not see the link between the two? But if Hirst is right, there is no link. If one is studying the history of settlement in south-eastern England, this is one thing; if one then studies the physics of the atmosphere in south-eastern England, this is another. The only link is the purely arbitrary one of the location of the study.

A discussion of the aims of geography teaching

The foregoing review was in part an historical perspective on what might be called the general aims of geographical education. It will readily be appreciated that the aims given were more in the nature of general goals for geography teachers to strive for, than statements of what geography as a subject could be demonstrated to achieve. Little if any evidence exists, for example, to enable a verification to be made of the statement that geography helps to develop tolerant attitudes. The same may be said for most of the other general aims of geography teaching which are of an extrinsic nature. In other words, if one chooses to justify the position of geography in the curriculum on the grounds that the subject contributes to something outside the education process, such as citizen-formation, then one is put in the very difficult position of being unable to offer very substantial proof that geography does in fact achieve such extrinsic aims. This, of course, would be true of many other subjects whose justification was similarly sought through the satisfaction of general aims. A further disadvantage is that such aims, because of their generality, give little precise guidance to the teacher in his day-to-day work, though they may give a general direction to his teaching. At best some of these general aims may be thought of as long-term goals which can act as criteria in the selection of teaching-learning activities that go on in the classroom. For example, studying the nature of Israeli-Arab boundary conflict is more likely to contribute to the formation of a world citizen than studying the growing of dates in a desert oasis. But the teacher will probably never know whether the students, to whom he taught such a topic, do become 'good world citizens'. In fact it is highly unlikely that teachers act in the way postulated. They tend to rely on more immediate feedback from their pupils which indicates whether a particular course of study is appreciated or not.

Trevor Bennetts (1973) has made a classification of the aims of geographical education as seen from a general education point of view and from the geographical point of view. His diagram is reproduced as Figure 5.1.

This is useful in the sense that it shows that one can begin either by assuming certain general education aims and noting how geography can contribute to these, or by looking at geography and deciding which aspects seem to be valuable educationally. It also shows that in order to be of much use to the teacher, the general aims have to be broken down into more limited or more specific objectives (Graves 1971). For example, involved in the aim of turning out a good citizen is the more limited objective of developing the idea that people in the world are interdependent and need to cooperate with one another. But even this is not specific enough, since in order to develop such an idea the teacher would need to plan certain learning experiences to demonstrate the validity of the notion of interdependence (Hart 1975). It could be that his specific objective would be to show that transport in Britain would be hampered without Middle East petroleum and that industry and commerce in Kuwait and Abu Dhabi would be very limited without

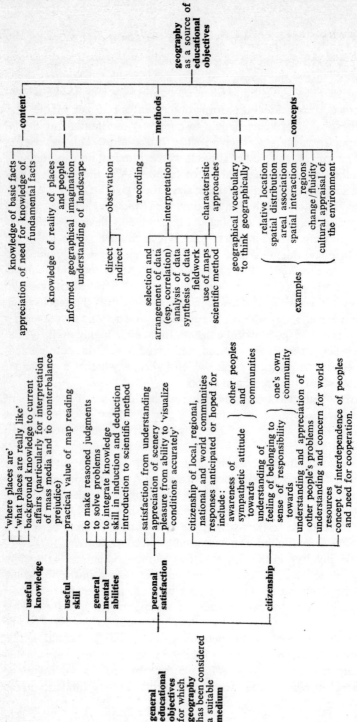

FIGURE 5.1. A classification of objectives that have been stated as appropriate for geography in secondary schools. (Bennetts 1973).

British and American goods. This has led some educationists to aver that the only useful objectives for the teacher are 'behavioural objectives', since these specify clearly the intended behavioural change in a student resulting from a programme of instruction. The argument is simply that, if instruction is to be efficient, then the instructor must know clearly what is to be achieved. This has analogies with industry. No production assembly line for an automobile can be efficiently run if the design of the car is not known in all its detail. Thus in writing instructional objectives it is necessary to specify:

1. the person who is to undertake the learning;
2. the behaviour which will indicate that the objective has been achieved;
3. the learning outcome or product by which the achievement of the objective can be evaluated;
4. the conditions under which the behaviour is to be performed, for example, with what instruments or books or data;
5. the criterion or standard to be used to evaluate the achievement, e.g. the extent of error in a measurement which is allowable (Clegg 1970).

Thus a behavioural objective in geography concerned with map skills might be 'Given a 1:50,000 map of the North York Moors, the students of the fifth form will draw a cross-section to indicate the profile of the relief from Pickering to Whitby on a horizontal scale of 1:50,000 and a vertical scale of 2 mm to 100 metres. There should be no more than three inaccuracies in the shape of the profile vertically and none in the horizontal scale.'

Behavioural objectives were developed in the U.S.A. and later in the U.K. in association with the introduction of programmed learning. Since programmed learning involves the breaking down of instruction into a series of relatively small steps, it follows that the instructional objectives must be clear and specific; the frame writer for the programme must know where he is going and what he is aiming at. Much was written about behavioural objectives in the 1940s, 1950s and early 1960s, but in fact every teacher who set out to teach a skill or concept to a particular group of individuals, must implicitly or explicitly have delineated certain specific or behavioural objectives, otherwise his instruction would have been erratic and capricious, and whatever learning took place may have been unintended and adventitious. Teaching is an activity, which if it is to be successful, involves the teacher in being crystal-clear about his objectives. This is why many teachers find that they have only properly understood a subject when they have had to teach it! There arise, however, certain philosophical difficulties if it is claimed that all objectives should be stated in behavioural terms (Sockett 1973). This will be taken up later in this chapter.

We can see so far that aims in teaching geography have been stated at various levels of generality and specificity. In general, it is usual today to use the term *aims* to refer to those long-term aims which amount to a confession of faith in the value of the subject in education. These general aims may be instrumental in the sense indicated earlier (e.g. geography facilitates international understanding) or they may be intrinsic in simply stating why learning geography is a worthwhile activity and therefore inherent to the concept of education. Most writers who have attempted to justify the teaching of geography have in practice given the subject both instrumental and intrinsic aims. For example, Fairgrieve's statement quoted earlier about geography helping future citizens to think sanely about political and social problems, clearly sees geography as having instrumental aims; but he also wrote, 'There is a claim from geography for a place in the curriculum, not because it pays, but because we cannot have an education worth the name without geography' (Fairgrieve 1926), which statement sees geography as intrinsic to education. Underwood (1971) appears to detect, in analysing statements of these general aims from 1871 to 1971, a tendency for instrumental aims to be emphasized at times when the subject is under stress, possibly because of the greater need to indicate to the community at large that geographical education is useful. He also makes the point that during times of stress for the subject, there is a greater convergence between the stated long-term aims of education in general and those of geography in particular. An analysis of the current aims for geography teaching stated in official documents put out by the education authorities of those countries of Europe which belong to the Council of Europe shows also a mixture of intrinsic and extrinsic aims, the latter emphasizing the citizen formation aspect of geography (Marchant 1971).

Whether the general aims are intrinsic or extrinsic the teacher of geography must, as we saw earlier, be able to translate them into operational terms. This means that he needs to think in terms of a series of specific objectives capable of being achieved with a particular group of students. The term 'objective', therefore, tends now to be used to indicate these short-term goals rather than the long-term aims mentioned above. Of course, such objectives need not all be of the same degree of precision as behavioural objectives. If a teacher intends to put over the idea that the larger the towns in a given area, the further apart they tend to be, he will probably not lay down specifically the kind of behaviour expected of his students, but he will probably have in mind some means of testing that the idea has been assimilated. Further, there is a continuum between long-term aims and behavioural objectives, that is, there are variations in the specificity of objectives which depend essentially on how distant the objective is. Thus if a teacher is embarking on a programme the ultimate objective of which is that students should understand an energy-exchange model of the general circulation of the atmosphere, he is setting up an objective which though having some degree of precision will need to be spelled out in terms of the set of specific objectives to be achieved on the way to a complete understanding of that model. The specific objectives on the way may be: the idea of an energy equilibrium in the atmospheric system, gains and losses being equal; the idea that surpluses of energy exist in the tropical areas and deficits in the polar regions; the need for some transference mechanism to enable energy surpluses in the equatorial areas to be transmitted to the polar areas; the concepts of total potential energy and kinetic energy and the transmutation of one type of energy into another; the ideas of giant convectional meridional overturning in the Hadley and Polar cells and of zonal (east to west) circulation in the mid-latitude areas; the functions of these air movements in energy transfers, and so on. The more immediate is the objective, the more specific it tends to be. Thus a teacher who needs guidance as to what to teach is better helped by a series of medium- or short-term objectives given to him than by longer-term general aims. On the other hand, the teacher with many ideas may feel restricted by too closely defined objectives.

From the student's or pupil's point of view, there can be no certainty about the outcome of any particular lesson or 'learning experience'. This is why the teacher's objective is often stated to be an 'intended learning outcome'. It does not follow that what is intended will in fact materialize. It may well do, and clearly the more specific and short-term is the objective, the greater is the chance that the 'intended learning outcome' will become the *de facto* outcome, particularly if the objective is a simple cognitive objective, like knowing the meaning of the term rain shadow. But in many cases what in fact happens is an 'unintended learning outcome'; what the student in fact learns is not what the teacher had foreseen. This does not necessarily mean that the teacher has failed, the student may well have seen an aspect of the problem put to him which had escaped the teacher's attention; he may have moved two or three steps forward in his thinking or had an intuitive flash which has enlightened a whole area of the subject. This is not surprising since it is one way in which knowledge makes progress. It would be illogical to ask students to think for themselves and yet insist that their learning should not deviate from the objectives set for them by teachers. Of course, the 'unintended learning outcome' may often be much more disappointing for the teacher, with very little learning apparently taking place or with the students acquiring a muddled idea of the concept taught. This may well be due to all kinds of factors, including poor teaching, but one has to remember that in grasping an idea many of us go through a stage when we are not too clear as to its meaning and significance and only gradually do we apprehend its full implication; it would be surprising if many of our pupils did not go through a similar process.

Classification of objectives

It will have been evident in this chapter that there is a need to classify the aims and objectives of geographical education and of education in general. I have indicated that the term *aim* might be used exclusively for the long-term desirable outcomes of education, while the term *objective* might be limited to the more immediate short-term intended outcomes of particular learning experiences. We have also noted that aims may be conceived as intrinsic to the process of education if education is defined in Peters' sense as 'initiation into worthwhile activities', but that probably most people, including the learners themselves, find it difficult to conceive of education in these terms and consequently think of aims as extrinsic to the process of education, that is that, for example, geographical education is aiming at producing 'graphicate' individuals who can handle mappable information.

Whichever view one takes of education, short-term objectives are a necessity since these postulate immediate targets for the teacher to aim at in his daily teaching (Pring 1973). Many attempts have been made at classifying such objectives. A simple division would be to think of geographical objectives as being either skills (e.g. ability to draw a plan to scale), or concepts (e.g. knowing the meaning of diurnal temperature range) or attitudes (e.g. being disposed to evaluating different ways of life over the world in terms of cultural and environmental influences rather than in terms of one's own culture). Although this is a useful classification, it does not go very far in structuring objectives, it merely indicates that they can be of different kinds. Any single learning experience could, of course, lead to the student achieving all three kinds of objectives.

A body of American psychologists and educators worked together in the years following World War II to produce a taxonomy of educational objectives which is much more detailed. The decision to produce such a taxonomy arose out of the need to classify objectives in order to construct tests to examine what kind of knowledge had been acquired or not by students. It was decided to subdivide the task by considering three kinds of objectives separately:

(a) cognitive objectives, that is those concerned with knowledge and abilities;

(b) affective objectives, those relating to emotive states or attitudes;

(c) psychomotor objectives, those concerning mechanical or manipulative skills.

The results of the work undertaken by the group were published in two handbooks, the first dealing with the cognitive domain (Bloom 1956) and the second dealing with the affective domain (Krathwohl *et al* 1964). No volume has yet been published on the psychomotor domain, though others have written on this topic (Harrow 1972).

If we take the cognitive objectives first, we see that they have been divided into six broad categories:

1. knowledge;
2. comprehension;
3. application;
4. analysis;
5. synthesis;
6. evaluation.

Using the taxonomy on geography may show the significance of each category. This has been done by Cox in Australia (1966), by Tomkins in Canada (1968) and by Monk in the U.S.A. (1971). *Knowledge* concerns the ability to recall facts, concepts, principles, trends, criteria and processes. Thus the objective may simply be that the pupil be able to recognize and name the $66\frac{1}{2}°$N line of latitude as the Arctic Circle, or the wind blowing over Madras in December as the North-east Monsoon. The second category, *comprehension*, involves the student being able to understand the literal meaning of a communication in whatever form it is presented (oral, written, graphical, etc.). Thus to make a précis of a descriptive account of a region, would be a translation of what has been comprehended. This category can be extended to include an interpretation and extrapolation of what has been understood. *Application* is a category describing the kind of behaviour which shows that a student has the ability to apply the knowledge he has acquired to a novel situation. For example, an application objective would be one which postulated a student using a knowledge of the gravity model to find out whether the vehicular traffic between two towns was directly proportional to the product of their population. Another would be the ability to calculate a location quotient for a particular industry in an area, given the necessary data. *Analysis* describes the kind of objective which requires the student to separate out the elements in a situation, or to sort out the interrelationships in ideas, or to tease out the kinds of principles implicit in a given statement. A simple example would be that sorting out the kinds of factors to be considered before a decision is taken about the route of a motorway. *Synthesis* describes a group of objectives where the student is asked to combine a number of elements to produce a whole or a pattern of some sort. Thus the production of a plan for the development of a recreational park in an area of derelict quarries would be an objective of this kind. The last category, *evaluation*, classifies all those objectives in which a judgement is made either from internal or from external evidence. A student set the task of assessing the validity of W. M. Davis' cycle of erosion theory of landscape evolution would have been set an evaluative objective.

A characteristic of this taxonomy of cognitive objectives is that it is arranged in a hierarchy of complexity. That is to say, that any objectives classified in the second category must also involve those classified in the first, any classified in the third must involve those in the second and first, and so on. Thus to ask a student to evaluate something is to ask him to perform a task involving all the other categories of objectives. To use the example quoted above, assessing the validity of the cycle of erosion theory of landscape evolution involves:

1. knowing the terminology used;
2. comprehending the nature of the problem posed;
3. applying the theory to various known landscapes;
4. analysing the implicit assumptions and principles used in the theory;
5. synthesizing the evidence for and against the theory until some

sort of pattern emerges about this evidence;

6. making a judgement as to whether the theory is worth using or not as a mode of explanation.

This characteristic of the taxonomy is a useful one because it yields a means of deciding whether any set of objectives is unbalanced, for example, by concentrating overmuch on knowledge and not enough on analysis, synthesis and evaluation. It is particularly useful as a means of evaluating questions set in tests and examinations, for examinations in geography have in the past been notorious for their tendency to test factual information and little else. Another use of the taxonomy is to enable, to some extent, a prima facie judgement to be made as to whether an objective is likely to be too difficult for a given pupil. In broad terms it is generally accepted that only a limited number of students below the age of fifteen can think in a hypothetico-deductive manner, yet hypothetico-deductive reasoning is implied in most of the objectives classified under analysis, synthesis and evaluation, consequently any such sets of objectives may be too difficult for younger students.

Unfortunately the story does not end there, for although there are prima facie reasons for believing that objectives classified under analysis, synthesis and evaluation may be too difficult for pupils who are not able to handle abstractions, it does not follow that all objectives classified under knowledge, comprehension and application *are* suitable for younger pupils, for within these more simple categories, there may be items of knowledge of varying orders of difficulty. Indeed, this is explicitly recognized by Bloom and his associates. The category knowledge is for example subdivided into:

1.10 knowledge of specifics
    (knowledge of terminology, knowledge of specific facts);
1.20 knowledge of ways and means of dealing with specifics
    (knowledge of conventions, knowledge of trends and sequences, knowledge of classifications and categories, knowledge of criteria, knowledge of methodology);
1.30 knowledge of universals and abstractions in a field
    (knowledge of principles and generalizations, knowledge of theories and structures);

and it is affirmed that category 1.30 is more complex than 1.20, 1.20 itself being more complex than category 1.10. It is readily acceptable that, for example, knowledge of a theory of atmospheric circulation is more complex than knowledge of the classification of air masses, which is itself more complex than knowledge of the terminology applied to winds. However, even within one sub-category enormous differences may become apparent in the difficulty presented by various objectives. Let us take the terminology applied to winds. A simple objective may be to define what is meant by a south-westerly wind; a slightly more complex objective would be to define a katabatic wind, and a very much more complex objective would be the definition of a geostrophic wind (Graves 1972). Thus, though 'knowledge of specifics' is a classification of objectives which are apparently simpler than those classified under 'knowledge of theories and structures', much depends on the specifics and theories. Some theories may be simpler to understand than some definitions of terms. This also shows that the categories used by Bloom and his associates are not mutually exclusive, but overlap to some extent. The ability to fit a definition to a particular term must involve 'comprehension' as well as 'knowledge' objectives. Similarly, at the complex end of the taxonomy, 'evaluation' as a classification of objectives covers a wide variety of objectives. Much depends on the problem posed, on the nature of evaluation required.

The affective domain proved even more difficult to classify than the cognitive domain. Whatever lip service may be given to the importance of affective objectives in education, there is an inevitable tendency for teachers to concentrate on cognitive objectives because these are more easily identifiable and measurable. However, Krathwohl, Bloom and Masia persisted in their attempt and eventually brought out a taxonomy again in an hierarchical order, the hierarchy being based on the idea of *internalization*. That is the idea that higher order affective objectives are marked by a greater degree of internal acceptance by and therefore of identification with the person learning them. The classification is:

  1.0   Receiving (attending)
     1.1 awareness
     1.2 willingness to receive
     1.3 controlled or selected attention
  2.0   Responding
     2.1 acquiescence in responding
     2.2 willingness to respond
     2.3 satisfaction in response
  3.0   Valuing
     3.1 acceptance of a value

    3.2 preference for a value
    3.3 commitment (conviction)
4.0   Organization
    4.1 conceptualization of a value
    4.2 organization of a value system
5.0   Characterization by a value or value complex
    5.1 generalized set
    5.2 characterization

As in the case of the cognitive domain, an attempt has been made to apply this taxonomy to objectives in geographical education (Styles 1972). In category No. 1, the objectives are those which lead a student to become aware that, for example, people live in different cultural and physical environments; which lead him to receive willingly information on different cultural environments and to select certain environments for closer and more detailed study. In the second category objectives may be those of getting students first to acquiesce in searching for specified information about agriculture in southern India, then to show willingness by searching out unspecified sources of information and finally to develop a keen interest in the agricultural problems of Tamilnad.

The third category might be exemplified by objectives of trying to get students (1) to accept as valuable the conservation of an area of natural beauty from holiday chalet development, (2) to express preference for the conservation of areas of natural beauty, and (3) to become committed to such a value, as evidenced by their joining a conservation association.

The fourth category classifies those objectives in which an attempt is made to get students (1) to develop certain values as abstract principles; the idea, for example, that resource exploitation is not automatically a good thing simply because it raises some incomes; (2) to relate their acquired values in such a way that they develop a personal value system, as in the case when land development proposals are habitually judged by their effect on the living environment, certain standards having been acquired about environmental quality.

The fifth and last category is that which encompasses those objectives which aim at making a student behave consistently and characteristically in line with a generalized value system which he holds. For example, such an objective might be to get students to react consistently to world incidents (such as the Israeli-Arab conflict) not by seeking culprits, but by trying to find ways of harmonizing the respective claims of the contestants in terms which will respect others' points of view. Students exhibiting such behaviour, would have completely internalized a whole value system and would have identified with it.

Although such a classification concerns the affective domain, it seems clear that the objectives indicated are in part cognitive. Thus to hold a certain set of values does not mean that one holds them or has acquired them in a completely irrational way. It is implied, in the last example given, that an individual who reacts consistently as a peacemaker does so not only because he is emotionally committed to peace, but also because he has rationally come to the conclusion that such behaviour is better calculated to achieve peace than by seeking out a culprit for public blame.

A problem which arises in considering the affective domain is, therefore, the extent to which value objectives are valid objectives educationally, and how far they are indoctrinatory. Fenton (1966) argues that there are three kinds of values: behavioural, procedural and substantive. Behavioural values are those which relate to the way a class conducts itself, namely they are concerned with the extent of order or disorder in the learning group. Obviously we tend to value order rather than disorder in a classroom because order enables learning to take place more easily and it makes possible discussion and rational argument. Procedural values are those concerned with the rules relating to the subject or area of knowledge being taught. Thus in geography we would teach a respect for rational discussion rather than emotive outbursts, and a respect for evidence in coming to some conclusion. In other words, we would value certain procedures in acquiring knowledge. Substantive values are those which imply belief in a particular way of life, or in a particular political system, or in a particular philosophical doctrine, or in a particular religion, and so on. To teach such values, Fenton argues, is indoctrination, but to teach behavioural and procedural values is not. To a large extent whether teaching substantive values is indoctrination or not depends, in my view, on how these values are taught. If the teacher intends that his students should adopt certain substantive values and deliberately prevents the students from comparing them with others, implying that his values are the only values to be acquired, then clearly such a teacher is guilty of attempted indoctrination. Whether he succeeds is another matter. It can also be argued that perhaps the separation of procedural values from substantive values is not as easy as Fenton implies. In so far as one subscribes to procedural values which imply respect for certain rules of debate and evidence, for experiment in science, and so on, then in effect one has affirmed one's belief in certain substantive values which imply that the search for truth should be disinterested and not in conformity to some previously held belief. Thus to my mind the real issue is not whether one teaches substantive values or not, but whether one indoctrinates or not. The teacher may well indicate what his particular value system is, granted his students know of others and have access to the evidence which enables them to make up their minds. In geography teaching the main dangers lie in teachers giving the impression, perhaps unwittingly, that other peoples in the world should be judged according to values which derive from the society from which the teacher and his students come. Such ethno-centric attitudes are only too easily acquired and though they can hardly be dubbed the result of indoctrination, yet they have an effect which is not dissimilar to attitudes acquired from indoctrination. Attitudes are often derived from other people's behaviour rather than learnt as a result of deliberate teaching.

Towards the end of the section of this chapter entitled *A Discussion of the Aims of Geography Teaching*, I indicated that whatever the objectives that teachers set for their students, the outcomes were perhaps as often unintended as intended. This, as we noted, was not only to be expected but also welcomed since progress in any field of learning was often made through chance discoveries and through intellectual development that no teacher could forecast. And, in a sense, these unintended outcomes are seen by many teachers as a necessary part of the process of education, in which developing minds are stimulated to think for themselves and in so doing arrive at ideas in no way prescribed in the curriculum's objectives. I can remember a 'lesson' in which I was teaching a class of sixteen-year old boys a means of measuring the degree of specialization of a particular industry in a region by the use of the location quotient based on employment statistics. An unintended learning outcome was that they proceeded to tell me what were the deficiencies of such an index. In some areas of learning it is seldom possible to prescribe an intended learning outcome in behavioural or specific terms. Consequently Elliot Eisner (1969) has argued that there are probably two main types of educational objectives corresponding to two aspects of the educational process. The first type may be called *instructional objectives*, that is, those objectives in which the intended learning outcomes may be specified in fairly precise terms, for example: the student shall be able to describe a central business district and indicate by what criteria it could be delimited. Such objectives have the job of specifying those skills and ideas which our culture possesses and which are deemed worthwhile passing on. The second type of objectives may be called *expressive objectives*, that is, those which do not prescribe precisely what the student is to learn, but describe 'an educational encounter' in which a student may be confronted with a problem though it is not known exactly what particular ideas, attitudes or skills he will derive from this encounter with the problem. For example, the student may be asked to investigate what he could do with a piece of waste ground in the locality of the school. The result may be entirely negative, but on the other hand he may have to consider such factors as the ownership of the land and, therefore, how far any decision on the part of the community to use this land is restricted by law; he may have to decide on the possible benefits of alternative uses for this land to the community; he may have to find out about landscaping this land to make it aesthetically pleasing; he may have to consider traffic and access to the land, and so on. Thus responses to an *expressive objective* will tend to be diverse and idiosyncratic. It is consequently impossible to measure the achievement of such an objective in the same way as an *instructional objective* is evaluated. In geography many such expressive objectives may be devised, particularly in human geography where planning of farm layout, villages, towns, road networks, and so on, may be suggested. These *expressive objectives* involve the students in using already acquired cognitive skills and concepts and can often be made to appear more exciting than the *instructional objectives*, since the novel situations in which students find themselves can lead them to be creative. No claim is made, however, that students inevitably become creative in such encounters.

Conclusion

If this discussion of aims and objectives in geographical education has been protracted, it is because the whole area of educational objectives is one of controversy linked to the continuing debate about the fundamental nature of education. We have seen that according to Peters' concept of education, an educational process can have no extrinsic aims and on this basis it can be argued that geography is learnt in schools because it is a worthwhile activity. It then needs to be demonstrated that geography is a worthwhile activity because, for example, it gives students cognitive perspectives such as a greater consciousness of their own and others' environment, such as the ability to make judgements based on such geographical organizing concepts as spatial distribution, areal association, spatial interaction, and spatial organization. Many of the older stated aims of geography teaching were in fact statements of why geography was considered worthwhile. It was suggested that the term *aims* should be reserved for such statements since it was seldom possible to verify them empirically. On the other hand, the kind of targets which a teacher set his pupils in his day-to-day work could be called *objectives* and these are more specific though few teachers ever go to the length of specifying such objectives in the behavioural terms suggested by programmed-learning experts. These specific objectives can be classified according to the schemes proposed by Bloom and his associates, though the extent to which such a classification is useful to the practising teacher is not always evident, except perhaps in warning him against the danger of using too many 'knowledge and comprehension' objectives to the detriment of those requiring application, analysis, synthesis and evaluation in the cognitive domain. Perhaps useful as a clarifying device is the subdivision suggested by Eisner which sees objectives as being *instructional* or *expressive* according to what aspect of the educational process the teacher intends to develop. Ultimately the quality of the educational process, whatever classification is used, depends on the kind of relationship established between those involved.

Part of the problem of discussing aims and objectives in geographical education lies in the differing concepts or paradigms of both education and geography that different people have. Broadly, the two main paradigms of geography are (1) the ecosystem or man-land relationship paradigm, and (2) the spatial organization paradigm (Pattison 1970). If one takes a view of education as initiation into worthwhile activities, then both paradigms are relevant; but if one views education as having an essentially instrumental role in economic and social life, then the spatial organization paradigm may seem more relevant and so the broad aims of geographical education may be seen as those of teaching those skills, concepts and principles subsumed within that paradigm. The teacher must choose. My own sympathies are with the broader view of education.

CHAPTER SIX

Curriculum Development and Geography

The curriculum problem

As we saw in Chapters 3 and 4, the curriculum in schools has developed gradually by a process of accretion. As new knowledge evolved, as new subjects were formed, so these were added to the curriculum: sometimes willingly, more often under protest. Occasionally subjects or subject content dropped out of the curriculum; or subjects changed their guise, as at present classics is changing its image from a mainly language-oriented subject to a culture-oriented field. The pressures which have led to a broadening of the curriculum have been largely social and economic, though in some cases they have been avowedly political. But although it is possible to look back over the history of education and see how the curriculum has evolved, on very few occasions is it possible to see a concern for its overall pattern or for some theoretical framework which would enable a curriculum to be built up rationally according to certain criteria or principles. When I began teaching in 1950, I do not believe that the staff of the school in which I taught ever discussed the curriculum operating in the school, except marginally, such as, what to do with the fifth and upper sixth forms after the examinations were over. Much more time was spent discussing the so called extra-curricular activities such as sport, dramatic productions and musical events which took place after school hours. It was almost assumed that the curriculum was in a stable state, unlikely to change and not worth discussing. True, this was in a traditional grammar school where able pupils offered little resistance to the academic education provided. The picture was a different one when I found myself head of a geography department in a comprehensive school, where the decision as to what to teach took on some importance. But it was still true that we spent little time discussing the curriculum as a whole, although the incentive to do so might have seemed greater. Still today it is not clear that (some notable exceptions apart) the staffs of a majority of our schools spend much time on curriculum planning, yet the curriculum problem is very much with us.

What is the nature of the curriculum problem? It is essentially that of deciding what shall be taught in a school, in what framework, with what methods and how evaluation of the learning may take place. This implies a somewhat altered meaning to the term curriculum from that which it has traditionally had in England. It was usual to refer to the curriculum of a school as the total range of subjects taught in the school. Thus one might refer to a particular school curriculum as consisting of English, mathematics, physics, chemistry, biology, history, geography, French, Latin, religious education, art and physical education. When referring to the content of instruction in any one subject, the term syllabus was generally used, and this was an ordered statement of what was to be taught within a subject in each year of the school course. Today the term syllabus tends not to be used in curriculum discussion, as the traditional syllabus statement is being usurped by a much more elaborate statement in which objectives, methods or educational experiences and evaluation techniques are all incorporated. Such a statement is now referred to as a curriculum plan. Clearly, to state that the curriculum consists of English, mathematics, geography, etc. does not say very much until one knows the kind of learning experiences which are proposed under each of these headings. But whatever terminology is used the curriculum problem remains: what to teach, how to teach it and how to evaluate the educational process. It is a problem which also involves questions as to who should decide on curricula and on what criteria.

Dealing with the curriculum problem

Education authorities and educationists have been aware for over one hundred years of the need to deal with curriculum change in some systematic way. In England and Wales the traditional method of coping with this problem was to set up authoritative committees which would look at evidence from many published sources, cross-examine various expert and professional witnesses and after due deliberation issue a report suggesting certain modifications in the curricular arrangements for schools. To go no further back than the first quarter of the twentieth century, one may recall such documents as the Hadow Report in 1926, the Spens Report of 1938, the Norwood Report of 1943, the Crowther Report of 1959 and the Newsom Report of 1963. All these make suggestions about the structure and organization of secondary education as well as about strictly curriculum matters. The Plowden Report (1967) was concerned with the curriculum of the primary school. Since 1964 the task of curriculum reform and development has been entrusted to the Schools Council for the Curriculum and Examinations, a body specially set up for that purpose but derived from two pre-existing bodies, the Secondary Schools Examinations Council (originally set up in 1917) which had the duty of overseeing school examinations, and the more recently created (1962) Curriculum Study Group of the Department of Education and Science. The result is that curriculum problems and curriculum development are under continuous review rather than under periodic review, though clearly reports emanating from the Schools Council can only do so from time to time. Another result of the setting up of the Schools Council is that money is being spent to finance curriculum experiment and curriculum design in a wide variety of fields. Before the advent of the Schools Council, curriculum experiment only occurred in a few 'progressive' private schools or in some state schools where strong encouragement was given to the staff of a particular school to step beyond the bounds of traditional schooling, though seldom were additional resources afforded to the school in question, with the exception of those schools involved with Nuffield Projects. Thus we are faced with what is quite a novel situation in English education, a series of curriculum development projects in which teams of teachers are actively experimenting with new curricula to find out whether they are capable of being usefully introduced into the majority of schools.

This recent development of institutionalized curriculum development is new only in the English context. In the United States of America, curriculum experiments were devised in the 1930s, the most famous of which was the Eight Year Study in which thirty high schools attempted to work a curriculum which was designed according to the apparent needs of adolescents in American society, rather than according to any established disciplines or subjects (Aikin 1942). Such projects were usually designed with the cooperation of curriculum consultants, evaluation experts as well as the teachers, school authorities and universities who in the above case waived traditional entrance requirements to enable potential university students to take part in the experiment without fear of subsequently being barred from university. Many curriculum development projects have been financed in the United States since the Eight Year Project, those most relevant to geography being the Earth Science Curriculum Project (1963-1967) and the High School Geography Project (1961-1970), all of which have been massively financed. In the U.S.A., though funds might be obtained from the government, the running of each project was in the hands of independent bodies. The High School Geography Project was, for example, largely in the hands of the Association of American Geographers. In the U.K., funding of curriculum development projects has been inevitably on a much more moderate scale, but the running of projects has also been farmed out to teams of specialists who in many cases put up the idea for the project in the first place. Those relevant to geography so far have been: 'Geography for the Young School Leaver' led by geographers (R. Beddis and T. Dalton) at Avery Hill College of Education, 'Geography 14-18' led by a team at Bristol University Department of Education (G. Hickman and J. Reynolds), and 'History, Geography and Social Science 8-13' led by W. A. L. Blyth at Liverpool University. Since September 1976, a 'Geography 16-19 project' led by M. C. Naish and based on the University of London Institute of Education has been in operation. These will be mentioned later in this chapter. For other international comparisons of innovations in education and curriculum development, reference can be made to the publications of the Centre for Educational Research and Innovation (C.E.R.I.) of the O.E.C.D.

Curriculum theory
So far we have seen that attempts have and are being made to solve the curriculum problem by
1. reflecting on the nature of the curriculum, seeking expert (including teacher) advice and making suggestions in reports;
2. experimenting with various aspects of the curriculum to see how far innovations are workable or under what conditions innovations can be expected to take root and be diffused among schools.
But an important question was asked in the opening paragraph of this chapter and still needs to be answered, namely on what theoretical

basis should a curriculum be planned? It is important to expose explicitly what are the assumptions made and processes implied in curriculum development rather than allow these to be unclear or implicitly assumed. In the U.K., possibly because it has been deemed important since the 1920s to allow practising teachers to control curriculum design and development and teachers are busy people with limited time for theoretical reflection, curriculum theory has been, until recently, implicit rather than explicit. In the United States, on the other hand, university and other educational experts have always been associated with curriculum development, with the result that at least from the 1940s onwards, a body of explicit curriculum theory has gradually evolved, though as in all theory building, not all theoretical frameworks have proved useful. It is important to realize that the term theory is here used in the sense of normative theory and not scientific theory (Moore 1974). Possibly the best known name in this field is that of Ralph Tyler (1949) who, as a result of his participation in the early U.S. curriculum development projects, wrote a small book *Basic Principles of Curriculum and Instruction* which has become a classic in this field.

Tyler stated that four fundamental questions needed to be asked when developing a curriculum:

1. What educational purposes should the school seek to attain? This is a question which as we saw in Chapter 5 always looms large in educational discussions, though answering it may not be as simple as might appear at first. It is symptomatic that Tyler spends virtually half of his book in discussing this question.
2. What educational experiences can be provided that are likely to attain these purposes? In other words what may schools plan to ensure that it is likely that the objectives are attained?
3. How can these educational experiences be effectively organized? This question relates to the way in which the learning experiences are structured in the curriculum so that basic concepts and skills in each field are gradually consolidated and related to one another in the curriculum.
4. How can we determine whether these purposes are being attained? This concerns the way in which an evaluation is made of learning to check whether the objectives set are being achieved.

This particular model of the curriculum process, that is of the way a curriculum might operate, is sometimes referred to as the linear model since it can be simplifed to the following:

Objectives→Planned learning experiences→Organization
→Evaluation

Its attraction as a model was that it leaves to teachers or education authorities the important decisions as to what are to be the objectives, the learning experiences and the kinds of evaluation to be implemented, while at the same time indicating the kinds of criteria on which such decisions should be made. Thus there is no apparent difficulty in applying such a model to geographical education and indeed one could argue that many teachers in their work do precisely this. They draw up a list of objectives contained in a syllabus or curriculum document which also contains plans for what shall be learned throughout the year, they draw up lesson plans and organize lessons or schemes of work which provide the learning experiences of their pupils and they organize periodic tests and examinations to

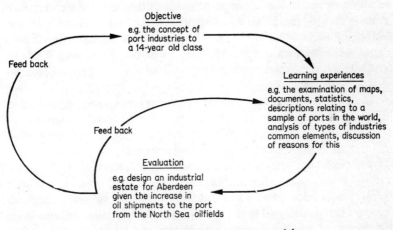

FIGURE 6.1. A curriculum process model.

evaluate the learning. Tyler's model of the curriculum process suited the English situation in which the values which guide the teacher in his choice of objectives have been implicit rather than explicit. But there is one important aspect of Tyler's model which needs to be looked at critically and that is the tendency to leave evaluation to the end. It is not clear from Tyler's book how often evaluation would take place in a period of a year or throughout a school course.

It would seem necessary, however, to see the whole curriculum process as dynamic so that as the learning experiences proceeded it would be possible to feed back into the process the results of evaluation which would tell the teacher whether his objectives had been achieved or even whether they were really appropriate to the learners and whether different learning experiences should be substituted for those provided. Such a curriculum process model would appear as a circular model (Figure 6.1).

In such a model the results of the evaluation could lead either
1. to a change in objectives and in learning experiences, or
2. to a change in learning experiences only.

Beauchamp (1961) investigated the field of curriculum theory and came to the conclusion it was 'a set of related statements that give meaning to a school's curriculum by pointing up the relationship among its elements and by directing its development, its use and its evaluation'. He made it clear that this kind of praxiological theory was really a tool to help action rather than a scientific explanation of all curricula. In particular he pointed out the need for a curriculum process model to indicate (1) what was to be the source of the objectives to be sought, (2) on what knowledge of educational psychology the learning experiences were to be based, (3) what kinds of evaluation instruments were to be used which were appropriate to the objectives sought.

The curriculum process model then becomes more complicated (Figure 6.2). This curriculum process model is effectively derived from one proposed by Wheeler (1967), and another proposed by Kerr (1968). A brief summary of these exists in Lawton (1973).

An interesting systems approach has been developed by D. S. Biddle (1974) from ideas suggested by Johnson (1969) specifically with geographical education in mind. It is an elaborate system taking into account factors external to the school, which he has called a Curriculum Development and Implementation System and which is illustrated in Figure 6.3. In this system, which, it is necessary to emphasize, is *not* a description of what actually happens, but what perhaps ought to happen if curriculum development were to take place under near ideal conditions, the large box occupying most of the diagram is an attempt to summarize the kinds of curriculum processes that could occur within the educational system. There are inputs to this from outside the educational system, that is, from society in terms of society's physical and human resources and in terms of society's cultural and

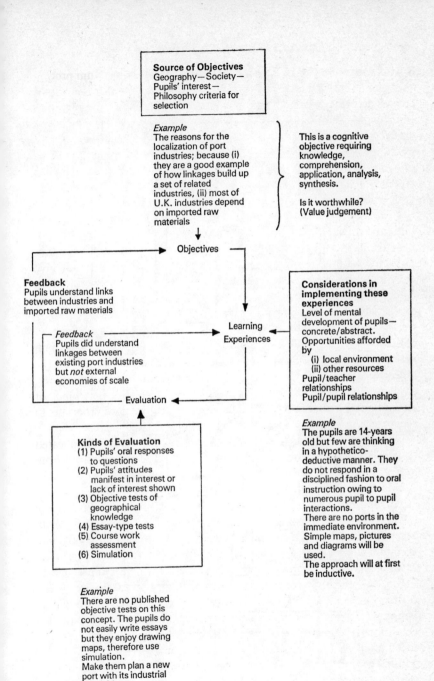

Source of Objectives
Geography— Society—
Pupils' interest—
Philosophy criteria for
selection

Example
The reasons for the
localization of port
industries; because (i)
they are a good example
of how linkages build up
a set of related
industries, (ii) most of
U.K. industries depend
on imported raw
materials

This is a cognitive
objective requiring
knowledge,
comprehension,
application, analysis,
synthesis.

Is it worthwhile?
(Value judgement)

Objectives

Feedback
Pupils understand links
between industries and
imported raw materials

Feedback
Pupils did understand
linkages between
existing port industries
but *not* external
economies of scale

Learning
Experiences

**Considerations in
implementing these
experiences**
Level of mental
development of pupils—
concrete/abstract.
Opportunities afforded
by
  (i) local environment
  (ii) other resources
Pupil/teacher
relationships
Pupil/pupil relationships

Evaluation

Kinds of Evaluation
(1) Pupils' oral responses
    to questions
(2) Pupils' attitudes
    manifest in interest or
    lack of interest shown
(3) Objective tests of
    geographical
    knowledge
(4) Essay-type tests
(5) Course work
    assessment
(6) Simulation

Example
The pupils are 14-years
old but few are thinking
in a hypothetico-
deductive manner. They
do not respond in a
disciplined fashion to oral
instruction owing to
numerous pupil to pupil
interactions.
There are no ports in the
immediate environment.
Simple maps, pictures
and diagrams will be
used.
The approach will at first
be inductive.

Example
There are no published
objective tests on this
concept. The pupils do
not easily write essays
but they enjoy drawing
maps, therefore use
simulation.
Make them plan a new
port with its industrial
area laid out.

FIGURE 6.2. A curriculum process model with a geographical example

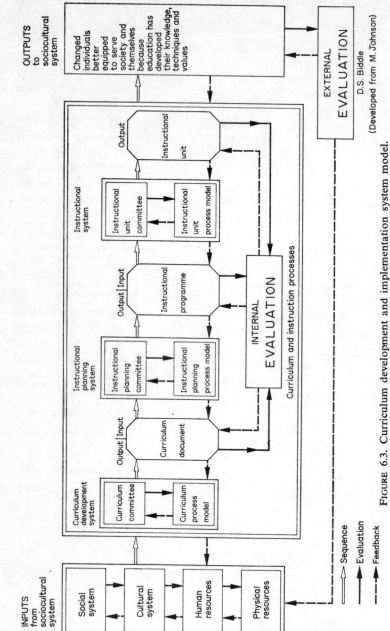

FIGURE 6.3. Curriculum development and implementation system model.

D.S. Biddle
(Developed from M. Johnson)

social values. Similarly, there are outputs from the educational system to society in terms of the transformed individuals. Within the educational system Biddle sees three sub-systems:

1. a curriculum development system which produces a curriculum document, i.e. a statement of general aims, content and learning experiences and intended learning outcomes;
2. an instructional planning system which produces an instructional programme, i.e. a more detailed programme of work produced at departmental level;
3. an instructional system which is at the classroom level and which produces teaching units based on the suggestions of the instructional planning system in the light of the known characteristics of the pupils to be taught.

This is a system for gradually refining what are general directives with regard to education in general and geography in particular to a state where these are operationally usable in a classroom. It is highly likely that in practice, the middle system (the instructional planning system) merges either with the curriculum development system or with the instructional system where these are at all recognizable in the present educational system in the U.K. or elsewhere. But let us concentrate on the curriculum process model (Figure 6.4) which attempts to show how a curriculum for geography might develop.

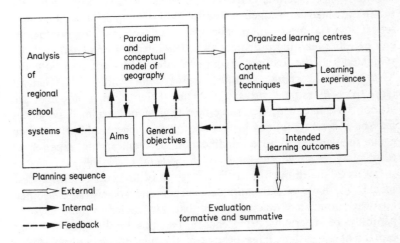

FIGURE 6.4. Curriculum process model for geography.

The left-hand box contains the inputs from the school system indicating the need for change as indicated by changes in society, research findings, teachers' and pupils' views, and so on. These apparent needs are fed into the next box which effectively is a small sub-system in which the various paradigms of geography are analysed in the light of these needs (labelled Aims=general aims of school system) and a paradigm is chosen which appears to supply the means of satisfying those needs. For example, it may be argued that given society's concern for environmental quality, then an ecosystem paradigm for geography may be a better one to use than a spatial organization paradigm. Also interacting in this sub-system are general objectives derived from within geography itself; that is objectives that impose themselves if a particular paradigm is chosen. For example, if the ecosystem paradigm is chosen for use within the model, then it follows that the whole idea of an ecosystem must be one of its general objectives. A particular paradigm and the general objectives which stem from it having been accepted, they are then fed into what Biddle calls the 'Organized Learning Centres' (the right-hand box) which I take to mean a sub-system in which the general objectives prescribed are used as criteria for selecting the content from geography (or from one paradigm of geography) to organize certain learning experiences intended to have certain learning outcomes. How specific are these learning outcomes and how detailed is the content will depend on whether this curriculum process model is seen as merely the initial stage in producing a curriculum document or whether it is seen also as a means of producing an instructional programme. In any case the learning outcomes (whether intended or actual) will be evaluated and the findings of the evaluation fed back into both the 'Organized Learning Centres' sub-system and the 'General Objectives—Paradigm' sub-system. Thus if the learning outcomes are (1) not those intended, then some modification of learning experiences may be necessary, (2) not in accord with the general objectives, then again this may lead to a modification of the learning experiences or possibly to a reconsideration of the general objectives.

Let us follow through a particular aspect of this curriculum process model. We have already assumed earlier that society is concerned about environmental quality (aims), that this has led to the ecosystem paradigm of geography being chosen, that this implies that the concept of an ecosystem must be *one* of the general objectives. If this is fed into the 'Organized Learning Centres' sub-system this means that appropriate content and techniques must be chosen such as, for example, the use of an area of heathland to illustrate the relationship between climate, soil and vegetation, and learning experiences using techniques of soil analysis, quadrat sampling of vegetation in the field with documentary evidence of the climate being analysed in the classroom, to show progressively after several such experiences that the relationship postulated exists or does not exist. The teachers producing the instructional or teaching units will need to go into detail as to the level at which the ecosystem idea is to be developed, on what scale, in which area the field work is to take place, what statistics are to be used, and so on. But clearly this is only a beginning; the ecosystem idea must be pursued so that it eventually reaches a point where pupils become aware of man's function in a large-scale ecosystem, of the kinds of action which lead to a disequilibrium in a particular ecosystem, of the criteria on which one may evaluate whether a particular change in an ecosystem is likely to be harmful or not. In other words the content and learning experiences need to be planned progressively throughout the school course, so that the general aim suggested (concern for environmental quality) may ultimately be achieved. This is no mean feat and it is perhaps not surprising that in the past teachers working on their own, attempting to cope with all the variables involved have not always succeeded. It is, therefore, suggested that teachers should get a lot more help in curriculum building than they have done up to now. This means in terms of Biddle's curriculum development and implementation system (Figure 6.3), that all stages up to the instructional system might be taken as having been prepared for the teacher. The teacher could then concentrate on what he is meant to be doing, namely teaching. This does not mean that teachers should not, if they so wish, participate in the decision-making going on in the other parts of the system; but the whole weight of curriculum development responsibility should not be on their shoulders alone. In many educational systems, teachers have never had this responsibility. It is in fact a peculiarly English phenomenon, though as John White (1973) points out, it is a phenomenon which only dates from 1926 for elementary education, though it is of older vintage for what we call secondary or post-elementary education.

To sum up this brief survey of curriculum theory in relation to geographical education we can return to Figure 6.2 and state that in building a geography curriculum we need to:

1. know the general aims of the education system (or school) which enables us to choose a paradigm for geography which in itself will suggest certain general geographical objectives. We have discussed objectives at length in Chapter 5.
2. devise learning experiences derived from the content of geography but taking into account such psychological considerations as the conceptual level of the content in relation to the perceptual and conceptual difficulties likely to be faced by students. These considerations will be examined in some detail in Chapters 7 and 8.
3. evaluate the outcome of learning experiences both in the short term (day to day) and in the longer term: each year at the end of a school course and so on. We shall be concerned with evaluation in Chapter 9.

Before we go on to look at the psychological considerations, let us briefly examine various curriculum development projects which have been concerned in one way or another with geography, bearing in mind what we have learnt about curriculum theory. This will give us some idea of the way practice has evolved in relation to theory, particularly as some workers in the curriculum field aver that any highly structured model such as Biddle's is difficult to use in practice.

Curriculum development projects in geography

A. *The High School Geography Project*

The first project I propose to examine is the High School Geography Project of the Association of American Geographers. This project arose because of a concern for the quality of geography taught in American High Schools, felt by many educators, but particularly by those who represented geography teachers, viz. the National Council for Geographic Education (roughly equivalent to the Geographical Association in the U.K.) and by those who represented the professional geographers, viz. the Association of American Geographers (roughly equivalent to the Institute of British Geographers). A joint committee of the two organizations was set up in 1958 and this body decided to develop a 'High School Geography Project' whose object would be to improve the content of geography courses and provide instructional materials for teachers and pupils. A one-year course was to be devised as an example which teachers could use or emulate (Graves 1968).

In 1961 a Working Group of professional geographers began to define basic ideas and skills of geographic enquiry which were thought suitable in the High School. These were formulated in an Advisory Paper used by thirty teachers who began experimenting with new ideas and techniques and met regularly to report their findings. An account of these may be found in Kohn's (1964) *Selected Classroom Experiences: High School Geography Project*. From 1961 to 1963 the project was under the overall direction of Professor William D. Pattison and funded by the Ford Foundation and the Fund for the Advancement of Education. In 1964 the project was taken over entirely by the Association of American Geographers, acquired a much enlarged grant from the National Science Foundation and a new director in Professor Nicholas Helburn who with his team was based on Boulder, Colorado. With the additional funds work on the project accelerated. Geographers from various parts of the United States and elsewhere in North America were commissioned to produce courses and materials on various themes. Eventually some six units were produced as shown in Figure 6.5.

The course was to be aimed at students in the 14-16 age range. The process for developing each unit was the following. The concepts, skills and values deemed important to be taught were structured into a course unit devised by professional geographers in consultation with school-teachers and educational psychologists. The unit was then tried out in a limited number of high school classes, usually in the locality where the unit was originally conceived. In the light of the reactions of students and teachers, the original course was revised by the team which had drafted it. The revised unit was then tested in classrooms all over the United States. Again in the light of comments from the trial schools and evaluators, the unit was edited, this time by the High School Geography Project (H.S.G.P.) staff. Then followed another nationwide testing of the course unit and a final revision by the H.S.G.P. staff. The final version was then sent off for commercial production (Gunn 1972). The units are shown in diagrammatic form in Figure 6.5 as being interlinked, because it was realized during the trials that no two schools would necessarily use the course units in the same order. So much depended on what had been done by the pupils beforehand. It was also realized that some units would probably be used independently, i.e. that they would not form part of the whole course devised by the H.S.G.P. team. The unit on Japan exemplified the project's approach to the geographical problems of a nation state.

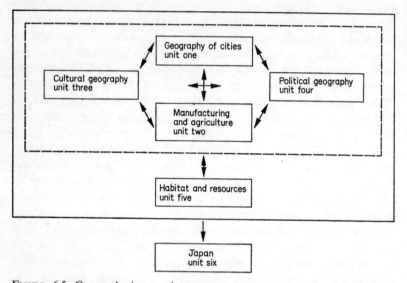

FIGURE. 6.5. Geography in an urban age: a one year course for students aged fourteen to sixteen (*Source*: Gunn 1972).

It may be seen that the evaluation aspect of the curriculum process was undoubtedly built into the H.S.G.P. There were many trials and revisions. Dana Kurfman (1972) avers that the steering committee of the project envisaged three evaluation functions:

1. that of helping to clarify the objectives of each part of the course;
2. the development of tests and questionnaires to judge the efficiency of the instructional materials;
3. the evaluation of the complete course before it was marketed. This was in fact never undertaken partly owing to pressure of time.

The first function was a useful one in that it forced course unit writers to be more and more precise about the learning outcomes that they were attempting to produce, that is, it induced them to become more specific. On the other hand it became clear that in the preparation of instructional materials which were used in trial schools, certain objectives which had not in fact been planned turned out to be of some importance. For example, in handling the Portsville materials (a map board on which the development of a port's urban area is simulated), students learned a good deal about historical factors which had not been specifically written in as some of the unit's objectives. In other words, there was some feedback, from the trials and their evaluation, which resulted in a change in the original objectives. These were never stated in behavioural terms; the task would have been daunting and would have resulted in some inflexible course units.

The second evaluation function, namely the development of tests and questionnaires to judge the efficiency of the trial materials, was only partly carried out. Various tests were created to measure the effectiveness of the *Geography of Cities* unit, but it rapidly became clear that, when concepts and skills were used more than once in a unit, it was difficult to attribute the understanding developed by the students to any particular materials or part of the course. Consequently more faith was placed in the questionnaire answers provided by students and teachers. Student opinion was useful in pin-pointing the aspects of the course which had proved effective and teacher opinion was invaluable in suggesting the kind of revision most desirable. A measure of student interest was apparently the most reliable estimate of the usefulness of a course unit.

What about the objectives of the H.S.G.P.? As we saw earlier, some attempt was made to outline these at the inception of the project in 1961, in the Advisory Paper. But if the curriculum process is similar to the one outlined in Figures 6.1 and 6.2, one can expect these objectives to have been progressively modified. The specific objectives to each activity within any one unit were stated in the Teacher's Guide, but there evolved a gradual realization that there were certain general objectives to which the project would subscribe. These were stated by Nicholas Helburn (1968) to be:

Students will work with a representative variety of facts or generalizations from all the regions of the world, including both physical and social topics. Students will also work with most of the broad abstractions of the field.
Students should understand certain basic abstractions. While there seems to be available no definitive statement of the abstract ideas of geography at any given level, the following have been given a high priority; ecosystem, man-land relations, sequent occupance, location, distance, pattern, spatial distribution, areal association, spatial interaction, diffusion, spatial hierarchy, region, and change through time.
Student training should focus on four skill objectives: an increased

awareness of place and its significance; an increased ability to deal with data in terms of their spatial characteristics; an increased ability to formulate appropriate problems which derive from that awareness; an increased ability to solve (or at least partially solve) those problems.

As a result of working with the Project's materials, the student will be able to ask—indeed, will want to ask—a series of questions that will help him to understand the contents of the world:

Where is it? Where in relation to others of its kind? Taken together, what kind of distributions do they make?

How did it get there? What was there before that made a difference? Whose decisions about the choice of location were important? How were these decisions made?

What factors influenced its growth in that place? What difference does it make to me, to society that it is there?

What else is there too? How are those things related to each other in place?

How is it connected to things in other places? What kinds of flow result?

The students' ability to formulate questions like these, to collect information and to select the relevant from the mass, to hypothesize answers, to recognise the tentativeness of those answers—this is the primary objective of the High School Geography Project.

One might add 'and so be it for geography in schools in general!' If one examines the various units in the course, there is little doubt that a genuine attempt is made to stimulate pupils in the direction indicated by Helburn. Another feature of this project is the very careful guidelines laid down for teachers so that teachers not familiar with the ideas of the project might yet be enabled to use the materials meaningfully in their teaching. But towards the end of its life, the project team found it more and more necessary to concentrate on the process of teacher education to enable the greater diffusion of the project's ideas to take place (Rolfe 1971).

B. *The Geography 14-18 Project* (*1970-75*)

This project began as a result of a group of teachers in the Bristol area discussing the changes required in school geography from 1964 onwards. Proposals were put to the Schools Council which eventually invited the University of Bristol School of Education to initiate a project. The original proposals were for a four-year project which would undertake the following tasks:

1. analyse current classroom practice in the light of changes occur-

ring in geography at university level and of developments in curriculum theory and curriculum development elsewhere (e.g. the High School Geography Project);

2. formulate objectives for geography teaching and identify relevant concepts and skills to be structured into a course of study;

3. prepare appropriate teaching materials as exemplars;

4. re-appraise the objectives as the project developed;

5. develop a set of criteria so that teachers might assess whether the learning experiences provided were suitable for the objectives proposed;

6. assess what changes in the education system would best promote such curriculum development, for example, through in-service training or through new examinations, etc.

This was to be done in relation to the average and more able students in the 14-18 age group. Another project, the 'Geography for the Young School Leaver' project was to be concerned with the 14-16 year age group with emphasis on those unlikely to stay at school beyond the age of 16 (Reynolds 1971). The project got under way in 1970 and ended in 1975. The project team under the direction first of Gladys Hickman and later of John Reynolds had its own idea of how curriculum development might take place. It felt that curriculum development should be seen as part of socio-cultural change; that it involved not only new knowledge to be acquired by teachers and passed on to pupils, but also changed attitudes on the part of teachers, inspectors, head teachers, examination boards, and so on. In other words, it rejected the idea that all that was required was the development of a course backed by materials and a 'teacher-proof kit' of instructions. It clearly did not wish to follow in the footsteps of the American High School Geography Project, but aspired to developing a *teaching-learning system* which became dynamic and therefore self-developing. The approach of the project team is best seen in the diagram in Figure 6.6.

The team agreed that curriculum development was best seen in terms of a system, in this case a *teaching-learning system*, hence the 'recognition of need for systems planning' in the first box. It saw the need to clarify what were to be the main aims and the means of achieving these aims in modern school geography. Some analysis was required of the kinds of factors within the education system and society which might impede or foster change so that appropriate action

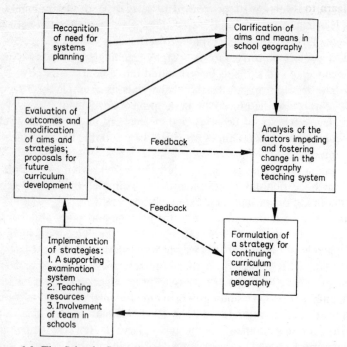

FIGURE 6.6. The Schools Council's Geography 14-18 Project's teaching-learning system.

might be taken, given the aims and means agreed upon. This proposed action was to be spelled out in the project team's strategy which was seen to involve a geography examination which would support the curriculum development process, the production of resources for learning and the involvement of the team in the trial schools. The learning outcomes from the schools would be evaluated with a view to feeding back the information into the next stage of the process so that appropriate modifications could be made in the objectives, in the analysis, and in the strategy (Figure 6.6) (Schools Council 1972a). Thus much stress was laid not just on innovation, but on institutional support for innovation. The team also accepted the idea that objectives should not be of the behavioural variety, but should be in Eisner's terminology both instructional and expressive and could not be completely predetermined by teachers. In the words of an Interim Working Paper: 'There is something contradictory about expecting students to learn to think for themselves, if they have to do this in a way that fits learning objectives set entirely by their teachers or examining boards' (Schools Council 1972a).

The project team made an interesting analysis of the interaction between

1. the way geography as a subject was seen;
2. the aims of geography in school and their assessment;
3. the kind of learning experiences provided in the classroom;
4. the way curriculum change should be managed.

Broadly the analysis is the following (Hickman, Reynolds and Tolley 1973):

Type A When geography is seen as a man-land study with the emphasis on regional description (i.e. the areal differentiation paradigm), aims tend to be those of giving information about the world for citizenship purposes, to make plain man-land relationships and teach map and graphic skills whilst assessment is largely to test factual recall and map reading; learning experiences tend to depend on the teacher as an expositor though he will use audio-visual aids, case studies and other aids. In such a situation curriculum change is managed through changes in examination syllabuses and textbooks.

Type B When geography is seen as a science with predictive powers (the spatial organization or ecosystem paradigm), aims tend to be those of stressing the contribution of geography to scientific thinking, and pupils are asked to learn certain principles and theories and to test hypotheses; assessment tends to be more rigorous, often with objective type questions; learning tends to occur with the teacher providing a sequentially developed course from the simple to the complex, the pupil's learning behaviour being closely determined by the precise concepts, skills and principles to be learned; problem solving is a common teaching technique. In such a climate, curriculum change tends to be managed by providing ready-made courses with materials which the teacher can use immediately.

Type C When geography is seen as a science, but a science in which the principles and ideas are seen as emanating not from a clinical laboratory situation but from a certain culture in which values and a value system are implicit, then aims tend to stress geography's contribution to a student's total sensitivity so that the concepts and principles he learns are related to other areas of experience and to the value system in which they have been developed; assessment is used for feedback purposes and individual work and course work are stressed more than periodic tests. The teaching-learning situation tends to be one where the teacher is a mediator who encourages inter-action between students and between himself and the students and provides problems and resources which help to reveal to the students the purpose of geography and the kind of enquiry pursued in this field. In such a situation the management of curriculum change is a more complex process involving consultation with the teachers, exam-ination boards and others in the education service, as well as the development of criteria for selecting subject matter and learning experiences.

It seems clear that the Geography 14-18 Project team saw them-selves as operating in the last situation described; though they recog-nized that the three situations mentioned above are stereotypes rather than descriptions which will fit all possible cases. Indeed, in many 'real-life' situations a mixture of all three (A, B and C) types of inter-action tends to occur but with the emphasis on one of them.

Let us see what happened in practice. It is important to bear in mind that the team saw as vital a change in the examination system at 'O' level because examinations and the curriculum had got into a vicious circle: examining bodies did not wish to change the examina-tion because they felt teachers would not be in sympathy, whilst teachers felt that there was no point in innovating if examinations remained as they were. Thus part of the institutional support consisted of providing an examination which would be in sympathy with the curriculum objectives of the project. The team negotiated with the Cambridge Local Examinations Syndicate which agreed to run the new examination on behalf of other G.C.E. boards. The main distinc-tion between this 'O' level examination and previous examinations is that only 50% of the total marks are allocated to a common examina-tion paper of $2\frac{1}{2}$ hours in which candidates answer four questions out of a total of twelve questions set. The other 50% of the marks are derived from course work which is internally assessed and externally moderated; the schools determine the rank order of their candidates. The examination questions are based on a core syllabus common to all schools which covers the established ideas and skills of geo-graphy. The questions set entail the interpretation, evaluation, analysis and synthesis of provided sources which include medium- and large-scale maps, atlases and other documentary sources. They are chosen to test the student's understanding of:

1. (i) the character of the local area and the British Isles;
   (ii) contrasts and similarities in economically developed and developing areas, e.g. types of markets;
   (iii) the working of physical and economic systems on a world scale, e.g. types of international trade;
2. (i) the processes underlying landscape and spatial patterns and how these may be expected to change;
   (ii) environmental interrelationships considered as systems and subsystems, so that the notion of multiple and cumulative causes is understood rather than simple deterministic relationships;
   (iii) decision-making and how this is influenced by the values and perceptions of decision-makers, in relation to spatial patterns and organization;
   (iv) the importance of the scale on which patterns and systems are considered;
   (v) how models of various kinds simplify complex geographical reality.

We shall return to this core syllabus later when we consider the operation of the project in a particular school.

The second kind of support that the project team attempted to provide was to use individual members of the team as *change agents*. This term is used to describe the role of the team member in his capacity as a catalyst in the process of curriculum renewal. In effect the *change agent* would participate formally in meetings with a school's geography staff and offer suggestions and help in formulating new curricula, though he would avoid being placed in a position where he would have to take all the decisions. The *change agent* would also take part in small group discussions in teachers' centres, at regional workshops and other meetings in order to sow the seeds of attitudinal as well as cognitive changes. The latter situations were more informal and teachers felt freer to raise their own problems, they were more willing to experiment and could assemble a greater variety of resources. It is, at this stage, difficult to evaluate how successful the *change agents* were, one problem being the relatively small resources at the disposal of the team, so that the impact of the *change agent* is likely not to have been very widely felt, though the further diffusion of the ideas of the project is likely to take place, in part through schools taking the project's 'O' level examination.

The third kind of action taken by the project team was that of providing materials focusing on key ideas which would start the students thinking for themselves and on examples which would start teachers preparing others and developing ideas initiated by the team. Four types of *exemplars* were provided:

1. an individual lesson or assignment;
2. a unit of a sequence of lessons;
3. a course planning structure, i.e. suggestions for developing a course;
4. a starter kit, i.e. a unit of 6-8 weeks' work to start off a course which teachers could develop.

Let us now look at how the project operated in the light of one school's experience, in this case a girls' independent school (Jones and Reynolds 1973). The school (Colston Girls' School, Bristol) agreed to become one of the project's pilot schools in the summer of 1971. During the academic year 1971-72 the school team of three teachers (Sheila Jones, Sheila Smith and Carol Speedyman) and John Reynolds of the project team, hammered out the aims and objectives of a new syllabus which was being planned. The broad aims were stated to be:

> ... to encourage/develop an awareness of the environment, giving an appreciation and understanding of that environment (both physical and human providing a bridge between science and the humanities ...
> ... it is hoped that the child [sic] has been stimulated to think (and act) rationally at local, national and international levels, increasing his/her tolerance and understanding of others.

The school team decided to construct a syllabus with a theme to minimize the tendency to emphasize factual rote learning and to enable students to understand the relationships between the various parts of the course. Water was chosen as a theme since it made possible the consideration of three systems: (a) water in the atmosphere system, (b) water in the drainage system, (c) water in the economic and social system. These three systems enabled ideas to be developed vertically within each system and yet also provided linkages horizontally between each system. After selecting examples from various scales of operation (local, regional, national and international), the team evolved the course content outlined in Figure 6.7.

FIGURE 6.7. Outline of course content and programme at Colston Girls' School.

1972-3 Sub-theme	Suggested topics/case studies	Course work
AUTUMN TERM *Water on and under the ground—* The known—Bristol 'Region' Outline of rock formation and earth movements: The Mendips ⎰ water on and The Cotswolds ⎬ under the Chalk Downs ⎱ ground *Water in the atmosphere* Local weather study Igneous rocks	*Refer to water and man* The local area and selected contrasts Dartmoor	
SPRING TERM *Water on the ground—* Rivers Rivers and man *Water in the atmosphere* Contrasting weather studies	River Basins—e.g. Severn, Trym, Rhine Water supply, Farming, Severnside	River Basin study = 1 unit
SUMMER TERM Glaciation and the sea	Dorset Coast, Leisure/tourism, National Parks, Mediterranean	*Easter Holidays* Field and laboratory investigations of soil = 1 unit Illustrated study of glaciated mountain area = ½ unit Problem solving exercise —conservation/ recreation = ½ unit

1973-4 Sub-theme	Case studies	Course work
		Start on individual study —discussion before end of Summer Term
AUTUMN TERM *Man and water—* Population and food supply *Water and the* Climatic *Atmosphere* contrasts	Climatic and physical limitations *Too little water:* Deserts ⎰ hot ⎱ tundra *Too much water:* Soil erosion Floods/control Monsoon Reclamation *Agriculture:* Subsistence Commercial Plantation—tropical *Forests:* Coniferous	Irrigation/agriculture study = 1 unit Essay related to population/food supply problems = ½ unit

FIGURE 6.7. (*Continued*)

1973-4 Sub-theme	Case studies	Course work
SPRING TERM *Man and water*— The known—Bristol	Urban life— *Water supply:* *Transport a* | motorways *b* | airports *c* | railways *Power:* *Industry a* | motor car *b* | aircraft *c* | chemicals I.C.I. *Pollution*—Sabrina project	Statistical transport exercise $=\frac{1}{2}$ unit Fieldwork transport investigation $=\frac{1}{2}$ unit Essay on urban problems $=\frac{1}{2}$ unit ———— Total 6 units
The unknown	*Sociological* *Other towns*	
SUMMER TERM *Man and water*— Rural areas	Population explosion Rural depopulation Countryside conservation	Individual study to be completed by end of Easter holiday $=$ total 4 units Final examination $=50\%$ 10 units of course work $=50\%$

The course extends over two years and involves three groups of girls in their fourth (15-year-olds) and fifth year (16-year-olds) at secondary school. The course is taught in the fourth year by three 40-minute periods plus two 35-minute homeworks and in the fifth year by one 80-minute period, two 40-minute periods and two 40-minute homeworks. The school staff team also spend 80 minutes each week discussing and planning exercises and work for the course, a task that was stimulated by frequent contact with the project team and with other pilot schools. Consequently exchanges of ideas and materials occurred frequently. One of the ideas of the project was that the course work and the core syllabus should be interlinked. Thus the possible structure of course work topics to be examined is shown in Figure 6.8.

The units in fact chosen for the school are shown in the right-hand column of Figure 6.7. It is clear that each unit of course work is a development of an idea contained in the core syllabus. For example,

FIGURE 6.8. Course work topics for pilot schools.

	Number of assessment units for coursework	
	Minimum	Maximum
I. *Regional or synoptic studies* (i.e. studies of the inter-relationships between complex varied phenomena in areal units at different scales, e.g. human landscapes, local areas, conurbations, politico-economic units)	1	4
II. *Practical environmental and sociogeographical problems* (e.g. studies of problems of development in less affluent nations, or urban planning of conservation, etc.)	2	4
III. *Innovation studies* (e.g. developing research aspects of geography) or other special interests, e.g. water supply, soils, etc.	0	3
IV. *Individual studies by students* ('projects', fieldwork, etc.)	4	4
Chosen units should total	10 units	

the field and laboratory investigation of soils is an extension of 2(ii) in the core syllabus, namely, environmental interrelationships considered as systems and sub-systems.

In general, what the school team has done is to use the ideas developed through discussion with the project team in a way which suited the expertise of the staff and the school and the local environment. This has resulted in a course which appears slightly to emphasize the physical aspects of geography. One may also wonder whether the detailed objectives are really contributing to the long-term aims, but it is difficult to be sure of this except in the long term and such a distant perspective is not yet available. In any event, if the curriculum process is working as in Figures 6.1 and 6.2, the feedback to the school team through the evaluation should facilitate a modification of some of the aims and objectives sought.

C. *The Geography for the Young School Leaver Project (1970-75)*

This project, although conceived at the same time as the Geography 14-18 project, arose out of the need to develop a curriculum in geography for adolescents who have compulsorily remained at school from fifteen to sixteen since the academic year 1973-74. It had, therefore, an apparently more limited task to undertake; the team appointed to this project (Rex Beddis, Tom Dalton, Trevor Higginbottom,

Pamela Bowen) decided that its main task was to produce appropriate resources for pupils and teachers, around certain topics or themes. Thus in this case the team decided what themes would be useful to teachers, whereas in the Geography 14-18 Project, the team attempted to make teachers in each school develop their own themes. The Geography for the Young School Leaver team used the following criteria for selecting their themes:

1. each topic should be of interest to the pupils at this point in their lives, i.e. it should involve them, if possible, creatively;
2. each topic should be exploitable in the local situation of each school;
3. each topic should be of more than transitory relevance.

The members of the team sought to avoid thinking of the target population as 'less able' and so isolate them from the rest of the school population, yet they had to be realistic in their assessment of the initial attitude of the young school leavers to school-work.

The team worked in general in the following manner. It made contact with schools to be clear about the conditions under which teachers worked, reviewed the sources of teaching materials available, decided on three main themes (1) Man, land and leisure; (2) Cities and peoples; (3) People, place and work; and began preparing a preliminary version of the first theme. Each theme contains five or six units, each unit being a self-contained sub-topic likely to keep a class employed for about a month of geography time on the school time-table. An example of some of the key ideas considered for Unit 2 of the *Man, land and leisure* theme is set out in Figure 6.9.

The project team provided ideas and resources in the form of a teacher's guide, work sheets, loose-leaf maps, photocopied extracts from journals and newspapers, photographs, slides, films and tape recordings; these were tried out in five pre-pilot trial schools. The theme and resources were then revised in the light of experience with these five schools and then trials were arranged in 280 schools in England and Wales. Regional meetings were held to discuss with teachers concerned the objectives of the trials and to review progress as the trials developed. To encourage the diffusion of the ideas of the project, newsletters were sent out and trial schools were arranged in clusters to make possible rapid communication and mutual encouragement among those involved in the trials and the possible spread of the ideas from an active diffusion centre (Geography for the Young School Leaver 1972). Further, local coordinators were appointed in a large number of local education authorities to stimulate dissemination and development of the project's ideals.

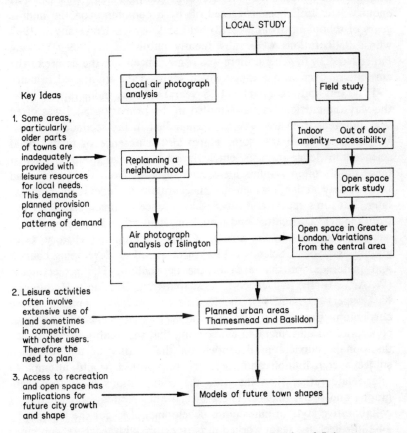

FIGURE 6.9. Key ideas for one unit of *Man, Land and Leisure*.

This project in its management of curriculum development resembles (on a much smaller scale) the American High School Geography Project. In terms of the analysis provided by the Geography 14-18 Project team, it is much nearer to Type B than to Types A or C, though the kind of geography it provides is not necessarily of the strictly scientific type postulated in Type B curriculum development.

D. *The History, Geography and Social Science Project for the Middle Years of Schooling* *(8-13)* *(1971-75).*

This project arose out of an enquiry conducted for the Schools Council on the extent of social studies teaching in the schools of England and Wales in the 8-13 age range (Lawton *et al* 1971). But that enquiry had itself been triggered off by a conference on the middle years of schooling (from 8 to 13) held at Warwick University in 1967 whose deliberations were subsequently published in 1969 (Working Paper No. 22). In general there was some concern for the nature of the curriculum over an age range which spanned the traditional primary (5-11 years) and secondary (11-18 years) schools, more especially as the way the curriculum was handled in the primary school was often very different from the way it was handled in the secondary school. In particular there was some alarm at the absence of much social science knowledge from the curriculum for that age group, given that these pupils often acquire ideas and attitudes from their peers and from society at large which are inaccurate but difficult to eradicate later. Lawton's report confirmed this absence of much social science from the 8-13 curriculum and made suggestions for developing certain courses. As a result, the Schools Council set up the History, Geography and Social Science 8-13 Project aimed at developing courses and materials for that area of the curriculum. The project team (W. A. L. Blyth, R. Derricott, A. Waplington, G. Elliott, H. Sumner, K. Cooper) accepted that the idea of *integration* as applied to the curriculum was ill-defined, that there was no generally accepted conception of an integrated curriculum, that the quality of any multi-disciplinary curriculum depended on the quality of an individual subject's contribution and therefore the project would attempt to inter-relate rather than integrate the contributions of history, geography and social science. The project team's strategy was to adopt a collaborative style of curriculum development. As for the Geography 14-18 Project, the team worked in partnership with teachers, conscious of the existence of four variables in each of the schools collaborating with the project, namely children, teachers, schools and environments, each of which had to be taken into account in order to develop courses. There was, therefore, no attempt to produce overall courses and themes with 'teacher-proof' packs.

The team, after a conference with teachers participating in the project's work, produced a document on objectives and key concepts which it believed would focus attention and help thinking in the development of curricula. The objectives which were to be sought were those which could be classified as (i) intellectual skills, (ii) social skills, e.g. the development of empathy, (iii) psycho-motor skills, e.g. manipulating equipment, (iv) attitudes, values and interest. In the case of the intellectual skills, it was thought important to develop the ability:

1. to find information, through reading, listening and observing;
2. to understand and interpret pictures, maps, charts, graphs, etc.;
3. to organize information through concepts and generalizations;
4. to communicate findings through an appropriate medium;
5. to evaluate information;
6. to test hypotheses and generalizations and to question the adequacy of classifications.

The key concepts were, in effect, means of focusing attention in the fields of history, geography and social science on aspects which would have maximum transfer value, that is on ideas which would be generally rather than uniquely applicable. The key concepts (I would call them organizing concepts in this context) were:

1. communication: the movement of individuals, groups or resources or the transmission of information;
2. power: the exercise of power over individuals, groups or resources;
3. values and beliefs: the conscious or unconscious systems by which individuals or society respond to natural, social and supernatural orders;
4. conflict/consensus: the ways in which behaviour is adjusted to cope with natural and social events;
5. similarity/difference: the classification of phenomena according to relevant criteria;
6. continuity/change: the distinction of phenomena in relation to time;
7. causality: the idea that a phenomenon may be attributed to occurrences preceding it (Blyth *et al* 1972).

It was felt that each of these key concepts would help teachers to relate one curricular area to another. For example, conflict in relation to pollution may be seen to have a geographical or spatial dimension as well as an historical and a social one.

The team working with teachers in some 31 schools developed over 100 units by the summer of 1973, a unit corresponding to half a term's work within the framework of secondary school time-table, or two to four weeks' intensive activity in some primary or middle schools. One example of a unit may be taken from one created by P. Tutchener at St Peter's School Wem. This unit is developed around the theme of fire, and is aimed at ten-year-old children. It is in three parts. Part I uses historical evidence of a great fire in the children's own town (Wem) in the seventeenth century; part II is concerned with the problem of fire in the present; part III is concerned with the scientific aspect of fire. The ways in which the objectives and key concepts are seen as operating are shown below.

FIGURE 6.10. Objectives and key concepts at St Peter's School, Wem. (*Source*: P. Tutchener, Wem.)

GENERAL OBJECTIVES

COGNITIVE
(a) Knowledge
    —of historical fact relating to the environment,
    —of methods used to record such facts,
    —of buildings past and present,
    —of properties of 'fire'—combustion, heat, inflammability, means of extinguishing,
    —of the fire service.
(b) Concepts
    —of a 'fact' as opposed to a hypothesis,
    —of change, and of there being a reason for change (causality),
    —of 'fire' (not simply bonfire, hearth fire, cigarette, cooking stove).
(c) Skills
    —in language—oral or written,
    —in reading,
    —in problem solving,
    —in researching and investigating,
    —in looking—critical visual examination,
    —in art work, pictorial and graphical representation,
    —in devising and carrying out experiments (problem, hypothesis, observation, deduction).

AFFECTIVE
(a) Attitudes
    —evaluation of the religious attitudes expressed concerning the fire,
    —what attitude to adopt towards attaching blame to the girl who caused the fire,
    —fire hazards—if household contains danger, there is also danger to others. Should houses be inspected? etc.,
    —towards utilizing fire—is it worth the risks,

(b) Interests
—in whose interests to prevent fires,
—in whose to utilize fire.

OBJECTIVES SPECIFIC TO THE SEPARATE DISCIPLINES

HISTORY

(1) To develop 'historical' thinking.
—notice fact of change since seventeenth century,
—see in existing seventeenth-century buildings a sense of continuity,
—appreciate a particular factor causing change, i.e. fire.
(2) To develop an understanding of human values.
—appreciate that Vicar's explanation of the fire was a value judgement,
—deal sympathetically with such values, recognizing the conditions and extent of knowledge prevailing at that time.
(3) To develop historical imagination.
—simulating the activities and panics of the burning town,
—possible story e.g. 'I was a boy living in Wem on the night of the fire ...'
(4) To develop critical thinking using the historical method.
—evaluating the evidence—how many accounts of the fire are there?
—do they differ?—how far can we trust them?
—how can we discover anything at first hand? e.g. must be reason why seventeenth-century cottages in profusion at Tilley but few in Wem.
—consider modern instances of conflicting reports of the same incident in different newspapers.

GEOGRAPHY

Substantive—man in his environment.
Methodological—perception, recording, interpretation.
—how many people in Wem at time of fire? How big was it?— reference to maps—can we conclude that houses packed together (thus aiding spread of fire)? How near to water?
—origins of street names as they were then,
—why did fire not spread to Tilley?

SOCIAL SCIENCE

(1) Methodological
(a) Cognitive
—scientific method—making assumptions and then testing it.
e.g. people didn't return to Wem because they found homes elsewhere,
people didn't return to Wem because they thought the fire might happen again,
people didn't return because they thought God was angry with it.

(2) Substantive
  (a) Cognitive
    —to develop understanding of nature of society.
      —society joins to provide fire service to protect all,
      —responsibility of householder to other people,
    —laws to protect children from fire in school,
      —laws proscribing fire lighting in fields etc.
        i.e. society reflecting the needs of man. (Note: contrast with
        old fire services which would turn back, without assisting,
        from buildings not bearing their plaque. Were they help-
        ing society? *All* the people?)
  (b) Affective
    —sociological curiosity
      —the fire service isn't just *'there'*—who pays, who runs it, who
      thought of it?
      —after simulation of Wem fire—discuss Why do people act
      as they do in such a situation? Do they always do the most
      sensible thing?

KEY CONCEPTS

Values and beliefs
  —'religious' interpretation of fire.
Conflict/consensus
  —how did the inhabitants adjust to their post-fire situation?
Similarity/difference
  —comparison of Wem and another town according to the specific
  criteria of seventeenth-century houses.
Continuity/change
  —'why were post-fire houses built of brick?'
Causality
  —attributing change in Wem to the effect of a particular phenomena.

The teachers have evolved resources for attempting to put over these
ideas from documentary evidence, from observation in the locality and
from materials provided in school.

The project team has published a handbook to help teachers further
develop programmes of work in this area of the curriculum; (ii) some
units designed to implement certain objectives; (iii) materials and procedures which have been found repeatedly useful. It is also intended
that a considerable amount of time and resources should be devoted to
a programme of diffusing the project's ideas and methods (Blyth *et al*
1976).

Other comments on geography curriculum development projects may
be found in Hall's (1976) *Geography and the Geography Teacher*, and
in Boden's (1976) *Development in Geography Teaching*.

Curriculum development and geography: a summary

Rational curriculum development in geography in the United Kingdom has only just begun. If an explanation is to be sought for this relatively late start, it is probably to be found in the reluctance of educationists to become involved in curriculum theory and course design and in the widely accepted value judgement that the teacher in the classroom is the best judge of what to teach as well as of how to teach it. As Taylor (1970) has indicated in his report *How teachers plan their courses*, the value judgement has led in practice to teachers concentrating on the content of courses, subscribing to general and unverifiable aims, neglecting the methods appropriate to the subject matter and to the aims postulated, and also neglecting suitable means of evaluating the course. If this is an accurate picture for teachers in general, it is probably valid for teachers of geography, since Taylor included geography teachers in his investigation. The problem is that the complicated processes necessary to the achievement of a worthwhile curriculum in geography require far more time and energy than the average teacher possesses.

It would seem necessary, therefore, to abandon the pretence that curriculum planning is mainly the teacher's concern and to establish strong curriculum planning teams for geography. These would consist of geography schoolteachers, university teachers of geography, and curriculum specialists in education who would hammer out a curriculum document consisting of general and more specific objectives, suggestions as to learning experiences to be provided, and indications of the evaluation procedures to be used. Such a document would give firm guidance to the teacher but would allow him to adapt his precise teaching methods to the students he is teaching, and to the environment in which he finds himself. If such a document were revised periodically, it would not become, like many examination syllabuses, a fossilized view of the subject as it was two decades or even half a century ago. Such a suggestion is not without precedent in the English-speaking world, in Australia and particularly in New South Wales, work has been developing along these lines for many years (Biddle and Shortle 1969) and well-structured curricula have been planned. Curriculum development projects in geography could then be looked upon as experiments in curriculum design which need to be reviewed periodically because of the changing conceptual structure of a discipline and because of the evolution of educational ideas. The results of such experiments would feed information into the design of a new curriculum document. This involves a greater measure of centralization than has been usual in the U.K. in the past, but centralization is not ipso facto an undesirable thing, particularly if it leads to greater efficiency in curriculum design, planning and execution.

CHAPTER SEVEN

Learning Problems in Geography: Perception

Introduction

The process of education never runs smoothly. All teachers become aware of certain learning difficulties which arise among the pupils or students whom they teach. In some cases the diagnosis is simple: the students have no intention of learning whatever the teacher intends they should learn. In other words, they lack the basic motivation to learn this or that idea or skill, and in the last analysis, it is this which is paramount in the learning process. No teacher can make a student learn what he does not want to learn. This fact has led some educationists to argue that no attempt should be made to teach a pupil anything about which he has not expressed some curiosity or interest. This is an extreme position which I find difficult to accept since there are many aspects of life and learning which few of us might have spontaneously been interested in, had it not been that a teacher awakened in us some response. Consequently I would regard it as part of the teacher's duty to attempt to stimulate interest in a field about which the pupil may have shown no great curiosity. We have to recognize, however, that we may fail and frequently do. It is perhaps one of the greatest disappointments faced by a young teacher, keen on geography as a branch of learning, to find that his enthusiasm for the subject does not evoke a similar response in all his students.

It is not my purpose in this chapter to delve deeply into the problem of motivation, because the number of variables involved is enormous and it is difficult to affirm anything which has general validity (Vernon 1969). For example, in any given classroom, not only may there be thirty to forty individual variations in basic motivation to learn geography, but each individual's attitude to the subject may be influenced by his own interaction with the teacher's personality, and by his interaction with other individuals in the class. It is a commonplace that pupils often take to a teacher rather than to what he teaches; in other words, motivation for the subject derives from the charisma of that particular teacher. Further motivation to work in school is to a large extent socially engendered. Thus the social background of the children, the area the school finds itself in, are both variables which may influence the ultimate attitude of the child to what he will or will not willingly learn. If attitudes in the community outside the school consider education to be an essentially instrumental process for preparing students to earn a living, then scientific and practical subjects may be favoured by pupils at the expense of the arts or social science subjects. Thus two teachers of equal teaching ability may find the task of motivating children to learn geography easy or difficult according to the schools in which they teach. There is no easy solution to this problem, particularly for those teaching in adverse social environments, and it would be dishonest to state otherwise. Only in a society where goals are clearly stated and the whole apparatus of the state is geared to achieving these goals, as in China and the U.S.S.R., is the problem of motivation at least partially solved (Taylor 1971).

Assuming that there is no basic resistance to learning geography, what kinds of mental operations are involved for the pupil? Learning geography implies the learning of certain concepts, principles, theories, and skills which are contained within the subject as it now is. But in acquiring such a body of knowledge, pupils are asked to observe landscapes and phenomena either directly in the field or indirectly through the media of maps, pictures, diagrams, written evidence, and so on. Consequently a problem is immediately posed, namely what do the pupils in fact observe? Is it what the teacher sees, or are they in fact seeing something different from the teacher? Most teachers will testify from personal experience that very often the question 'What do you notice in that picture?' brings forth an answer which is different from that anticipated. We therefore have in any learning situation, a problem of perception which immediately arises—that is, the teacher must be aware that students will not necessarily see what he sees in a landscape or in a map. What a student in fact sees will be influenced by his previous experience, by the kinds of concepts he has acquired, and by the sorts of theories he may hold. For example, if I call the Forge Valley in North Yorkshire a glacial overflow channel, I am not only indicating that I have observed a valley-like feature and that I have a concept of such a feature, but that I also have a theory as to its formation. Thus what I perceive is not an objective reality which may be put into words, but an interpretation of what my senses perceive in terms of the kind of conceptual framework which I have acquired over time. Thus conceptualization and perceptualization inter-react. What is perceived helps the individual in his concept formation but equally his existing concepts to some extent guide what he perceives. As Piaget has pointed out, learning involves *assimilating* experience into one's existing conceptual framework and *accommodating* one's conceptual framework to new experiences. If new experiences (e.g. in classroom lessons) do not unduly disturb the conceptual framework of the child, then there is an equilibrium in the mental system. But if new experiences prove difficult to assimilate within the existing conceptual framework, then a disequilibrium sets in, manifest by the pupil making certain typical errors, and the process of equilibration can only occur when the pupil changes his conceptual framework to accommodate the new experiences (Piaget 1961). To take the example of the Forge Valley cited earlier, if my conception of rivers is that they run from high ground to low ground gradually cutting into the surrounding land to form a valley, then my first encounter with the course of the Derwent river must yield me an experience which it is difficult for me to assimiliate completely within my present conceptual framework, for the Derwent would appear to have cut through an escarpment of Corallian limestone instead of flowing eastwards out to sea near Scalby (Figure 7.1).

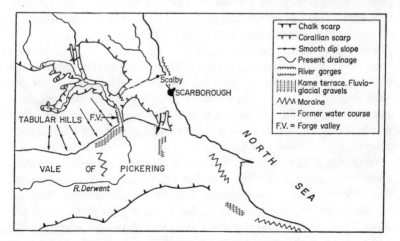

FIGURE 7.1. The flow of the River Derwent.

It is, therefore, necessary for me to alter my conceptual framework to take into account a possible blockage of the eastward route of the Derwent river resulting in the pounding back of water until it overflowed over the scarp of the Corallian at a low point into the Vale of Pickering, and in so doing, gradually cut a gorge now called the Forge Valley. By postulating such an event I am now able to assimilate this new experience and my mental system is in equilibrium once more; I have accommodated my mental structures in a manner which enables me to make sense of this experience. It may well be, of course, that later experiences may cause me to revise my ideas further.

Having raised the issue of the interaction between perception and conceptualization, I am going to concentrate for the rest of this chapter on problems relating to perception.

Environmental perception

If one considers that learning geography must to some extent, if not to a large extent, be based on direct experience of the environment in which the student lives, then it would seem important to understand how the student perceives his environment. If the teacher is seeking to enlarge his students' perceptions of their environment, then it is necessary for him to know what these students' present perceptions are. Of course the extent of a child's environment and the nature of his perceptions are a function of his age and experience. Visual perception is derived from the effect of light on the eye's retina which transmits a series of impulses to the brain. The all-important operation of interpreting these impulses occurs in the brain. Consequently a young baby seeing patterns of light and shade, of colours and movements, makes very little sense of these compared with the kinds of interpretations given by an adult. Similarly, a person blind from birth who is suddenly given his sight, may have to spend some considerable time trying to make sense of the visual impressions which now assail him, since until then, he has relied entirely on his senses of hearing, touch, smell and taste.

Gradually a child begins to become aware of his immediate environment in his room, in the home and in the immediate neighbourhood, this process being helped considerably by the stimulation provided by the people in his environment, that is mainly his parents and siblings. This process is also helped as speech develops, since naming and classifying objects is a way of interpreting the environment. The speech learnt will tend to conform with publicly accepted meanings since by so doing the child can begin to operate on his environment in a way which is meaningful to others as well as to himself, and he is more likely to be successful in obtaining what he desires (Vernon 1962).

But what do children of school age in fact perceive in their environment? Although there is a growing literature on environmental perception (Goodey 1972) and mental maps (Gould and White 1974; Spencer and Lloyd 1974) much of it is concerned with the adult's view rather than the child or student. Probably the best known work in this field is Kevin Lynch's *The Image of the City* (1960) in which residents' perceptions of central Boston, Jersey City and Los Angeles were analysed to find out what parts of these cities were well known to them and which parts were not, what stood out in the environment, what was missed and what was liked and disliked. Research in environmental perception is largely concerned with such matters as: perception and environmental quality, hazard perception, urban images, perception from certain routes, perception of barriers, micro areas and personal space, perception of far places and lastly preferential perception. It ought to be pointed out that in a sense the word perception involves two slightly different processes and therefore different percepts according to whether the person perceiving has had direct experience of what he perceives or whether he has had vicarious experience only. There is bound to be some discrepancy between my mental images of Addis Ababa, a city which I have visited, and that of a person who has never been there, although he may have read about it and seen pictures of the city. In geography we are often called upon to give students images of far away places which they have never visited and we must therefore expect these images to differ from our own (if we know the place). These students' mental images will still be to some extent based on analogies with environments which they know from direct experience. But even if two people have both had experience of a certain place, there is no guarantee that their perceptions will be identical or even similar (Yi-Fu Tuan 1974).

The number of studies which have been made of children's perceptions of their own environment is relatively limited, though in this as in other areas of child psychology Piaget was a pioneer. However, Piaget's studies were principally concerned with the child's conception of space and his ability to carry out mental operations involving spatial relationships. These will be looked at in Chapter 8. Here I will be concerned mainly with what children notice in their own environment. Few simple studies of this kind have been undertaken, possibly because researchers have been more interested in children's ability to map data or interpret maps and photographs. Two studies which have been undertaken use photographs as a means of finding out what the children know of their environment. The first undertaken in the U.K. in Leeds was an attempt to find out (inter alia) what children aged 7-11 years actually saw in their home area, which in this case was an industrial area with textile mills, clothing and engineering factories, terraced houses, roads and a canal. They were asked to state what they saw in a photograph of the area (Bayliss and Renwick 1966). The children's responses showed that they had little difficulty in naming the main items of their environment pictured in the photograph, though particular things within the *cultural landscape* tended to be picked out and no general statement was made about the area. Indeed, only five of the ninety-five children involved thought that a hill (shown by rising ground in the background) was worthy of a mention. In other words, observations tended to be of particularities rather than generalities in the townscape. The second investigation was essentially concerned to find out (1) which features of the environment around a school the nine- and ten-year old children could recognize, and (2) which features of the environment they marked on maps which they were asked to draw of their journey from home to school (Calland 1973). The investigator accepted Lynch's idea that significant features of the environment would probably be landmarks, edges, districts, paths and nodes. He photographed a number of these features, mostly outside a one-mile circle centred on the school, with a few features located over three miles away. He then asked twenty-four children who lived within a mile radius of the school, whether they recognized the features shown, and later discussion took place about them. In general the total percentage of firm recognitions, that is the percentage of locations accurately named by children, was around 15%, though some children had an idea that they had seen the features but could not name them. There was a tendency for the distance-decay principle to operate, the further away the feature the less likely it was to be recognized, though anomalies existed owing to the smallness of the sample tested. Most features recognized lay within a circle centred on the school whose radius was $1\frac{1}{2}$ miles. It seemed also that a recently cut dual carriageway road (of the motorway type) was effectively acting as an edge to the perceptual field of the children. The maps children drew of their journey from home to school tended to show that they had a clearer idea of what the environment contained at both ends of the journey rather than what existed in between. Certain buildings stood out, such as a hospital, groups of shops; road features like junctions and roundabouts (Lynch's rotary) and the 'motorway' where it impinged on a child's route. On the whole, the ten-year old children tended to put in more information than the nine-year olds. It seemed clear that at this age children are conscious of landmarks, edges, nodes and paths but not of districts or areas.

There have been, to my knowledge, no other studies of older children's and adolescents' perceptions of their local environment. In general one may hazard a guess that as children get older, so their perceptions become more selective; what is observed and noticed particularly depends on developing interests and the growing conceptual framework which is being acquired. My son as a primary school boy used to observe all sorts of things which I as an adult ignored. When he became a student of architecture his observations in the landscape were much more concerned with buildings and environmental quality. Similarly a student who becomes interested in geomorphology begins to see the natural landscape in a new light and observes features on a journey which others do not find significant. Thus many students, as they mature, acquire a 'set', that is an inclination to perceive the environment in certain ways, even if that set is no more than a tendency to observe certain types of motor cars. A review of the literature on environmental perception may be found in Wood (1970), in Saarinen's contribution of *Focus on Geography* (Saarinen and Bacon 1970) and in Yi-Fu Tuan (1974). One important point that teachers need to understand is that children's or adults' images of the environment are 'real' to them even if they do not correspond to some 'objective' reality. The teacher has to start from the images held by children, not from his own.

The perception of photographs and pictures
Studies of what children in fact see in photographs have been made from time to time and have brought out useful information about children's perceptions of landscapes of which they have no first-hand knowledge. Two investigations were undertaken by Long (1953, 1961), the first with primary school children and the second with secondary

school children. The pattern of the first study was to present children
with three photographs of essentially rural landscapes and to ask
them to describe what they saw. No attempt was made to guide the
children or to prompt them. Their spontaneous comments were
recorded and analysed. It appeared from this analysis that the photographs were not seen as a 'composition' but rather as an agglomeration
of individual features; the height and size of landscape features were
never suggested and many errors of scale could be inferred from
statements made by the children; the recognition of features therefore
tended to depend on their shape rather than on size. An interesting
aspect of the findings was that children expressed feelings of pleasure
or of anxiety on seeing certain of the landscapes depicted. They
seemed able to imagine themselves in the area shown and to react
accordingly. In the second study carried out in English grammar
schools with students aged eleven to sixteen years of age, two
approaches were used: that of undirected search for features perceived, and secondly, a directed search, the students being asked
certain questions about the landscapes in the photographs. The
undirected search revealed that the secondary school children did
not observe more features than primary children, but they seemed
more aware of what were 'geographically significant' features. In
other words, they had become more selective in what they observed.
They tended to observe man-made features of the landscape more
readily than natural features, though if invited to search for such
features they did find them. In general the conclusion of these
studies was that if photographs are to be used as evidence in
geographical study, then students must be trained to search for
relevant features and particularly should be trained to compare the
size of objects pictured in the photograph to develop a sense of
scale.

It is important to bear in mind that being sensitive to photographs
and pictures is to a large extent dependent on the culture in which
the student is brought up. Pictorial representations of three-dimensional
reality are a convention, but one with which most people in the
developed world are familiar through long exposure. However, children
and adults from cultures where such representations of reality are
rare, may not interpret such pictures in the same way as we do. This
is particularly true of the conventions used for perspective, so that
a large animal which is drawn small in size to give the illusion of
distance may be seen as literally small but near, whilst much smaller

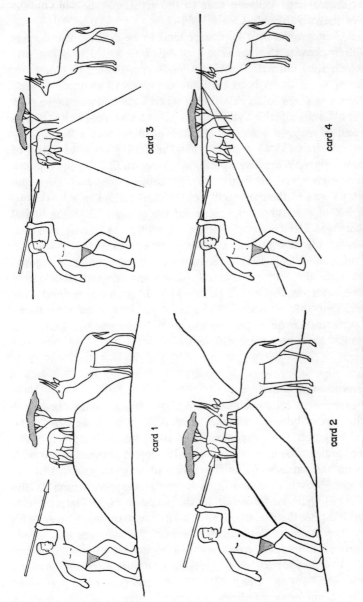

FIGURE 7.2. The effect of representation on perception. (*Source:* Mundy-Castle 1966.)

animals drawn large because near to the artist may be seen as the bigger of the two (Mundy-Castle 1966).

Aerial photographs of a landscape tend to be difficult to interpret by children because they present a point of view which is not that from which they normally look at a landscape, though this problem may lessen as air travel becomes more popular. An example of such difficulties was given in an experiment when forty children (aged 6-11 years) in a Cambridgeshire village were shown a vertical aerial photograph and a map on scales of 1:5000 of their own village. Only fourteen children (35%) realized that the area shown was that of their own village. When twenty children who studied the photograph first were each asked to identify fifteen features once they knew the photograph was of their own village, the total failure rate was 30%, that is, out of a possible total score for the group of 300, the actual total score was 210. In fact the failure score (90) was heavily weighted by the relatively high failure scores of a group of children below the age of nine years (Dale 1971). Above the age of nine, children seemed to have little difficulty in correctly describing most of the simple features shown on the aerial photograph. It must be remembered, however, that this was a photograph of an area known to them. Their performance on a photograph of a landscape not known to them might have been very different.

The perception of maps

Dale's experiment briefly summarized above was as much concerned with children's abilities to make sense of a map as well as of an aerial photograph, since the vertical aerial photograph is, in a sense, a rather special version of a map. He also provided the children with a map on the same scale as the aerial photograph and asked for preferences. Most children seemed to prefer the photograph to the map, though their performance in the recognition of features tests did not indicate their marked superiority over those children who chose to use the map. Performance on both the map and the photograph seemed to improve considerably after the age of nine. This is a finding partly supported by a more elaborate series of experiments conducted by Blaut and Stea (1971). These workers asserted that, since a map's essential characteristics were those of possessing a scale, a projection and a set of abstract signs, a vertical aerial photograph could be conceived as being a map, for though it may possess no

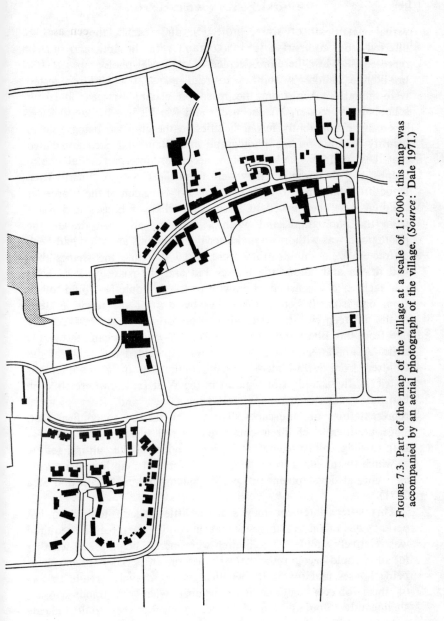

FIGURE 7.3. Part of the map of the village at a scale of 1:5000; this map was accompanied by an aerial photograph of the village. (*Source*: Dale 1971.)

verbal statements of scale, projection and legend, these may be inferred from comparing the photograph with the area and objects represented. They therefore decided to use aerial photographs to test pre-literate children's abilities to read maps. The children tested were initially taken from the reception classes (six-year olds) of schools in Worcester, Massachusetts and Rio Piedras in Puerto Rico. There were apparently few difficulties in the children being able to identify features on the photograph and Blaut and Stea concluded that these children could therefore accurately interpret aerial photographs, and that whether they were from the U.S.A. or Puerto Rico made little difference to their performance. Nineteen of the Worcester children were then asked to trace the outline of houses and roads from the photograph and when a number had been drawn, the photograph was withdrawn and after the children's attention had been distracted for a minute, they were asked to name the shapes they had drawn and colour the houses red and the roads yellow. After this each child was asked to draw in pencil the route he would follow from one isolated house to another by way of the roads. Sixteen of the nineteen children were able to perform all tasks satisfactorily and from this Blaut and Stea claim that six-year olds can read iconic maps. A similar kind of experiment was conducted with six-year old children from an isolated peasant community in a mountainous district of the island of St Vincent in the West Indies, where children had no contact with maps, television, films and other pictorial representations of landscapes. The results seemed to confirm that, since pre-literate children could read aerial photographs and that map-reading ability seemed to be independent of the cultural setting in which the children lived, 'a "natural" form of map learning occurs as a normal development process in young children' (Blaut and Stea 1971).

This latter statement may seem a little difficult to accept, but perhaps one ought to remember that the kind of map reading required was relatively simple. The children were merely being asked whether (a) they could recognize certain shapes on an aerial photograph as being houses and roads, (b) whether having drawn a crude tracing of these objects they could remember what the tracings (once significantly coloured) stood for, and (c) whether they could indicate how to get from one house to another by road. They were being asked to handle representations of concrete objects of which they would have had direct experience. On the other hand, it is salutary to remember that when the 58 St Vincent children were asked to identify features on the aerial photograph, the mean score per six-year old child was only 1·4 features, but with the 107 Worcester children the mean score was 6·4 features per child. The claim that map-reading ability is possibly one which develops naturally in widely differing cultures needs to be qualified considerably. It would seem on the evidence presented that it develops more rapidly in some cultures than in others. However, it seems to me that the essential conclusion concerned with perception which may be gleaned from this experiment, is that young children do not have great difficulty in perceiving what the more discrete shapes and lines represent on an aerial photograph, especially *once they realize what the photograph is meant to show.*

When one moves away from the perception of simple shapes on an aerial photograph or map to the perception of more complicated documents like atlas maps and topographical maps, many problems arise in interpreting the wide variations in performance which exist between different learners. Psychologists have tended to argue that there exists a kind of primary mental ability which they have called a 'space factor' the extent of which would determine how well learners would cope with map-reading or the reading of geometrical and machine drawings. Indeed in the U.S.A. Thurstone (1944) wrote a book on the study of perception in which he specifically identified

1. 'perceptual speed' as a variable, that is the ability of a subject to notice and identify quickly details in tests requiring him to match shapes and pictures;
2. the ability to perceive embedded shapes, that is, shapes inextricably mixed up with other shapes, which require close analysis before they can be visualized as being separated from their matrix.

In England, Macfarlane Smith devoted a great deal of his research work to studying the spatial aspect of mental ability and published an overview in his *Spatial Ability* (1964). Neither of these studies was specifically concerned with map-reading or interpretation. More general studies involving geography were reported by Heywood in 1938 and by Taylor in 1960. Heywood in a small investigation in which he tried to find out what mental factors were involved in the geographical work of boys and girls, seemed to be able to detect the existence of a spatial ability factor as conducive to a good performance in geography. Taylor, on the other hand, found that the

general factor (g) was far more important in explaining good performance in geography than any spatial factor. But these studies although
relating to geography were not closely concerned with the perceptual
abilities of children. Satterly (1964) was more specifically concerned
to find out whether performance in map-reading could be associated
with certain psychological variables. He tested sixty students aged
fourteen to fifteen in a secondary modern school in England, giving
them a battery of psychological tests for ability in spatial concepts,
spatial skill and perception, and a series of tests of map-work
performance. The scores on the two sets of tests were used to
calculate product moment correlation coefficients to indicate the
degree of association found between each of the variables. The
results showed that in general there was a statistically strong and
significant correlation between the psychological variables measured
and performance in map-work tests. In other words, the students
who got high scores in tests of spatial ability tended to get high
scores in tests of map-work. Satterly then carried out further analysis
of his data to find out whether any one psychological test could best
predict performance in map-work. The results of this analysis
indicated that a test for the perception of embedded shapes was the
best single predictor of map-work ability.

This particular finding of Satterly's is one which seems to accord
with experience outside the experimental situation. A topographical
map is, after all, a mass of embedded shapes in which roads stretch
across contour lines, railways, canals and urban areas, in which discrete symbols like those for a church or a windpump may be surrounded by other symbols, in which the shape of contours seems
infinitely variable, in which information may sometimes appear buried
in a jungle of colours and shapes. Thus the student who seems to have
the ability quickly to disentangle perceptually the kinds of shapes
which he requires in order to make sense of certain aspects of the
map information, who is also able to discriminate between similar
shapes (e.g. cutting and embankment symbols) is likely to be the
good performer in map tests. But this only leads to a further question,
namely: why are some people better able to perceive shapes even
when embedded? Satterly carried out a further analysis of his data
in order to find out what factors appeared to underlie the correlations
which he found between the psychological tests and the map-work
tests. Of the two groupings of factors which seemed to stand out as
being closely related, there appeared to be one corresponding to

perceptual reasoning (the ability to perceive spatial relationships) and another corresponding to the achievement of a spatial concept, that is the ability to internalize spatial relationships and operate on them mentally. We shall consider the attainment of spatial concepts in Chapter 8.

Another perceptual problem which children and adults encounter when studying maps is that of disentangling the figure from the ground. It is a well-known phenomenon in the psychology of perception that although children very quickly learn to distinguish a figure or shape which stands out from a background, there are many cases where attention may focus on either the figure or the 'ground' if both are equally meaningful or meaningless. In Figure 7.4 either the central white figure or the two black 'grounds' can be focused upon so that two completely different interpretations may be given to the figure.

FIGURE 7.4. Alternating 'figures'.

A similar problem faces a child or adult who is unfamiliar with the configuration of a particular country or region if it is represented in black and white or any two contrasting colours. The child may have no clue as to what is the land and what is the sea, neither will he necessarily know whether the map is conventionally positioned with north at the top unless the cardinal points are clearly marked. This problem is illustrated in Figure 7.5 where the sea is shaded but the land remains white. Some will inevitably interpret the shaded area as the figure (the land) and the white area as the 'ground'. Such figure-ground problems are less apparent when several colours are used or when there are different intensities of shading on the map.

The problem of perceiving differences in intensity remain as do those of interpreting what each shading is meant to represent.

Barbara Bartz (1970) who has done much research on the legibility and interpretation of maps, makes the simple but important point that for many learners the most important quality which they look for in a map is its clarity. A map which contains too much information is liable to be misread and will not serve its primary function, since

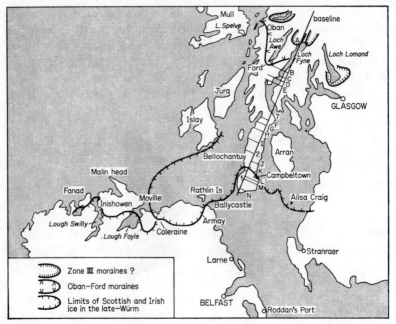

FIGURE 7.5. A shoreline diagram and late-Pleistocene ice limits in the north of Ireland and south-west Scotland. (*Source*: Dury, G. H. (Ed.), *Essays in Geomorphology.*)

perceiving what one is looking for will be difficult and time-consuming. The problem of legibility concerns symbols as well as the type used on the map. Certain symbols stand out more clearly and readily bring to mind an appropriate stereotype; for example, the symbol for a church on a medium-scale British Ordnance Survey map or that for a railway. Others seem to fade discreetly into the background and are less easy to apprehend, such as parish boundaries, or rough grassland. A perceptual-conceptual tendency is that children in particular tend to concentrate on limited aspects of the map information.

This we saw happened when they studied pictures or photographs. Thus an instruction to study a map does not automatically ensure that students will scan the map for broad distributions and patterns; rather will they tend to examine special limited aspects of the map or micro-patterns. It is important that teachers be aware of this tendency, since often when a topographical survey map is used as evidence in a geography lesson the teacher will want to bring out broad patterns of relief and how these may affect the distribution of man-made features. Thus instructions have to be explicit, otherwise teacher and pupil will be looking at different things.

Sandford (1967, 1970, 1972) investigated the perception of an atlas map by English grammar school boys and followed this by a study of children's conceptual understanding of atlas maps. Here we shall be concerned only with the first investigation. The technique was a simple one: a group of boys aged from eleven to eighteen were given an atlas map of the continent of Asia and asked to write down in twenty minutes what the map told them about Asia. The replies were analysed to see if any significant patterns emerged. This unguided perception of an atlas map yielded the information that the students scanned an atlas map in a variety of ways, the most common of which was to start somewhere near the centre of the map and to move from west to east (as one would read a book) or to move around the coastline in a clockwise direction, or occasionally to move in a north to south direction. It could be inferred that the starting point of the scanning was to some extent determined either by the boldness of the type or by familiarity with a particular name on the map.

It would appear that training in the use of an atlas map is something which needs to be reinforced. The problem of the symbols used is also present on an atlas map as on a survey map, since some symbols seem to be perceived and understood easily (e.g. a town or a river) whilst others are not. The comprehension of symbols is made difficult by the fact that different atlases use different symbols.

Summary
Geography like other subjects attempts to develop students' mental abilities both in the cognitive and the affective sense. Teachers in attempting to stimulate the mental faculties of their charges need to be aware of the kinds of learning problems which are likely to face students, some of which will be specially relevant to the subject

which is their concern. In the case of geography it is particularly important to note that perceptual difficulties are very likely to arise either in the direct observation of the environment or in the study of secondary evidence, particularly photographs and maps. In the case of the direct observation of the environment it seems clear from what evidence is available so far, that primary school children do perceive certain landmarks, nodes and edges but are little aware of areas. The extent of their observations is limited by the resources of their environment and by any marked barrier which makes access to a neighbouring area difficult. A distance-decay principle seems to operate in that they recall fewer features of their environment the further these are located from their home base; older children tend not necessarily to observe a much greater number of features, but their wider experience sometimes leads them to have a wider perceptual field and their mental 'sets' lead them to become much more selective in their observations. This would accord with the development of deductive reasoning whereby some albeit unconscious, hypothesis-testing may develop.

In the perception of secondary evidence, it seems clear that whether students are looking at photographs or maps, they tend to look at particular features, not at wholes or 'gestalt'. To get pupils studying macro- rather than micro-patterns requires careful training. Recognition of individual features on photographs or maps depends essentially on the shape rather than the scale of the feature, and on maps in particular identifying features may be rendered difficult by the 'figure-ground' problem, especially as it concerns the difference between land and sea, but also on the perception of map symbols. Individuals differ significantly in their ability to perceive what is on a map, this being related partly to some perceptual speed factor and partly to their capacity to conceptualize space. It is to this conceptual aspect of learning geography that we now turn.

CHAPTER EIGHT

Learning Problems in Geography: Conceptualization and Logical Thinking

Introduction

As we noted in Chapter 7, the relationship between perception and conceptualization is a close one. A child's inability to make out whether the map he is looking at represents an area which is mostly land or mostly sea, may be classed as a perceptual problem. But it is equally true that what he does perceive is as much due to the concepts he holds about what the lines and patterns on a map represent. As in every branch of learning, the problem of concept acquisition and concept growth is acute in geography, and is intimately linked with the development of language and with the pupil's experience of the world. A primary school child who explains that an island is a raised piece of pavement in the middle of a busy road is indicating that his experience of the term 'island' has been in an urban context and that he has acquired the language to describe this experience. The fact that in a geographical context, the term is normally used to mean an area of land entirely surrounded by water is irrelevant to that child's experience. He may be given a formal definition of an island, but this may remain little more than verbiage until he has been able to see an island either by direct observation or by means of pictures.

In this chapter we shall examine the problems of acquiring concepts in geography and especially those concepts which are concerned with location, spatial distribution and spatial relations, since these are particularly the concern of geographers. We shall also look at the ability of pupils and students to handle these concepts in the process of reasoning about spatial relations. The importance of concepts is paramount since they form the basis on which our whole pattern of thinking develops. The concepts of geography and their inter-relationships are the substance of the geographer's view of the world.

Concepts

It is necessary first to make clear in what sense I am using the word concept. I propose to use it in a sense which is generally acceptable to psychologists, that is to describe a way in which the mind structures particular experiences such that these experiences become classified and evoke a similar response. A child very quickly learns to distinguish certain aspects of its immediate experience from others. For example, it soon learns to distinguish men from women, birds from cats and dogs, cars from bicycles, and so on. It acquires a concept of each of these experiences and reacts to them in certain specific ways. It may or may not be able to use words to describe these concepts. Concepts may be acquired independently of the language used to represent them. In early life children form many concepts though they can seldom express these in words. Contrariwise, children may later use a number of words which are either empty of meaning for them or to which they attribute a meaning which is not the publicly accepted one. As children develop their use of language, so this language can play a part in conceptual development and this part becomes more and more important as one moves away from the acquisition of concepts representing concrete objects to those representing ideas. To sum up, a concept is basically a classificatory device which enables the mind to structure reality in a simplified manner by concentrating on the essential attributes of certain experiences. All volcanoes are different, but they have certain common attributes (cone shape, craters, lava and/or ash lithology) which enable us to group all hills of this type under one concept. This is the public concept of a volcano. It is true that any person's private concept may vary in a thousand different ways. I may have a mental picture of Vesuvius when the word volcano is mentioned, you may have a mental image of Popocatepetl. This does not matter since we are agreed on the essential attributes of a volcano.

Problems arise in communication when either there is no agreement about the public meaning of a concept or where there are two or more distinct concepts which are represented by the same word. Clearly there is no universal agreement about the concept represented by the word 'geography', which is why people are often talking at cross purposes when they are discussing geography. There are, of course, innumerable differing personal views of what geography is. Similarly, the term 'region' is one which needs qualifying if discussions using this term are to be fruitful, since there are several different concepts which use the same term. Hence the need to distinguish between 'formal regions' and 'functional regions'. It is to minimize these misunderstandings that physical scientists agree to give a formal definition to certain terms so that all workers in the field shall, during the lifetime of that definition, use the same concept. This does not mean, as is implied by the previous sentence, that once a term has been defined it remains fixed conceptually for ever. As knowledge progresses, so the kinds of concepts used may change. Some concepts may no longer be deemed very useful and may disappear, whilst new ones are evolved. For example, within the field of geography the concept of 'grade' as devised by W. M. Davis in 1902 to describe the condition of balance between erosion and deposition attained by 'mature' rivers is now thought by some geomorphologists not to be a particularly serviceable concept and is not being used by present-day research workers (Dury 1966). On the other hand, a phenomenon may be observed, studied, classified and renamed where the old name seemed less suitable, as is the case in the study of the movement of the upper layers of the earth's crust, which is now called the study of 'plate tectonics' rather than 'continental drift'.

It will be clear from this elementary analysis that concepts may be of very different kinds. The simplest concepts are those used to describe things or objects: river, beach, canal, hill, farm, shop, street, and so on. These are the sort of concepts the referents of which can be seen or observed. Certain concepts, however, refer to things or events which cannot be observed in their entirety. Or put in another way, it is difficult to get experience of these concepts directly. For example, the term market as applied to the stalls in a town's main square is easy enough to conceive, but when it is applied to the money market or the foreign exchange market, it is much more difficult to get the necessary experience of the concrete events which give rise to the concept. Similarly, when the scale of the object referred to is enormous by human standard, it may prove difficult to acquire a concept of it, as in the case of the term continent as used in geography. Further, certain concepts refer not to things or events but to ideas developed by man. These concepts can never refer directly to observed phenomena, they are what Gagné (1966) has called concepts by definition. A simple one often used in geography is that of 'density of population'. One cannot observe a 'density of population' since it does not exist in reality. Density of population is a defined relationship between population and area and may be expressed as number of people per square kilometre. Other such concepts would be: relative humidity, the location quotient, the connectivity index, and so on. These concepts usually express relationships which have been structured in particular ways to suit a human purpose, usually to suit research and explanation in that field. The distinction between a concept which can be acquired by observation and one which can only be acquired by a process of human communication is fundamental in the learning of any subject including geography. Lastly, the term's 'organizing concept' is sometimes used in geography. This term denotes a complex of inter-related concepts pertaining to one aspect of the subject. For example, the terms 'locational analysis', 'areal association', 'spatial interaction', are organizing concepts.

Concept acquisition in geography

Children acquire a large number of concepts during the process of physical and mental development and most of these concepts are undifferentiated as far as the children are concerned. They do not know that the concept of weight belongs to physics, nor that of tree to botany, neither do they know that rock is a geological concept. Many of the concepts which are used in geography children pick up during their experiences in and out of school, sometimes because of deliberate action on the part of the teacher, sometimes by chance. Few of us can remember when or how we came across and began to use such concepts as rain, cloud, stream, valley, hill, mountain, town, village, and so on. These concepts form part of our mental make-up from an early age. Which particular concepts we learn depends a good deal on the sort of environment we live in. An English, American or Western European urban child is likely to acquire many common concepts used to describe a town and urban phenomena.

He will come across shopping centres, residential areas, industrial areas, traffic, roundabouts, car parks, railway stations, etc. A rural child may be more familiar with rough pasture, wood, grass ley, heifer, steer, hogs, silo, combine harvester, and cattle market; he may also be more sensitive to concepts describing the relief features of a landscape than an urban child whose landscape is built up.

Evidence about which of those concepts used in geography are acquired at various stages in our life is scanty. Vass (1960) attempted to find out whether it was possible to determine the age at which the teaching of physical geography could be fruitful because children had acquired many of the basic descriptive concepts. His experiment showed that there was a steady growth in understanding of certain basic concepts in physical geography from eight years to fifteen years; but he found it impossible, on the evidence he had, to suggest an age at which physical geography might begin to be taught. Perhaps the most useful evidence to come out of this study was that the concept of 'relief' as applied to the landscape was generally ill-understood. This indicates that all concepts which encapsulate a variety of more simple concepts are difficult to acquire. Another concept offering similar difficulties is that of drainage.

Lunnon (1969) was concerned to find out whether the growth in understanding of certain geographical concepts by primary school children was gradual and how far this growth was related to mental age, chronological age and the socio-economic class to which the children's parents belonged. He used ten concepts (river, mountain, beach, farming, trade, desert, season, soil, cloud and map). His method was to test for comprehension of the concept in two ways: by asking each child what he understood by the word representing each concept (a verbal test), and by showing exemplars and non-exemplars of the concept in pictorial form and asking the child to indicate which was an example of the concept (a pictorial test). The 140 children tested ranged from five to twelve years in age.

The scoring of the children's performance showed that growth in understanding of those concepts occurred gradually, but was fastest in children aged between five and eight years and was more related to chronological than to mental age. If one tries to account for this finding, it is probably that the explanation lies in the simple fact that the older children have had the necessary experience to enable them to assimilate those concepts. Children whose parents were in the highest socio-economic group did perform much better in both the verbal and

pictorial tests than those whose parents were in the lowest socio-
economic group; further, the differences were much more marked in
the verbal than in the non-verbal tests. In other words, children from
the higher socio-economic group have a distinct advantage when it
comes to handling these concepts linguistically. On the other hand, the
test showed that, with all socio-economic groups, a grasp of a particular concept when tested non-verbally was acquired earlier than when
it was tested verbally. This simply means that children often have a
concept of a farm, or beach or river, long before they can explain
verbally what a farm, a beach or a river is. Acquiring a concept is one
thing, being able to verbalize about that concept is another and
requires a degree of linguistic sophistication not normally possessed by
young children, particularly those coming from homes where the
'elaborated code' (language which is not context-dependent) is not in
common use. Another finding which is of interest is that some of the
concepts tested, such as soil and trade, were not fully grasped by the
older children. This has to be understood within the limits of what the
experimenter would accept as a full grasp of the concept, but it demonstrates once again that the more complex the concept, whatever the
apparent simplicity of the word used to describe it, the less it is likely
to be understood at an early age.

In view of these findings it is surprising that few text-books used in
geographical education are in any way carefully graded in the concepts
which they present to the pupils. Milburn (1972) who investigated the
terms used in primary and secondary geography text-books in England
noted that, not only were about half of the terms introduced without
being defined, but there seemed no clear rationale behind the introduction of a term at any given stage, neither was it clear that authors
were aware that, for example, the terms *river basin* is more complex
than the term *confluence*. Further, text-book writers were often fond
of using a variety of regional terms, like Sudd, Paramos, Selvas,
Campos, Fjeld, which picturesque though they may be, add a considerable load on the memory without necessarily enlightening the
mind. If the concept to be understood is that of a tropical rain forest,
it is not conceptually significant that this goes under different local
names in Brazil, Zaïre, Indonesia or Eastern Malaysia.

It would therefore seem necessary for those concerned with geographical education to become much more aware of the cognitive
hierarchy within the discipline. The concepts used in geography might
be classified under such headings as:

1. *Concepts by observation:*
   (a) simple descriptive concepts, e.g. stream, tributary, factory, river mouth, department store, wind, etc. many of which are concepts acquired in ordinary everyday experience but which can be reinforced in the geography curriculum;
   (b) more difficult descriptive concepts, that is either
      (i) those which it is difficult to experience directly because of their scale or location, e.g. a continent, a cirque, tundra;
   or (ii) those which require the understanding of two or three other concepts, e.g. an aquifer (a rock, porosity, water), functional zone or area;
   (c) very complex descriptive concepts requiring the understanding of a large number of related concepts, e.g. the level of the water table, relief, drainage, central business district, urban hierarchy;
2. *Concepts by definition:*
   (a) simple defined relationships between two variables, e.g. density of population, location quotient, index of integration in a network;
   (b) more complex defined relationships in which three or more variables are involved, e.g. the concept of geostrophic wind involves an understanding of the relationship between air movement, the pressure gradient and the coriolis force.

It would take up too much space to attempt to work out in detail a cognitive hierarchy for all the concepts used in geography. The diagram (Figure 8.1) gives an indication of the kind of hierarchy I have in mind. Some concepts may be learnt 'in parallel', as for example where certain concepts all refer back to an earlier notion. Thus river mouth, source and tributary all refer back to river and only have meaning (in that context) when the concept river is known, but it does not matter whether river mouth is learnt before tributary or *vice versa*. On the other hand certain concepts are learnt 'in series' in the sense that logically prior concepts need to be known for the new concepts to be acquired. For example the concept of a river basin is meaningless to anyone who has no notion of the way networks of streams collect water from an area and feed it to a main stream and so out to a lake or a sea. Similarly the idea of antecedent drainage will only have meaning to those familiar with the idea of a drainage basin and with mountain building. Descriptive terms indicating a classification of a river or drainage patterns, like dendritic drainage or trellis

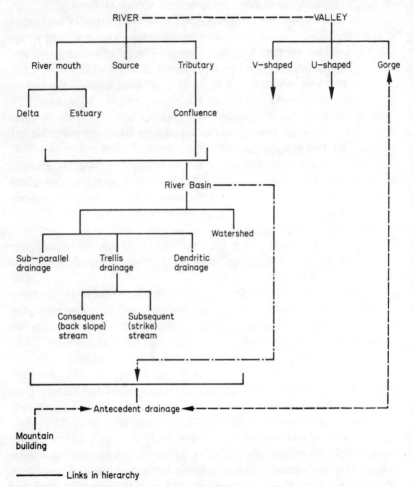

FIGURE 8.1. Concept hierarchy in a river network.

drainage, may or may not enter into the hierarchy depending on how detailed the work being done on that topic.

Such a hierarchy will have links with other hierarchies. For example the concept 'valley' may be linked subsequently to V-shaped valley, glaciated valley, or gorge, each of which will be linked to concepts which seek to explain the formation of such valleys. Thus the term 'gorge' can be linked to the idea of antecedent drainage.

It is important to note that in the diagram (Figure 8.1) there is a clear distinction between most of the concepts which are simple descriptive concepts and the term antecedent drainage which is an explanatory concept subsuming a hypothesis about the way in which a particular drainage pattern may be explained. For example when it is stated that the Brahmaputra river basin is a case of antecedent drainage, one is stating that the present river pattern may be explained by postulating that the Brahmaputra river system existed prior to the formation of the Himalayan Mountains.

Such a concept is at several degrees of complexity removed from the concept of, for example, dendritic drainage. I am not therefore suggesting that once the concept of river basin is known, then the idea of antecedent drainage is next in line to be taught. It is much more likely that there will be a long period of time when other ideas are being learnt before the teacher will deem it appropriate to teach the concept of antecedent drainage.

Concept development and Piaget's model of mental development

How far children and students are able to assimilate and accept these concepts as part of their mental equipment depends on their mental development. If we accept Jean Piaget's classification of the stages of mental development, we obtain the following pattern (Beard 1969):

I. During the sensori-motor period (0-18 months) the baby is getting to know his immediate environment tactually and visually, and develops the ability to repeat certain actions, e.g. grasping a small hanging ball or toy.

II. During the period of concrete operations of classes, relations and numbers (18 months to about 12 years), the child develops the ability to use language and to think conceptually. This long period may be subdivided into:

(a) the pre-conceptual substage (18 months to $4\frac{1}{2}$ years). These are the nursery education years, when the child begins to use language and to represent things symbolically through words, playing, drawing and later by writing. There is evidence from his language that he is not yet able to form true concepts. In other words his use of words to describe things is inconsistent; he has not yet understood, for example, that certain men may be classed within the concept 'father', but not others. The same would be true for many objects within his environment. He is not clear as to what attributes are essential to a concept. Thus during this nursery education period one would expect a child to begin trying to classify his environmental experiences, but one would hardly expect him to be very successful. Similarly one would not expect him to reason logically. He would be quite capable of holding contradictory beliefs such that the sun moves independently (from morning to evening) but also moves because the child moves (as when travelling by car or in a train). We shall return to spatial relations later.

(*b*) the intuitive substage ($4\frac{1}{2}$-7 years). These are the years when children really begin to form simple descriptive concepts based on their growing experience of their environment. Trees are correctly described and understood to be different from bushes, and again different from grass. Trees, bushes and grass are given as examples, but which particular concepts they will acquire will depend on their environment and particularly whether this environment is urban or rural. During these infant school years children's thinking tends to be very much influenced by their immediate environment and by immediate stimuli. They find it difficult to review a situation mentally, but need the presence of the objects about which they are talking and thinking. Their thinking is essentially egocentric in the sense that events are interpreted as all being related to their needs or actions. Consequently it is difficult to attempt to make them conceive of a situation (e.g. in a distant land) in which they are not involved. Further, children in this stage find it difficult to understand the relationship between the parts of a whole and the whole. A simple illustration will bring this out. When my children were in that age bracket (5-7 years) we used to spend our holidays in a small town in south-eastern France. We travelled from England by car and therefore had to cross virtually the whole of France from north-west to south-east. Therefore one could argue that my children not only lived for some time in St-Rémy-de-Provence and knew it to be a very small town, but also had the experience of travelling two days across France in order to get there and another two days when it was time to return. Yet their conception of France was the town of St-Rémy-de-Provence; it was the place where they stayed. They did not conceive of France as a huge area in which St-Rémy-de-Provence was a very small part. The roads along which we travelled to get there were seen as a kind of narrow strip of land joining England (home) and France (St-Rémy-de-Provence). Gustav Jahoda (1963) demonstrated this same difficulty with a group of Scottish children of a wider age range, Stoltman (1971) with American children, and a similar experiment was carried out by Towers (1974) with a sample of 9-year old children with broadly similar results. An international study (Stoltman 1976) confirmed this to be a general tendency.

During this period, it is also relevant to geography to mention that relative terms such as bigger than or smaller than present difficulties. Big and small tend to be seen in absolute terms, the exact nature of the absolute being dependent on the child's experience. Similarly, the concept of the conservation of quantities is not accepted, whether this applies to numbers, areas, volume or weight. Thus to say that Great Britain is smaller than France but has about the same population may not be very meaningful to children at that stage.

(c) the concrete operations substage (7-12 years). During this period 'operations' become true mental operations in the sense that they are internalized. In other words the child can begin to work things out 'in his head' without necessarily needing to manipulate them physically at every step in the thought process. For example, if asked to arrange in order coloured columns in cardboard representing the petroleum production of a group of countries, he can do this relatively quickly without needing to measure laboriously each column against every other. More specifically, children who are reaching the end of the stage of concrete operations learn to deal with:

(i) a hierarchy of classes. Not only are they able to form concepts, but they realize that certain concepts include others. Thus they begin to understand that the land surface of the earth may be divided into continents, that each continent contains a number of states ($C = S_1 + S_2 + S_3 \ldots + S_n$), that each state is often subdivided into provinces, departments or counties, etc. ($S = P_1 + P_2 + P_3 \ldots + P_n$). They usually begin to understand what are in fact pairs of sub-classes, for example, detached houses and houses that are not; grassland and arable land, motorways and other roads. When children can operate mentally in this way they are said to have understood the 'law of closure or composition';

(ii) orders of succession or magnitude; that is, they are able to arrange data in order according to the size of each item of the data. This can apply to lengths, areas or volumes. This is important in comparing the size of countries, or the production of particular commodities, or the respective sizes of populations;

(iii) the idea of complementarity, that is that if a population is made up of two types, say French-speaking and Flemish-speaking Belgians, then if one subtracts all the French-speaking Belgians, only the Flemish-speaking ones are left. This may seem to us very obvious, but it is an idea which is not always grasped by children of this age. A further complication is to consider other ways in which the Belgians may be divided, e.g. rural-living and urban-living Belgians; or again Belgians over 21 and those under 21. Children who are able to handle such 'substitution' will realize that no matter how they subdivide the Belgians, their total numbers at any one time will remain constant. Children will then understand that if $Fl + Fr = B$, that $B - Fl = Fr$, or that operations can be reversible;

(iv) symmetrical relationships. This follows to some extent from (iii) Children realize that the distance between point A and point B is the same as the distance between point B and point A. Or put another way, they understand that even if the return journey from Birmingham to London seems shorter (or longer) than the outward journey, there can be no difference in distance granted the same road was followed. Another aspect of these symmetrical relationships may be illustrated by stating that if the Severn Bridge joins England to Wales, then it also joins Wales to England. The same is true for relationships between individuals or between countries. Thus at the stage of concrete operations a child may be capable of understanding that all members of the E.E.C. are partners and that each partner stands in a similar relationship to other partners.

Associated with this ability is the understanding that an operation followed by its converse is annulled, for example, a point five kilometres east and then five kilometres west is 0 kilometres away;

(v) the multiplication of classes, or put in another way, the ability to classify things according to two or more criteria. Thus if we ask a pupil to name countries in Western Europe with populations of less than ten millions where French is spoken as one of the languages, we are asking them to select countries according to three criteria;

(vi) the multiplication of series, that is the ability to use two or more criteria each arranged in series to select a given item. The best example of this is the ability to locate places on a map by means of a reference system such as the national grid on British Ordnance Survey maps. The numbers 075 634 involve using two series of numbers (eastings and northings) in order to locate a point on a 1 : 50,000 (or some other scale) map. It goes without saying that this ability is best developed by using a simpler reference system when first introduced, such as letters for eastings and single numbers for northings.

It might seem, when reviewing what mental operations children can perform in the stage of concrete operations, that little remains for them to learn. However great is the mental development which occurs in this period, one needs to bear in mind the great variability which exists between one child and another. Thus not only will there be great differences at any one age between the totality of mental operations that pupil A can perform compared with pupil B, but whereas pupil C may be ahead of pupil A in his ability to classify things, A may be ahead of C in his ability to conserve quantity. Various aspects of mental operations will develop at different rates in different children. Further, whereas many have believed that by the age of twelve most children will no longer be thinking in concrete terms, much of the evidence which has accumulated since the 1950s suggests that many adolescents and adults go on thinking in concrete terms for many years, particularly when faced with a novel or unusual situation.

What are the limitations of the thinking of pupils and students in the stage of concrete operations? First they find it very difficult to argue from verbal propositions. For example, to set before them the following proposition and ask them to resolve it is usually asking for too much: Canada is larger than the U.S.A.; Canada is smaller than the U.S.S.R.; which is the biggest country? It would be a different matter if they were presented with an equal area map of the world showing all three countries, or if they could see a globe. Since they think in concrete terms, a purely verbal proposition is asking them to undertake a mental operation for which they are ill-equipped. Secondly, they will tend to reject a premise which seems to contradict their experience. For example, to ask them 'If there were no atmos-

phere around the earth, would it still rain?' is to court the answer
'yes' because they cannot easily conceive of what is an essentially
hypothetical situation. Thirdly, they do not understand the meaning
of general laws; they are firmly anchored in their thinking to concrete
particular instances and consequently cannot explain an event in terms
of the workings of a general principle theory or law. To ask for a
general explanation of the fact that it rains less in the Eden Valley
than on Scafell Pike is, when children are still thinking concretely,
somewhat premature. This does not mean that children will not give
an explanation, but it will be in terms of the particular events with
which they might be familiar, such as clouds apparently 'bursting' on
the hillside of Scafell. Fourthly, and arising out of what has been
written so far, children at this stage cannot easily give verbal definitions. We saw that Lunnon's experiments demonstrated that children
acquired concepts long before they could accurately describe these in
verbal terms. Thus the general inability to give a definition is a manifestation of the difficulty that children of this age group have in explaining what 'the general case is'. They may be able to recognize
instances of a meander, or a beach, or a cliff when they see one, but
to delimit precisely what a meander, a beach or a cliff is in verbal
terms is usually beyond them. This is why to teach them to repeat
definitions learnt by rote is of little avail, for they cannot carry out the
mental operations which would make such definitions meaningful.
This also applies *a fortiori* to 'concepts by definition' as indicated
earlier.

III. During the period of formal operations (12+ years) the adolescent develops the ability to think in an hypothetico-deductive manner
and not to be imprisoned by his immediate environment or experience.
He is able to conceive of things which are not physically present, and
therefore to argue by assuming certain premises and working out
mentally their implications. For example, he can begin to work out
the answer to a question which begins 'If the sea level were to be
raised by ten metres, what would happen to the size and shape of the
land surface of southern Britain?' Problems which are put to him may
be solved by internal processes of thinking as well as by physical
experiment rather than by trial and error. For example, if he is asked
what kind of weather conditions will produce the environmental lapse
rate shown in Figure 8.2, he will probably proceed by looking at the
nature of the curve, decide there is a temperature inversion near
ground level, note that normal lapse rate resumes above the inversion,

look at the temperatures recorded on the curve at various levels, and
in the light of the evidence, deduce that the weather is probably anti-
cyclonic, with rapid cooling of the earth and therefore in early evening
or at night and given the level of temperatures and the location, that
it is winter. Of course, this presumes a student already has many
mental skills and knowledge at his disposal.

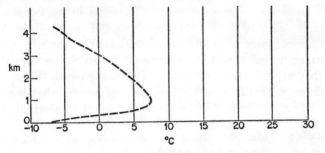

FIGURE 8.2. Lapse rate.

Regularities or possibly laws may be inferred from evidence provided, in other words inductive thinking will occur. For example, a
comparison of the monthly mean temperatures of, say, Winnipeg and
the monthly mean rainfall might lead to the conclusion that rainfall
is highest when temperatures are highest and that this might be
explicable in terms of the greater capacity of warm air compared with
cold air to contain moisture. Or again, the tendency for the tropical
deserts to exist in areas of high atmospheric pressure might lead an
adolescent to an understanding of the tendency for descending air to
hold and absorb moisture compared with ascending air. The student
who is evolving towards the state of formal operations becomes aware
of the need for and importance of precision in defining concepts. He
becomes conscious that in order to define an object or idea, not only
does one need to show how it differs from other objects or ideas, but
which particular attributes single it out as a class of objects or ideas.
He begins to realize, for example, that to define a cirque as 'an armchair hollow in a mountain side' is perhaps insufficient. A further
characteristic of the stage of formal operations is the acceptance of
the theoretical notion of infinity, clearly a notion which cannot be
directly experienced. Also there develops the understanding of 'relations between relations'. Let us take a simple example: the concept
of relative humidity which is used by physicists, meteorologists and
geographers. This 'concept by definition' is not a simple relationship—

it is *not*, for example, the percentage saturation with water vapour of any given volume of air. It is 'the ratio of the mass of water vapour per unit volume of air to the mass of water vapour per unit volume of saturated air at the same temperature' (Ubarov *et al* 1966). Thus relative humidity depends on the ratio of two masses of water vapour relating unsaturated air and saturated air, but that ratio is itself dependent on the temperature of the air. Therefore to understand the concept of relative humidity involves being able to conceive mentally of 'relations between relations' as Piaget puts it. Another example taken from human geography is that of taking a decision about, say, the location of an industrial plant. Neglecting all the non-rational elements in a decision, let us assume that a decision about the location of the plant is to be taken on the basis of economic factors alone. The costs to be considered are raw material transport costs, labour costs, sales costs and transport costs to market. Now if 90% of all costs are distribution costs (transport to market), then no great problem arises, the plant must be located in the market area as in the case of the soft drinks industry. But situations are seldom as clear-cut. To locate near the market may reduce distribution costs, increase raw material and labour cost and reduce sales cost. To locate near raw materials may reduce raw material costs, slightly reduce labour costs, but greatly increase distribution and sales costs. Clearly one is dealing with a multi-variate situation in which the variables change in value in various directions according to the possible locations chosen. To attempt to reduce one set of costs by changing locations may result in another set increasing, and so on. Thus an individual dealing with such a problem needs to keep in mind the various relationships involved. If he is in the stage of formal operations, he is able to build a mental model of the operations required in order to arrive at a minimum cost solution. In fact, the most clear-cut evidence that a student is in the stage of formal operations, is when he shows the ability to solve (or attempt to solve) a problem by putting forward various hypotheses and rejecting them until he has found one that seems useful for the purpose of dealing with that problem.

As Rhys (1966, 1972) has shown, we should not be too sanguine in our expectations concerning students' ability to think in a hypothetico-deductive manner. This is an ability which grows but slowly, and ultimately much depends on the complexity of the problem to be solved. A problem in which only two variables need to be considered may still need hypothetico-deductive reasoning for its solution, but it is much more likely to be tackled successfully by a sixteen-year old than one involving five variables. It is very important for teachers of geography to understand this, because of the tendency for 'real-life problems' to be multi-variate and therefore essentially complex. Thus in secondary school geography it would seem sensible to tackle in the lower forms hypothetical situations in which the problems have been considerably reduced in complexity, and in which only one or two variables are considered, and then gradually increase the number of variables as one moves into the sixth form. Let us take the problem of locating an hydroelectric power dam. It may be that at first the only variable that need be considered is an appropriate site for anchoring the dam. Then the shape of the valley behind the dam may be introduced. Later the extent of the catchment area may have to be considered. Then the régime of the rivers supplying the water to the reservoir behind the dam; still later, the influence of the climate of the area needs to be evaluated in terms of the respective supply of water and rates of evaporation from the reservoir; but that is related to the shape of the reservoir. Then there is the question of the distance between the generating site and the consuming areas—whether one considers the High Dam at Aswan or the Daniel Johnson (Manic 5) Dam in Quebec, the real-life situation involves all the above and many other considerations, but there is clearly no need in schools to deal with all these complexities, in fact, to attempt to do so is to court failure.

It may be useful to conclude this section on Piaget's model of mental development in relation to concept attainment and logical thinking by recalling that Bruner expresses similar ideas in a somewhat different way (Bruner 1967). Whereas Piaget indicates that mental development must pass through the three stages indicated (sensori-motor, concrete operations and formal operations) the last representing a fully adult form of thinking, Bruner prefers to see the human mind as having evolved three modes of representing the environment and events in it. The first mode is through action, in which we operate on the environment in a way which is pragmatically successful as when we have learned to ride a bicycle and to drive a car. This Bruner calls the *enactive* mode of representation. The second mode which he calls the *iconic* mode of representation is one which depends on certain images based on our immediate experience which we develop which enable us to cope with certain specific situations, but which are not generally applicable. We may have a set of mental images acquired from previous journeys which enable us to get from A to B but no generally applicable system to enable us to find our way in a variety of circumstances. The third mode is the *symbolic* mode of representation in which the mind is able to think in symbols which mentally replace actions or images and are much more flexible and economical. If we use the symbolic mode of representation, then we are able to deal with situations of which we have no direct experience, as for example, being able to plan journeys to areas we have never visited before. The useful aspect of Bruner's formulation is that though he recognizes that children and adolescents will pass from the enactive mode through the iconic to the symbolic, he also recognizes that someone who has passed through all three stages may still use the enactive or iconic mode of representation when this appears appropriate. Indeed, as we are all aware, most skills cannot be learnt by other than the enactive mode of representation. Field-sketching, map-drawing, diagram drafting, can only be learnt by attempting to do just those things no matter how symbolically one may be able to think. Similarly, when an adult is coping with what is a general problem, he will often want to look at a concrete instance of it in order to grasp its implication. In other words, he is using the iconic mode of representation in conjunction with the symbolic. Supposing one puts forward the general proposition that in a rapidly developing industrial society, putting a by-pass road around a town will be self-defeating unless one takes care to prevent ribbon development from occurring on and near the by-pass. Is it not natural to think of a concrete case, like the Kingston by-pass in south-west London, or the Sidcup by-pass in south-east London, to review the validity of the proposition? Bruner also looked at the problem in terms of what could be taught to children who were mainly using the enactive or iconic modes of representation. His conclusion was expressed in the often quoted phrase that 'any subject can be taught effectively in some intellectually honest form to any child at any stage of development' (Bruner 1960). This was, in effect, a means of stating that since a child in the stage of concrete operations (iconic representation) cannot apprehend the meaning of general laws or theories, he must be approached through particular instances or cases, that is, he must be approached in a way that has meaning to him. Bruner's view was that because children may have ways of viewing experience which do not include the symbolic mode of representation, this should not debar them from learning certain subjects which state their propositions in highly symbolic terms. The onus should be put on teachers to present those subjects in a manner which is consonant with the pupil's view of the world. The same subjects can be presented in gradually increasing degrees of abstraction as the pupil enters the stage when he begins to represent the world symbolically—hence the so-called spiral curriculum. This is also true of concept development. As the student's experiences of the world are enriched, so he refines his concepts until these become more precise, and ultimately new and more abstract concepts are grasped.

Gagné's conditions of learning

The American psychologist, Robert Gagné, has suggested that there are eight types of learning which each require different 'conditions of learning'. Each type of learning is of a different order of complexity from the others, and all eight may be arranged in a hierarchy, starting with 'signal learning' at the bottom and culminating in 'problem solving' at the top. He suggests that when a student is engaged in a problem-solving operation, it is necessary for him to have learnt certain 'rules', to have acquired certain related 'concepts', which themselves have had to be learnt through a process of 'discrimination', and such a process is dependent on the student having learnt a series of 'chains or associations' (verbal or non-verbal) which are themselves dependent on learnt 'stimulus—response connections' which may or may not be the result of 'signal learning'.

Let us illustrate each of these with an example taken from the learning of geography. *Signal learning* has occurred when a pupil reacts in a characteristic way to a particular signal. For example the sight of an atlas map may cause him to react by manifesting pleasure. This kind of diffuse emotional reaction is typical of signal learning and is often the result of conditioning in the Pavlovian sense and is therefore involuntary. This is why it may not be essential to the higher echelons in the learning hierarchy. In cases, like the present one, when the atlas map can stimulate a pleasurable sensation, then it could be argued that such a reaction will be favourable to more complex learning processes in geography. Creating the pleasurable response may be the difficult part of the process; perhaps the atlas is associated with a smiling kindly teacher, perhaps with the prospect of an interesting period, or simply because the teacher rewards all students who have an open atlas when he enters the room.

Stimulus-response learning is of a voluntary kind. For example a teacher may point on a wall map to various symbols and extract the verbal responses indicating what each symbol represents. Thus pointing to a thin blue line may provoke the response 'river', to a black dot 'town', to red broken line 'frontier', etc. Learners are stimulated by the teacher's action in pointing to particular features, they learn to discriminate between symbols by the teacher indicating whether the response is correct or not. They then learn to respond correctly. *Chaining* is the learning which occurs when two or more stimulus-responses are linked together. The teacher may be able to link a series of stimulus-responses together such that children may learn that 'a river runs from its source to its mouth'. *Verbal associations* are very common forms of learning, which are really a variant of chaining. In geography pairs of words often become associated like, dormitory town, urban hierarchy, fault-scarp, peri-glacial process. Verbal associations may be much more complex—as when a formal definition is learnt and the words are linked together in a sequence as for example when a pupil learns—'An isohyet is a line joining all points having the same mean annual rainfall.' Of course, such learning may be meaningful or not to the learner.

So far stimulus-response and chaining types of learning are fairly simple low-level types of learning; to operate at a higher intellectual level it is necessary for the student to be able to discriminate between various stimuli and responses and between chains of these. For example on field work in towns, many young students learn to discriminate between the various stimuli offered by suburban houses and note that some may be classified as terrace houses, some as semi-detached and others as detached houses.

Discrimination is therefore basic to *concept learning* as we have already seen, since a concept is a way of classifying experience according to certain selected attributes which need to be distinguished from other non-preferred attributes. Hence to learn the concept terrace house is different from learning the concept Georgian house because although many Georgian houses are in terraces, the learner is discriminating by selecting the attributes which make a house a terrace house rather than those which make it Georgian. There is therefore a prior need to have at one's disposal the means of identifying those selected attributes, which has involved a good deal of stimulus-response learning and chaining about various architectural features of houses.

Rule learning is the term Gagné gives to a chain of concepts. Thus if students are learning that 'detached houses tend to be found in the areas of a suburb where incomes are high', they are learning a chain of concepts which are linked together in a meaningful statement. Sometimes the 'rule' is much more closely articulated in a relationship as when one defines the 'location quotient for any industry in any region as the percentage of workers in that industry in that region divided by the percentage of workers in that industry for the whole country'. Clearly the ability to learn the rule and apply it meaningfully is dependent on the relevant concepts being known. *Problem solving* according to Gagné is the ability to use the 'rules' and concepts at one's disposal to tackle situations which are new to the learner and require thinking out. Thus deciding on whether the employment structure in a region is balanced or not may lead a student to employ those 'rules' (or relationships) he knows to arrive at a solution to his problem. For example he may decide to calculate the location quotient for each industry in a given region and from the results obtained come to some conclusion.

It is clear that problem solving, although at the top of the learning hierarchy, may itself be at very many different levels. In secondary schools, the geography teacher is largely concerned with elementary problem solving which implies that 'rule' learning and concept learning are also of great importance. But Gagné's contribution to the understanding of the learning process is to point out the prerequisites of each type of learning and therefore the different conditions under which each occurs.

Level of learning in relation to climatic explanation
An interesting series of experiments was carried out by Ward (1972) with a view to finding out how the understanding of climatic relationships changes during the period of adolescence (14-21 years in this case). After surveying textbooks of various kinds at different intellectual levels, he decided to select eight fundamental climatic relationships for investigation. These were:
1. rainfall—relief;
2. rainfall—altitude;
3. temperature—relief;

4. temperature—altitude;
5. temperature—latitude;
6. temperature—season;
7. temperature—continentality;
8. rainfall—continentality.

These relationships formed that part of the study of climate which is concerned with the interaction between the atmosphere and the land at the earth's surface. No attempt was made to investigate the understanding of world climatic regimes or of the dynamics of atmospheric circulation. He then postulated that the generalized relationships expressed would have five distinctive attributes. They would involve:

1. spatial patterns, e.g. patterns of temperature or rainfall distribution;
2. spatial interaction, e.g. interaction between the sun, the earth and the atmosphere;
3. time, e.g. climatic data results from observations over time;
4. process, e.g. processes which yield patterns of temperature or rainfall distribution;
5. movements, e.g. processes which result in characteristic movement.

Some or all of these attributes might be present in an attempted explanation of a problem involving these relationships.

The three problem situations given to the 'subjects' involved a particular climatic distribution and required them to interpret the spatial patterns shown by using appropriate concepts and generalized geographical principles. For example the first problem involved examining a diagram like the one in Figure 8.3 and explaining the effect of topography on rainfall distribution. It might be argued that to *under-*

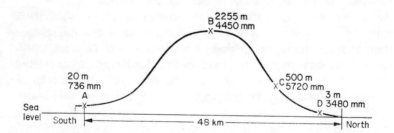

FIGURE 8.3. Rainfall distribution and relief: a hypothetical case.

stand the pattern, such concepts as prevailing wind, windward slope, relief rain, rainshadow and zone of maximum rainfall might be used. To give a satisfactory *explanation* it might be necessary to have an understanding of the following variables : average rainfall (the dependent variable), slope, aspect, altitude, direction of the prevailing wind (the independent variables). It would also be necessary to understand and use the processes of precipitation, condensation, evaporation and adiabatic cooling.

The tests actually given to the subjects were : firstly questions posed directly on the diagrams attempting to elicit an explanation of the climatic patterns; secondly a generalized essay type question ostensibly not on the diagrams but in fact related to these by the kind of problem posed; thirdly a series of multiple choice tests designed to discover whether the subjects had available the knowledge necessary to answer the problems originally set.

The analysis of the responses made by the subjects (159 students from selective secondary schools and colleges of education) seemed to indicate a general growth in ability to deal with the problems posed from the 14-year olds to the 21-year olds. Elementary responses occurred when students identified data as exemplifying a generalized relationship, for example : the diagram (Figure 8.3) shows that rainfall is greater at higher than at lower altitudes. Elementary explanatory responses invoked a principle to account for a particular distribution, e.g. air which is forced to rise cools adiabatically and precipitation may occur. At a more sophisticated level, responses may include sequences of atmospheric processes. For example, air which is humid and is forced to rise over a mountain range cools adiabatically; this means that the air temperature may fall to a point where the water vapour within it condenses; if the water vapour coalesces around dust or other particles in the atmosphere, raindrops will form and these may then precipitate as rain if they are heavy enough. At the highest level of response, subjects are able not only to give detailed explanations, but also to argue around a problem and possibly offer alternative explanations. As the subjects who were tested included fourth formers (c. 15 years), no fifth formers, sixth formers (c. 17 years) and first and third year college of education students (c. 18 and c. 21 years), there was a clear cut distinction between the 15-year old fourth formers who offered mainly descriptive responses and the older age groups who offered more explanatory responses.

Such findings are in harmony with the general theory that hypothetico deductive thinking develops gradually among adolescents. An important further finding was that, though knowledge of climatic concepts and processes tended to increase with age (as measured by the multiple choice tests), in individual cases, students could be found who scored highly on the knowledge tests, but whose responses to the problems set did not show a high level of understanding as measured by the number and quality of the explanatory statements made. In other words, though these students possessed the necessary concepts and principles to respond to the problem set, they did not perform in explanation at a level commensurate with their knowledge. This was interpreted as an indication that specialized knowledge alone was no guarantee that advanced explanations could be given. The ability to apply generalizations was necessary as well as certain qualitative changes in reasoning abilities which enabled students to synthesize several principles and concepts and marshal these in appropriate explanatory strategies.

A further finding of some interest was that higher levels of understanding were more frequent in rainfall-relief, rainfall-altitude, temperature-relief and temperature-season relationships than in the others (temperature-altitude, temperature-latitude, temperature-continentality, and rainfall-continentality). My own hunch is that this difference is not significant in fundamental terms, but merely reflects the pattern of teaching. For example though geography teachers recognize the principle of adiabatic cooling, they seldom enter into a detailed explanation of the physical processes which result in this cooling. In other words geographers have traditionally given relatively weak explanations of some relationships and strong explanations of others. It may therefore be appropriate to suggest that since no rational basis exists for such distinctions, geographers might consider giving strong explanations of all these relationships.

Spatial conceptualization and map-reading

Geography is inevitably concerned with spatial location, spatial distribution, spatial association and spatial interaction, whatever the predilection of individuals for a particular paradigm of geography. Consequently, it is of some moment to understand the way in which children and adolescents apprehend space and spatial relations. This section is, therefore, related specifically to that part in Chapter 7 which dealt with children's perceptual difficulties in dealing with maps and aerial photographs, though its purview of the subject will be somewhat wider.

The first question which needs to be answered is 'What is space?' This may appear a fatuous question since I have been using the term 'space' throughout this book without any apparent need to question its meaning. It would seem that we hold a view of space which is operationally viable, since we probably all know what we mean by such phrases as 'an open space', 'a space for your car', 'little space between the lines', or even 'outer space'. We also seem to be able to go from A to B (home to work or school) without too much difficulty, and on occasions undertake quite complicated journeys. In other words we operate in 'space' without undergoing too many traumatic experiences. Yet if we pause to ask ourselves what space is, we may find some difficulty in precisely defining the concept. For Newton, space was a kind of infinite container of objects. But as Leibniz pointed out, there is some logical inconsistency in that if the objects are removed, then there is nothing left—and yet the container image seems to presume space as being something. Consequently, Leibniz preferred to think of space as an idea created by the mind in order to structure the relationships between objects. If the objects are removed, space disappears. In other words, space is subjective and relative. Kant attempted to bridge the gap between these two views by assuming that though space stems from the mind, it is nevertheless structured by the mind in a particular way; he seems to have held 'that the human mind has built into it a spatial schema which serves a purpose analogous to that of the graticule of a map projection' (Richards 1974). To many people, the spatial geometry of the mind is Euclidean; that is, our mind structures the relationships of objects in space in terms of the 'carpentered' world in which we live, with vertical and horizontal lines, with right angles, with squares, rectangles, triangles, circles and spheres. For most purposes this kind of geometry works well, but we need to be clear that it is only one of the ways in which spatial relationships can be mapped. Other kinds of geometries exist, for example, the geometry of topological space, the geometry of curved space and the more general geometry of Riemannian space (Harvey 1969). Thus we are now in some sense nearer to the position held by Leibniz, in that space is now seen as being essentially relative, depending on the kind of mental 'graticule' used to apprehend it. There is no absolute space, and therefore one can expect that people's notion of space will differ considerably according to the cultural background from which they come, and in the case of children one might expect that at various stages of their mental development, they might well have different perceptions of space. It is also true that, in so far as man becomes conscious of these different geometries, he will tend to use the geometry which best fits his purpose. A simple example is the case of a topological map of a motorway system which shows clearly the connectedness between various towns linked by the motorways, but does nothing to represent their relative positions and distance from one another in terms of parameters like angles in degrees and kilometres.

Let us now look at the ways in which children and adolescents think of space. We are indebted to Piaget and his collaborators for much of the work done in this field (Piaget and Inhelder 1956; Piaget, Inhelder and Szeminska 1960). To use Piaget's terminology, what we are really interested in is the child's mental representation of space. It is not until the end of the sensori-motor period that the child begins to note the relationship between objects and therefore it is not till then that the child begins to develop an internal representation of space. His mental 'graticule', whatever its nature, does not begin to develop until he is about eighteen months to two years old. Next, the child's conception of space appears to develop in accordance with a mental system which is essentially topological. Early in the stage of concrete operations, the child begins to conceive of the environment in terms of objects being connected to one another, he can distinguish closed figures, but cannot easily represent shapes. Later, the child develops an internal system which represents projective space; that is, he is apparently able to represent three-dimensional objects in two dimensions. For example, he will tend to represent houses in elevation. On the other hand, the ability to represent perspective develops later. Children in the stage of concrete operations find it difficult to conceive that the spatial relationships between objects vary according to the point of view of the observer. Eventually, the notion of the perspective of an observer develops and the next stage occurs when the child acquires notions of Euclidean space. He is then able to represent objects as they are in terms of their respective positions, scale having been taken into account. This seldom occurs before the child has reached the stage of formal propositional thought.

This is an essentially simplified account of what, for many research workers, is an immensely complex subject. Part of the problem is that children's mental representations of space can only be known from what they do or say. Hence many experiments have been dependent on children's manipulations of parts of a model, e.g. the reconstruction of a model of a village, or from the way children draw spatial distributions and relationships on paper. For example, an experiment carried out by Lowe, a primary school headmaster in Shropshire, was of this nature. It tended to show that children's abilities to represent their journey to school on a map matured slowly from representing individual features to several features in order, and some eventually were able to draw a nearly correct plan. But it might well be argued that their spatial concepts could be ahead of their ability to represent these concepts physically in models or on drawings, just as most children's understanding of a concept is usually ahead of their ability to describe this concept in verbal terms. Consequently, while children may well find accurate map-drawing difficult, they may yet be able to read a map without difficulty. It must be admitted, however, that empirical evidence on this point is conflicting (Marsh 1966) and not conclusive (Feldman 1971). What it is important to know, nevertheless, is that children's ability to represent space in the conventional Euclidean framework is an ability which develops late rather than early, and is preceded by mental representations which are first topological and then projective. Indeed, if we probe our own childhood memories we can probably find examples within our own experience. When I first came to London as a boy of ten, I can clearly remember having a mental map of a local park which consisted of a series of connected paths by which I found my way from home to the football pitch. But I had at first no overall Euclidean view of the park. This topological view tends to be the one we adopt first when we arrive in a strange town. Many adults, in fact, do not get beyond this view. A tourist in Paris may have a mental map of the city which consists essentially of the bus or Metro links between the Arc de Triomphe, the Place de la Concorde, the Louvre, Notre Dame and Montmartre. Similarly, our early efforts at drawing were certainly projective and some of us had great difficulty in developing perspective. Again, our ability to draw a plan to scale showing objects in their correct positions in respect to one another, was one which developed slowly and for some of us painfully!

How far can this body of knowledge be applied to understanding the ways in which children's geographical learning can proceed? Clearly learning geography involves an ability to read maps and to represent data spatially by plotting this on maps. Further, the ability to perceive spatial patterns and relationships is one which is immensely useful to a geographer. Let us begin with map-reading.

Most of the maps which are used in geographical education are either atlas and textbook maps or medium- and large-scale survey maps. The first group may be drawn on a variety of projections, but usually represents a wide range of phenomena on a very small scale. The second group approximates to the Euclidean framework and can be on a very large scale as in the 1:1000 maps. What we are concerned to find out is whether, given the child's developing concepts of space, these maps used in geographical education have meaning for him, that is, can he interpret them so that they yield information which is valid at his stage of mental development?

As we saw in Chapter 7, Blaut and Stea (1971) believe that children develop an ability to deal with map-like information as early as five or six years, granted there is no necessity to read words or formal symbols. Prior (1959) felt that large-scale maps (25 inches to the mile) could be used with understanding by children of ten to eleven years. But in both cases the maps used were maps of the localities in which the children lived or went to school. This is confirmed by Dale's (1971) investigation, who felt that 'the prime difficulty for children in reading a map or aerial photograph was in forming a mental picture of the area which could be keyed into the relevant map form'. In fact, Prior specifically pointed out that when the area shown on the map was one of which the children had no direct experience, then they made many mistakes in map reading. Thus it would seem that children can begin to use a Euclidean type of map before they can actually draw Euclidean relationships themselves, but that while they are in the stage of concrete operations, the kind of map information which they can use is limited to that representing areas or landscapes with which they are familiar. This would accord well with the general Piagetian postulate that children in the stage of concrete operations are not able to handle a hypothetical situation—and a map of an unknown area approximates to such a hypothetical situation.

What kinds of map-reading problems arise which are to some degree the result of the slowly developing ability to conceptualize space? In spite of the apparent interest in this topic aroused by psychologists, the number of research studies yielding useful information is limited. Rushdoony's (1968) review of the American literature is disappointing; he admits there is a lack of extensive research on map-reading *per se*, but nevertheless seems to aver that 'children's errors or misconceptions were more a lack of systematic teaching than children's inability to read maps'. In Britain few studies have been made specifically concerned with this problem apart from those already mentioned. The British sub-committee of the International Geographical Union's Commission on the Teaching of Geography (now Geographical Education) did undertake in 1959 an investigation of map-reading abilities in selected schools in England. The aim of this survey was to try to find out whether particular map-reading skills could be assigned to certain age grades for teaching purposes. Although the results of the survey are only tentative, two points are worth mentioning. First, few children seemed to understand the scale aspect of maps before eleven years, and secondly, orientation continued to present difficulty even to adolescents of sixteen years. These findings tend to accord with American experience as reported by Bartz (1970). Perhaps of general interest is the difficulty that many adolescents (and adults) have in distinguishing east and west orientations of a map, so that an instruction to look at the western section of map often leads to students looking at the eastern section. There is not the same degree of confusion between north and south. It is tempting to argue that this is due to difficulties in distinguishing left from right (when north is at the top of the map), but there is little evidence to indicate that this is so.

Heamon (1973) carried out a series of experiments in which he tested primary and secondary children's ability to (a) generalize distributions on maps, e.g. the distribution of built-up areas on a map, (b) compare two distributions, e.g. the distribution of woodland in relation to other features (for instance high ground). These experiments were prompted by Piaget's idea that 'centration' (the tendency for children to concentrate their attention on a limited number of stimuli) decreases from childhood to adulthood. Heamon did find that fourteen-year old children were better able to represent the outline of, say, a built-up area on a map, than younger children, and also much better at seeing the connection between two distributions. Teachers will no doubt recognize this as the familiar tendency for younger children to examine micro-features on a map rather than macro-features and to remain unaware of apparently significant correlations between two patterns which may be quite evident to an adult.

A small-scale experiment carried out with C.S.E. (sixteen-year old) candidates to test their map-reading ability brought out the difficulty that many had in identifying on a map features shown on an aerial oblique photograph. The problem here is one of taking into account the fixed scale of the map compared with the variable scale of the photograph (Ilsley 1969). Thus although a vertical aerial photograph sometimes presents perceptual difficulties, it is much nearer to a map than an oblique aerial photograph, which is more like a view from a hill top or mountain. The mental operations required to correlate map information with that on an oblique aerial photograph are too difficult for most adolescents.

Smaller-scale maps like atlas maps present even greater difficulties since they involve translating information about large areas from some symbolic form into a meaningful conceptual form. Most pupils and students will have had no direct experience of the areas represented on atlas maps, so that any conceptualization must be by analogy, vicariously, or by inference. I have never been to the Altiplano of Bolivia, thus any mental image I have of this area is derived (i) by analogy from any other high plateau area I may have visited, (ii) vicariously from any other people's descriptions and from visual records, or (iii) by inference through knowing something of the effects of high altitude, intermontane conditions, and so on. It is, therefore, important that pupils looking at atlas maps should be made aware of the limitations of the information these represent. Sandford's (1972) research has shown how often secondary school students, let alone primary school children, are unaware of the limited nature of map information, so that either they make unwarranted inferences, or naïvely assume that a map shows all there is to be known about a country or area. In general it can be argued that the younger the children are, the less likely is it that an atlas map will be meaningful to them.

Summary

We have seen that the concepts which are taught in geography can vary considerably in order of difficulty. The simplest are those which describe features or processes which can be observed at first hand and are within the learner's experience of the environment he lives in. The most difficult are those which Gagné calls concepts by definition or principles which express relationships of an abstract nature. The distinction is an important one for teachers since the former may conceivably be learned by a process of discovery or simulated discovery, but the latter must of necessity be taught in some more direct manner. Further, whilst the concepts by observation may be learned in the early stages of mental development, concepts which are formally defined by language and other symbols (e.g. mathematical symbols) are unlikely to be understood until mental development has reached the stage when the learner can reason in an hypothetico-deductive manner. Thus the growth in understanding of higher-level concepts in geography is bound to be a slow process related to mental maturation and the development of sophisticated language. In understanding this, Piaget's model of mental development is a useful tool, even if the inability of children to make deductive inferences in the stage of concrete operations is now being questioned (Bryant 1974). It helps the teacher to understand how children's and adolescents' views of their environment change and what kinds of mental operations in handling information they are capable of at various stages. It shows how important it is for the teacher to be aware of what the learner's perceptions and concepts actually are. This is not to say that Piaget's model may not be superseded but merely to indicate that it is the most useful we have at present.

In realizing, for example, that secondary school students cannot easily handle multivariate problems in geography, one needs to be aware that they may nevertheless be able to handle some higher-level concepts which reveal the essential nature of geography, such as the concept of the field of influence of a shopping centre. The fact that students may not be aware of such concepts is simply a reflection that they have not been exposed to them in geography lessons. Slater (1970) has shown in a study of school students aged eight to eighteen in Iowa that the curriculum content of geography did not seem to provide the stimulus necessary to cause the pupils to operate mentally at a level appropriate to their stage of development according to Piaget's theory, neither was there any evidence that these children had acquired any of the basic underlying concepts of geography. In other words, the students were probably being fed with a kind of descriptive factual geography that did not enable them to sharpen their minds or ask penetrating questions.

Part of the process of mental development which is specially relevant to the learning of geography is that which relates to the development of spatial conceptualization. We have seen that the way in which spatial relationships are conceived varies with age and experience. From an inability to represent objects in space, a child in Western society seems to develop through a process in which he can represent spatial relationships in a topological manner and in a projective manner until he acquires the mature ability to conceive of spatial relationships in terms of the Euclidean framework. Since space is a relative and subjective concept, it follows that not all cultures would necessarily conceive of space in Euclidean terms. Knowledge of such development is, however, important to teachers since this will affect a student's ability to read and draw maps. In general it may be stated that large-scale maps (or aerial photographs) of the home or school area may be understood by upper primary school children, but that maps of other areas on a large or small scale will only be meaningful when spatial conceptualization and mental development have advanced considerably into the stage of formal propositional thought. This, of course, is not a reason for not using maps, but it is a warning that understanding will develop but slowly and must be based on experience of using a map 'in the field'. Asking children and adolescents to draw maps representing areas they know at first hand, is a useful way of finding out not only what their perception of the environment is, but also the extent to which their spatial concepts have developed.

Lastly, the whole process of conceptual development and of the growth of logical thinking is closely related to the development of language. Whilst some concepts may be acquired without language, the more refined and the more abstract concepts are dependent on inter-personal communication. Thus geographical education needs to be developed with the use of all possible forms of communication, but particularly by the use of spoken and written language. Hence the importance of 'expressive objectives' which allow the student to state in his own way what he feels. Further, the various formal 'languages' which have been developed over the course of time (the languages of mathematics, of science, of logic) need to be used when these seem appropriate to the student and to the learning task.

CHAPTER NINE

Evaluation in Geographical Education

Introduction

I spent many years preparing candidates for examinations in geography and often wondered when the results came out why certain students failed. On the other hand I rejoiced when some passed whom I had not expected to be successful. There was obviously a discrepancy between my estimate of candidates' chances of passing an examination and the examiners' assessments of these candidates. The process of examining was a mysterious one cloaked in a good deal of secrecy and it was impossible to obtain detailed information about the performance of candidates. I then joined the examiners and began to be involved in the marking of scripts. Soon the discrepancies between my estimates of pupil performances and their actual results disappeared. Being privy to the examination process, I was now aware of what chief examiners were after, I knew how pupils could score high marks or how they could act foolishly by choosing certain questions on which no one ever scored a maximum mark. In other words, I was aware of the immediate objectives of the examination and of the methods used to quantify the performance of candidates in attempting to reach these objectives, consequently I could feed back this information into my teaching. I hasten to add that neither I nor my pupils were ever aware of which questions would be set in the examination—but we became aware of the objectives of the examination and its assessment procedures.

The anecdotal beginning to this chapter is essentially to emphasize the points made in Chapters 5 and 6 that educational objectives, learning experiences provided for the students, and evaluation procedures are necessarily all part of the curriculum process. If there is a disjunction between any one of these three aspects, the educational process is likely to go awry. We have already examined objectives and learning experiences in some detail and it is now time to focus on evaluation.

The meaning of evaluation in education

Although evaluation has been thought of so far as if it were synonymous with examinations, it is in fact a term of much wider connotation. Essentially evaluation is a process where 'valuative' information about an educational activity can be made available to those able to take decisions about this activity so that it may be modified in the light of what has been revealed (Stufflebeam 1971). By 'valuative' information is meant information to which a value statement is attached. If, for example, a teacher reports that a lesson he has given on fishing around the British Isles awoke little interest among his pupils, he is simply reporting pupil reaction; but if he goes on to indicate that he does not think the topic worth teaching, he is making a value judgement about an educational activity which may subsequently affect his practice. It is this wider sense of evaluation that I wish to discuss in this chapter as well as the narrower sense of evaluation of student performance. It can, of course, be argued that evaluation of student performance contributes to the wider evaluation of educational activity, but it is often true that examinations and tests simply serve to grade students in rank order. This rank order may then be used to indicate on a certificate that a student has 'passed' or 'not passed' the examination. Such information is, however, seldom used to modify the curriculum, indeed the opposite has often been the case: established external examinations have been looked upon as setting objectives to teachers and students, so that curriculum change has been difficult without a change in the examinations. We have seen that the Geography 14-18 Project found it necessary to incorporate a changed examination system into its curriculum development proposals in order to feel certain that some curriculum changes would occur.

Thus, in general, it is useful to separate curriculum evaluation from the grading and testing of students. I shall deal with each in turn.

Curriculum evaluation

It is now generally accepted that, if teachers are still the prime movers in curriculum development, they nevertheless need help in this task. This help may come in the form of ideas to try out, of materials to experiment with, of curriculum-planning guides and of curriculum evaluation. But what does curriculum evaluation imply?

In the first place one must ask if the curriculum evaluation is provided for teachers alone. It would seem reasonable that if a curriculum development project is under way, some feedback mechanism should operate to allow those involved in the project to benefit from any concurrent evaluation being undertaken. Thus the evaluation is both for the teacher using the project and for those directing it. But evaluation will certainly interest those funding the project as well as the education authorities responsible for the curriculum. Consequently evaluation as a process is provided for all those who have some direct decision-making interest in curriculum development. For example, in the case of the Geography for the Young School Leaver Project of the Schools Council, evaluation of what was happening in the various trial schools was of great interest to teachers in these schools, to the project team, to the consultative committee for the project, to the local education authorities where the project was being tried out, and to the Schools Council itself. In fact, no formal evaluation of the project as such was undertaken, and the consultative committee found itself in the position of having to make its own evaluation on the basis of reports from the project team and from elsewhere.

In the second place, it is necessary to ask what kind of information should the evaluation of a curriculum provide for the decision-makers? This may vary considerably from case to case. It is possible that those who have to make decisions about a curriculum have some precise questions which need to be answered. For example, is the case study method the best way of putting over the idea of farms as a system? In most cases, however, the decision-makers will not have a list of precise questions to which they require an answer. It can be safely assumed, nevertheless, that the decision-makers will want to know

1. whether a proposed curriculum is feasible in the circumstances in which it is proposed to develop it. For example, is it likely that a curriculum on development problems in tropical areas may be a non-starter for children in inner city comprehensive schools in England?

2. whether the procedures developed by the project team are effective. This is a difficult question to ask because it has both

long-term and short-term implications. It is also true that different value systems may be involved by those within the project team and those outside it about procedures. For example, in relation to the Geography 14-18 Project, it was clear that the curriculum development model used by members of the project team in which they saw themselves as 'change agents' supporting teacher-based curriculum development, was very different from the model held by certain members of the Schools Council's Geography subject committee. Evaluation procedures, had they existed, might have thrown light on the effectiveness of the team's procedures. Evaluators might also consider procedures not used by the project team.

3. whether the curriculum in question has some educational value for the students for whom it has been devised. This in itself is an enormous question, but one about which information must be provided. It may well be that the decision-makers will not agree with the values enumerated in the evaluator's answer to this question. Their decisions will then reflect this disagreement, but at least the various issues raised by the question will have been considered. It is only recently that such a searching question has been asked about the examination syllabuses put out by various examination boards for the General Certificate of Education and for the Certificate of Secondary Education. If the merger of G.C.E. 'O' level and C.S.E. examinations takes place, opportunities may be afforded to plan curricula in the light of such evaluation.

Evaluation may occur along a continuum which begins at the inception of a curriculum development project, through the development stages, to the operational stage when the curriculum is working in schools as part of the normal programme. Scriven (1967) suggested that evaluation of a curriculum might be divided into two parts: *formative evaluation* to indicate the kind of evaluation which might take place during the development of a curriculum and would therefore be particularly useful to those undertaking the development, and *summative evaluation* to describe the kind of evaluation which would occur at the end of a project's development to give an overall view and make a judgement about its effectiveness and worthwhileness. This terminology was taken up by Bloom *et al* (1971) in the *Handbook of Formative and Summative Evaluation of Student Learning* and has been extensively used in the literature ever since. It is true that it is useful to know precisely when an evaluation exercise has taken place during the life of a curriculum development project. To that effect, the Schools Council's team of evaluators (Tawney 1976) has suggested that the terms *concurrent* and *subsequent* evaluation might be more accurate. It remains to be seen whether this terminology will be adopted. Clearly summative evaluation as conceived at present is only summative of a development at a particular stage. A project team's curriculum may go on being developed by teachers subsequently to the formal end of a project and evaluation of such development could then take place.

To sum up, curriculum evaluation is seen as a process of giving information to decision-makers about the feasibility, effectiveness and educational value of various curricula. As Macdonald (1976) indicates, there are various political stances which may be taken by evaluators. They may look upon themselves as the servants of those who have power over the education system, and merely provide information as to the efficiency of a particular means of achieving objectives set by the authorities (bureaucratic evaluation). A second stance (called autocratic evaluation by Macdonald), is for the evaluators to look upon themselves as experts whose advice would normally be accepted by the policy-makers, though it may not on occasions. The third stance is one in which the evaluators recognize that values in education are likely to be pluralistic and that it is no part of their task to recommend a particular course of action. Rather do they see their role as that of giving information about the curriculum development process to all who require it. In this sense much information must be available in a form readily understandable by non-expert users, and this distinguishes it from research information which is often esoteric. One can infer that Macdonald has a predilection for this type of evaluation which he calls democratic evaluation. At this stage one may well ask how this evaluation may take place.

Methods of curriculum evaluation

Since a curriculum is a process whereby students attempt to achieve certain objectives by undergoing learning experiences which are assessed in some way, it is reasonable to suppose that the act of evaluating a curriculum must concern itself with all three aspects. Yet when Tyler (1949) first set down his thoughts on the matter, he felt that evaluation was the simple process of measuring changes in the behaviour of learners. The argument is straightforward. If you intend that a group of fourteen-year old students should learn that glaciers erode landscapes to produce U-shaped valleys, corries, hanging valleys and also deposit morainic materials, then at the end of a teaching-learning sequence you can probably find out by testing whether they have or have not learned these facts and processes. If the objectives have not been achieved, then one can enquire why, try other procedures and then test again. This is sometimes called the 'engineering paradigm' of evaluation, for there is an analogy between measuring the output of a factory and productivity per man, and measuring the output of an educational institution. It is also a process akin to scientific experiment in agriculture whereby a field of maize is grown without any fertilizer and another identical field of maize is treated with a specific fertilizer and the two outputs are compared. In educational experiments, a control group of students is compared with an experimental group, the latter group having been given a special 'treatment' in the form of, for example, a different method of instruction. An important characteristic of this method is the need to keep all conditions likely to affect learning constant, except for the one variable which is being experimented with. Scriven (1967) is a supporter of this method of evaluation and goes to great lengths to ensure the comparability of conditions between control and experimental groups.

Whilst the scientific experiment type of evaluation is a hallowed technique used in educational psychology, it is doubtful how far it can be of great use to curriculum developers and teachers in general. In the first place, this 'paradigm' assumes that objectives are known and accepted to be worthwhile (or alternatively it can ignore the worthwhileness issue). But many curriculum development projects do not begin by having clear-cut objectives, indeed part of the process may be precisely that of developing such objectives. Further, if objectives are of the expressive type, then it is not possible to measure them as an output, since they will differ from individual to individual. In the second place if the experiment is to yield valid results it must either use small samples and all the controls indicated above, which makes it most unlike a real curriculum development situation, or it must use a large randomized sample which involves a major exercise in data collection which is expensive. In the third place, a general characteristic of curriculum development is that the situation in the project is ongoing and therefore changing continuously; but such a situation cannot be assessed by the classical experimental methods.

Consequent upon the difficulties of using the 'agricultural experimentation' paradigm of research, it has been suggested by some evaluators that a method based on the 'social-anthropology research paradigm' or the phenomenological approach is more useful. This 'paradigm' is more concerned with describing and interpreting what goes on in curriculum development than in measuring and predicting. It has been labelled *illuminative evaluation* by Trow (1970). It involves being able to describe what goes on in the 'instructional system' when a curriculum is being implemented and being able to disentangle the complexities of the 'learning milieu'. For example, illuminative evaluation involves being aware of the way the objectives which have been set by a project team may be rearranged and modified by the teachers implementing the project, such as when long-term aims which may have been concerned to develop an understanding of ecological relationships get transformed into a series of short-term aims in which the net effect is the learning of series of facts about plants, climate and soils. Illuminative evaluation also involves being aware that a modification of the instructional system may trigger off changes in the learning milieu which may considerably affect the curriculum. For example, the decision to teach a topic such as transport networks by the use of small group work and discussion, may lead to a change in rapport between members of the class and their teacher, which in turn leads to modifications of the curriculum derived from pupil suggestions. Thus chain reactions may be set in motion which need to be observed and recorded.

Illuminative evaluation, then, in no way sets out to copy traditional or classical research design. Its main techniques are first the observation and recording of what actually happens when curriculum development is undertaken, secondly the interviewing of those involved, thirdly, if necessary, the use of questionnaires and tests and of documentary evidence. These techniques are akin to participant observation research methods which are increasingly used in social psychology (Hargreaves 1969, Nash 1973), though many educational psychologists do not entirely approve of such methods. Clearly such techniques are very dependent on what the observer chooses to observe and on the interpretation he puts on what he records. In this sense the conclusions reached are subjective, though these may be checked against those of other evaluators in the same or similar positions. But one needs to note that even in classical experimental situations, interpretation is still subjective and the data that the researcher chooses to collect is governed by the hypothesis he wishes to check. True the hypothesis is either accepted or rejected in an objective manner, but the possibility of testing a particular hypothesis depends very much on structuring the experimental situation accordingly. Putting it in another way, there are certain questions about the process of curriculum development which cannot easily be answered by the classical experimental method largely because one cannot create the necessary 'laboratory conditions'. Illuminative evaluation is not so limited in the questions it asks, though the answers given may lack the precision obtained from scientific experiment. Illuminative evaluation can, if necessary, make use of achievement tests, attitude tests and questionnaires, though always with the caveat in mind that there will be certain limitations to these techniques.

Lastly, the evaluator using illuminative evaluation needs to bear in mind that the ultimate report he writes will serve different needs. The teachers and inspectors or local authority organizers will want to make decisions as to whether the experience described is generalizable in other schools. The funding authorities will want to know something about the relationship between money expended and the findings. Those involved in the project will want some feedback which will enable them to profit from the evaluator's insight. The evaluator merely provides the evidence from which they will take decisions.

Unfortunately, the two main geography curriculum development projects undertaken for the Schools Council in England and Wales were not officially evaluated though evaluators did monitor some of the activities of the G.Y.S.L. team. Consequently it is difficult to give a British example of curriculum evaluation in geography. Similarly, although the History, Geography and Social Sciences 8-13 Project had an evaluator attached to it and it seems clear from the literature (Blyth et al, 1976) that he undertook a good deal of formative evaluation by interacting with the project team, and that he gave advice on how teachers could evaluate their own teaching and the pupils' learning, there is as yet (1977) no overall statement available as to how he carried out his task. The American High School Geography Project was evaluated by Dana G. Kurfman (Kurfman and Richburg 1970) and reference is made to his evaluation techniques in Chapter 6. It is made clear that his evaluation was essentially illuminative evaluation. In fact, when he tried to find out which parts of a unit of the project were most effective in teaching certain concepts, he found that since the concepts and skills recurred more than once, it was difficult to be sure which sections were the most effective, and he ultimately came to rely much more on student and teacher opinion (*see also* Renner and Slater 1974). Thus Kurfman adapted his evaluation techniques to the developing situation in the High School Geography Project. It is interesting to contrast his description of the evaluation he carried out (with the help of the Education Testing Service at Princeton) and the essentially theoretical statement made by Temp (1970) in a book edited by Kurfman in which Temp exposes the essentially classical doctrine of evaluation as research.

The evaluation of student learning

One of the ways of evaluating a curriculum is to assess the learning that students have achieved. I have already indicated that this can only be part of the total process of curriculum evaluation. Nevertheless, it is an aspect of the curriculum which looms large in Great Britain, Australia (Biddle 1968, Biddle and Deer 1973), and also in North America. A recent statement on the curriculum emanating from the Schools Council (Schools' Council, 1975) seems to indicate that there is little doubt that assessment of pupils and students will continue to play an important part for many years to come. It is not my purpose here to repeat in detail what I have written elsewhere on the topic of examinations (Graves 1972). Suffice it for me to indicate what seems to be a balanced view of assessment in geography and to point to some possible future developments. There is, in any case, an extensive literature on assessment in geography (Senathirajah and Weiss 1971; Kurfman 1970, Salmon and Masterton 1974; Marsden, 1976).

The qualifying examinations of the General Certificate of Education and of the Certificate of Secondary Education are likely to develop further in the directions in which they are going at present. That is, from being essentially dependent on the essay type of question (structured or unstructured) they are moving to a situation in which a multiplicity of techniques are being used: objective tests of various kinds (multiple choice, completion, matching pairs, true-false, etc.), structured essay questions, open-ended questions, and so on. Further, these examinations are coming to rely less and less on the candidates' remembered information and more on evidence supplied in the format of the question. A good example of such questions are those devised by the Geography 14-18 Project team for their experimental O level examination in 1974.

In a recent newspaper advertisement [see Figure 9.1] the town of Pontypool claimed to have certain advantages for the location of industry.

Discuss the extent to which factors such as the ones listed in Figure 9.1 apply to:

(a) *one* industrial location in your local area;

(b) *one* industrial location in another part of the British Isles or overseas.

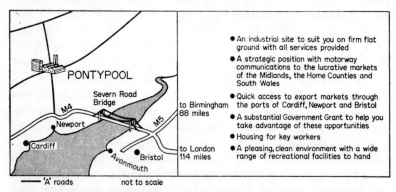

FIGURE 9.1. Diagram from the *Geography 14-18* experimental O level examination. (*Source*: Cambridge University Local Examination Syndicate)

The possible merger of G.C.E. and C.S.E. examinations in England and Wales makes inevitable the use of a wide variety of examining techniques owing to the wide ability range of candidates to be tested. Trials of such examinations were held in 1973 and 1974, for a number of examination boards, and these are being analysed. These methods of examining candidates' performance are an improvement on what was normal until the 1960s, since objective tests can sample a wide area of the syllabus, and these and other types of questions can be set to test the candidate's understanding and application of geographical skills and principles, rather than his memory for facts. It must be remembered, however, that objective tests are only objective in their marking. Someone has to make a subjective judgement as to what to include in the test.

A development which has occurred in recent years and is likely to develop further is the use of school-based examinations generally known, from their C.S.E. association, as Mode 3 Examinations. Essentially this type of examination overcomes the criticism that external examinations impose a constraint on the school curriculum, since it is an examination of what is taught in the school geography curriculum set by those who teach it for those who are learning. It may use any of the examining techniques currently available, but the examination has to be moderated. This means that the standards of the examination must be seen to be equivalent to other examinations for the same subject at a similar level. The techniques of ensuring satisfactory moderation are not yet very refined and the exercise at present is best seen as one of making an informed judgement about the comparability of candidates' performances in what are different examinations testing a different body of knowledge (Schools Council 1971; Deale 1975). This problem is inevitable in so far as each school is encouraged to develop its own geography curriculum which must include the evaluation aspect.

Assessment of student learning, if it is to fit into the curriculum process, cannot simply resolve itself into an examination in the last year of secondary education. It needs to be a recurrent event throughout school life affording feedback information as to progress to both student and teacher. If the course work undertaken by the pupils is of a searching type, then this in itself provides a means of assessment. For example, if fourth-year secondary school students have been working on the problems of raising agricultural productivity in India, one can set them course work by asking them to advise on a similar problem in Latin America. Given the environment conditions, given the cultural background, can they transpose the situation and analyse it in a similar manner? Their response will indicate how far they have grasped the principles involved. Again, if one is trying to find out how far they have progressed in their ability to obtain information independently of the teacher, it is possible to set them searching for information contained in resources held within the geography room, which they need to answer certain precise questions.

It may be necessary, however, to set a whole-class test to find out how well they have understood certain concepts or principles. It is in such a case that the teacher needs to be expert in constructing his tests, since presumably he does not wish them to be simply tests of factual memory. It involves him in devising many items and testing them to find out if they work. Such tests need to be developed over years in relation to a particular geography curriculum, so that eventually the teacher may have a battery of useful geography tests. Very few achievement tests in geography are commercially available in Great Britain, and too many of these are essentially factual. Tests available in North America are not necessarily suitable for British conditions, some are designed for social studies curricula, many are geared to primary school work, and most are not of a very high quality in terms of the thinking they test (Wood 1970, Buros 1965). It is probably better to use a test of geographical relationships which has not been technically evaluated for validity and reliability, but which effectively stretches one's students, than to use a test which may be reliable but which merely tests remembered facts.

Evaluating attitudes and values
A field which has only been investigated to a moderate extent in Great Britain is that of evaluating attitudes to geography. There were a number of studies in the 1940s and 1950s (e.g. Long 1950, Honeybone 1950) in which attempts were made to see how far particular techniques of teaching geography were viewed favourably, or unfavourably by pupils. Honeybone, for example, found that the use of pictures among grammar school pupils seemed to enhance interest and made for more effective teaching. Long demonstrated the close link which existed between interest and attainment in geography among grammar school pupils, though she pointed out that there probably existed a chain reaction in that as knowledge increased so did interest. Contrariwise there was a strong correlation between lack of interest and lack of knowledge. Long (1971) carried out a further study which examined among a sample of 1800 secondary school students aged 13-15 of a wide range of ability, their attitudes to various activities undertaken in classrooms in geography. This investigation revealed an immense range of likes and dislikes, though it may be generalized that the students concerned preferred graphical means of expression to written work, and particularly disliked note-taking either from the chalkboard or in dictated form. It seemed that individual and group work was appreciated and, in particular, exercises which allowed students to find out information for themselves. The use of large-scale and medium-scale topographical maps for geographical exercises was not universally appreciated, some students enjoying such work immensely, others disliking it, particularly girls. Jones (1974) has pointed out that in the G.C.E. and C.S.E. examinations about half the pupils entering for English (a subject offered by nearly all candidates) in these examinations, offer geography as a subject. In absolute terms about 120,000 candidates

sit for C.S.E. geography and about 170,000 sit for G.C.E. geography. Jones posed the question: why do students choose and not choose to study geography for an examination? In a minor investigation carried out by questionnaire in eight comprehensive schools in south and west London and in two grammar schools (one in London and one in Surrey), it became clear that neither parents nor peer groups had much influence on the choices made. The main reasons given were that a knowledge of geography was considered useful (or not useful) and that geography had been found interesting (or not interesting) in the past. Thus those candidates who decided to offer geography in C.S.E. or G.C.E. examinations appeared to do so mainly on the grounds that the subject might be useful and interesting to them, whilst those who rejected geography did so for the opposite reason. There were other aspects revealed by the questionnaire, namely that some did not choose geography because they found it a difficult subject and some because they had not enjoyed work with their geography teachers.

Whilst this further highlights the importance of interest in geography as a factor leading students to continue studying it (a not unexpected finding, as Jones points out), it gives no clue as to why geography should or should not appeal to certain students. Indeed since about half the candidates for these examinations choose to do geography, it might be argued that the same result would have been obtained by chance, i.e. if subjects had been chosen in a random manner. But this cannot be true, because most elective subjects are not taken by the same proportion of candidates. In fact, geography in England and Wales turns out to be (apart from English literature in the G.C.E.) the most popular of the subjects not regarded as quasi-compulsory.

At this stage one may well ask whether there is any point in evaluating attitudes to geography. It is possible that such investigations might further confirm that 75 per cent of all secondary school students dislike working with medium-scale maps. Would this then be a reason for not incorporating the use of such maps in the curriculum? To my mind the answer is an unequivocal no. The education process cannot be likened to the production of goods for a market subject to the results of market research. This general point has already been made earlier. Another view is that attitudinal investigations might lead to information which may help teachers to sugar the pill. For example, it might be found that though map-work *per se* was disliked, if it is associated with a favourite topic (e.g. development problems in the third world) then it will be acceptable to the pupils as necessary if unpleasant. Yet another view is that by probing into attitudes to geography it may be possible to discover that an unfavourable attitude to certain aspects of geography may stem from certain misconceptions or from certain cognitive difficulties which may be ironed out.

The problem associated with all investigations into attitudes to geography or parts of geography, is that of isolating the factors or combination of factors held to be responsible for certain attitudes. Thus, while it may be relatively easy to discover whether children hold or do not hold a particular attitude, it is much more difficult to find out why. Thus, while tests like those using Likert scales, or those using Osgood's semantic differential may well afford some measure of student interest in geography, they are not particularly useful in making a diagnostic assessment. The teacher has some information about his success or lack of success in interesting his students in geography (though in many schools this will be evident without the use of attitude tests!), but he is reduced to trial and error if he wishes to improve a negative situation. An elaborate probing exercise would be required to illuminate such a situation and this has, to the best of my knowledge, not been done yet (Carswell 1970).

What is clearly important is to find out the kind of values that geography as a subject purveys. For many decades geography was taught as though its content was neutral in the sense of not upholding any particular set of values beyond the procedural values mentioned in Chapter 5. I tried to indicate in that chapter that value teaching was inherent in any teaching-learning situation, for the subjects we teach are but human views of reality, not 'truth' in any absolute sense (Kuhn 1962). Cowie (1974) has also demonstrated that geography is a value-laden subject although this has not always been recognized. She shows that the very act of engaging in geographical study and teaching presupposes that such an activity will be to the benefit of man and, therefore, that the value assumption here is that life is good and should be developed in conjunction with the earth's resources which are perceived as being finite and worth conserving. Further, it is clear that much of the content of geography is permeated with values. There are, for example, innumerable expressions of religious, economic and social values in the spatial arrangements of the cultural landscape, whether this be the layout of a monastery, the functional zoning of a city or the characteristics of residential areas. Equally the methodology generally used in geography rests on the value assumption that there exist spatial regularities which may be investigated and explained in a rational manner using scientific methodology. Finally, the kind of teaching strategy employed by the teacher betrays his or her adherence to certain values. For example, a teaching strategy which emphasizes process as against content, is expressing the value that what matters is not the student's knowledge of a precise geographical fact or theory, but his ability to acquire such knowledge through developing enquiry skills and through a growing intellectual curiosity. In passing, it may be worth mentioning that so far most British examinations in geography seemed to have held the opposite value, namely that what mattered most was the content of geography.

I ought to add that geography in common with other subjects is concerned with the kind of values implicit in human relationships. Thus, the very way the teacher responds to children, his attitude to other members of staff and to people coming into the school, all these help to foster certain values within the school. Moreover, geographers have always felt a certain responsibility for the attitudes of children to foreign peoples, though the extent to which they can in fact influence children in such attitudes is apparently limited (Carnie 1972).

Value teaching is important not only because it is inevitable, but because a society in which individuals seem unable to develop firm value systems rapidly becomes an amoral society, with all that that implies for the quality of life in that society. But does this mean that geography teachers should incorporate in their curriculum the teaching of substantive values associated with geography? Cowie (1974) uses Rokeach's (1972) idea that any value held involves a choice in favour of that value, a conscious commitment to that value and action demonstrating this commitment. If this is accepted then clearly the choice element in the process of acquiring a value is an important one which cannot be by-passed. In other words, the process of value teaching is first and foremost one of helping a student to make a choice between values, rather than the direct teaching of certain substantive values. Thus, a series of lessons on local urban renewal can demonstrate that in deciding on a particular development plan a choice has to be made based on values about the aesthetic quality of the built environment, about how people should or should not be manipulated, about traffic flows, about social class mixing, and so on. Similarly, students can be made to express their commitment to some of these values by defending publicly their acceptance of these in a discussion, and they may act upon their conviction by taking part in activities in the local area designed to promote a particular solution to an urban renewal problem.

It has been necessary to return to the field of objectives in order to consider the problem of evaluating the learning of values in geographical education. The kinds of objectives postulated above are not the straightforward instructional objectives which could be expressed in behavioural terms, since the precise outcome of any value teaching cannot be anticipated. Neither the kind of choice made nor the commitment can be forecast. Consequently such objectives are more in the form of expressive objectives, though they could be conceived as being less open than the expressive objectives postulated by Eisner in relation to, for example, literature, on the grounds that the general objective set (how to undertake urban renewal) may be the same for all students, the constraints set by the availability of resources may again be the same, but the actual outcome in terms of the solutions chosen may be different. Given the value of these objectives, it is not possible to evaluate them by means of standardized tests of one sort or another. It would, therefore, seem that 'illuminative evaluation' of the kind used in curriculum development projects is more appropriate though its extent and its refinements will necessarily be limited in the ordinary teaching situation.

Conclusion

In reviewing the evaluation of geographical education I have deliberately kept the scope of the discussion wide, since the main purpose of this evaluation is not the grading of pupils, but the improvement of the curriculum. What has transpired is that though the techniques of educational research and student assessment have become more and more refined, such techniques are not particularly suitable to curriculum evaluation in general and to the evaluation of the geography curriculum in particular, especially if we bear in mind the growing realization that value teaching is of great importance in our society. On the other hand the phenomenological approach of 'illuminative evaluation' is more likely to be of immediate use.

The assessment of student learning which is part of the curriculum process is moving more and more towards the logical position of being course work assessment. Nevertheless, the hold of external examinations on the educational system in Great Britain is such that it would be sanguine to expect them to wither away rapidly. Consequently, examining techniques are being further refined to make them more valid and reliable. Such techniques are well documented elsewhere (Marsden 1976).

CHAPTER TEN

Geographical Education: Conclusions and Personal Perspectives

Inevitably I am the product of the educational and social systems in which I have lived and though I would claim a certain degree of autonomy, I am aware that my views cannot be seen as independent of their context. Therefore in attempting to sum up, I am conscious of the many influences which have been at work in shaping my conclusions. This kind of introspection is not unhealthy, but useful in analysing the nature of the education process. Indeed, when I look back over the years and examine how my views on geographical education have changed, I am conscious that this mind-opening process (if it be so) owes much to my own teachers and colleagues. Thus I find it relatively easy to accept Peters' view of education as a process which helps to transform the learner's view of the world in the kinds of ways which he has described. At the same time I am conscious that this is not a universally held view of education and that tension arises within the school system because of the different views of education held within it. The main alternative view of education as an instrument for shaping future members of society is one which appeals to common sense and appears to be accepted by many 'consumers' of education even though some may be disappointed with the product. The problem with this second view of education is that it appears to be essentially conservative in outlook and it is in practice unworkable, except in an extremely regimented society. It is conservative because it is concerned with existing society and existing knowledge, and not with new societies and creating new knowledge. It is unworkable because at least in the primary and secondary stages of education it is not possible to shape individuals so that they will fall into a series of occupational and role niches. Even in higher education the notion of courses being shaped by the needs of society is hardly a reality.

In rejecting the instrumental view of education, I am not, however, indicating that what goes on in schools need have no relevance to society outside. This would be impossible. Schools are a product of our society and to a large extent reflect its values and preoccupations. Rather am I saying that the process of education within schools should lead students to see beyond what is to what might be, to question established views and practices, to suggest new solutions to old problems, and see problems in situations which others accept as unproblematic. Postman and Weingartner (1971) expressed the same idea in *Teaching as a Subversive Activity*. The converse, a school which *merely* trained in certain skills and knowledge because these were directly required by society, would not be an educative community. Thus, whether schooling is education or not, depends on the quality of the process going on within the school; not on whether the content relates or does not relate to society. Clearly, the ability of teacher and taught to relate to common experiences will be paramount if anything useful is to be achieved, so that education cannot easily take place in 'ivory towers'.

I, therefore, accept that education can be seen as initiation into activities which are educationally worthwhile in that they introduce the pupil to various activities which give him an insight into the ways in which men have viewed reality. John White (1973) makes a distinction between those activities which logically cannot be understood without engaging in them and those about which it is possible to achieve some understanding without actually undertaking them. In the first category he puts communication, pure mathematics, exact physical sciences, appreciating works of art and philosophizing. In the second category he places such activities as learning a foreign language, games, and vocational activities. White makes the simple point that, if he is right, then category I activities must be compulsory since no pupil could possibly understand what they are unless he partakes in them. Category II activities may be encouraged, but should not be made compulsory, for, granted a student has engaged in category I activities, he can always find out what category II activities are like at second hand. He also argues that some ability to integrate knowledge acquired into a particular way of life is necessary to give what Peters has called cognitive perspective, and that such integration is not possible without some knowledge of practical kinds of understandings like that of political, social and economic institutions. These practical understandings, he goes on, should form part of the compulsory curriculum. He mentions geography in this latter context.

> Our student will have to know something about economic affairs—about industry, domestic and international trade, taxation and income distribution. He will have to know something about social, legal and political institutions; and about natural, geographical features relevant to socio-economic matters, resources of food and power, for instance. (White 1973, p. 57).

I am somewhat wary of accepting this view of the function of geography, even if it is placed among the compulsory group of curriculum activities, for it would seem to indicate a perspective of geography as an essentially information-giving subject about 'geographical features relevant to socio-economic matters'. Granted that for 'practical understandings' it would be sound that the examples used should relate to the kind of information that White mentions, but the kinds of activities that geographers consider worthwhile are the establishment of concepts, principles and relationships which are transferable from one context to another. Perhaps the argument is a semantic one and need be pursued no further.

It does, however, raise the issue that geography as a subject is frequently misunderstood by the non-geographer for reasons which are easy to see. First, geographers are not agreed among themselves as to the essential nature of their subject and secondly, it has in academic institutions straddled the arts and the sciences. It is not unusual for a subject in the early phases of its development to be unclear as to its essential function. One can point to biology and the various social sciences for evidence of past difficulties of a similar nature. In general subjects begin by being descriptive and classificatory and gradually evolve to the state of proffering explanations by the use of models, theories and laws. Geography is clearly at the moment passing into this explanatory phase, particularly in relation to human geography. If one accepts Kuhn's (1962) concept of a paradigm as 'universally recognized scientific achievements that for a time provide model problems and solutions to a community of practitioners', we can recognize that geography is moving from a situation where most geographers accepted the 'explanatory description of landscapes' paradigm, to one in which several possible paradigms are competing for supremacy. It is necessary to abstract climatology and geomorphology from this issue since both those subjects have long ago accepted the physical sciences paradigm as that most appropriate to research in these fields. In human geography, however, it would seem to me that two main paradigms are available but that the scientific community of geographers has not yet chosen between them. They are (1) that which sees geography as a 'science of spatial organization' and is exemplified by Abler, Adams and Gould's (1971) book *Spatial Organization*, and (2) that which sees geography in a somewhat wider context and might be termed the 'ecosystem view of geography' and is exemplified to my mind by Peter Haggett's (1972, 1975) *Geography: a Modern Synthesis*. The spatial organization paradigm (Figure 10.1) is the clearer break

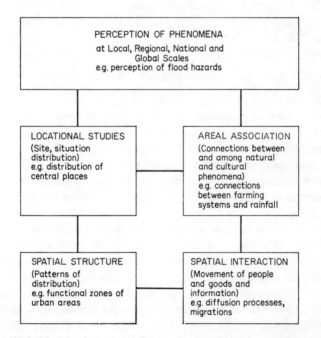

FIGURE 10.1. Model of the spatial organization paradigm of geography.

with tradition whilst the ecosystem paradigm (Figure 10.2) attempts to embrace some of geography's traditional concerns, as well as those relating to spatial organization. It is difficult to be sure which of those two will eventually dominate. My own predilection is for the ecosystem paradigm since it affords a smoother passage from the older to

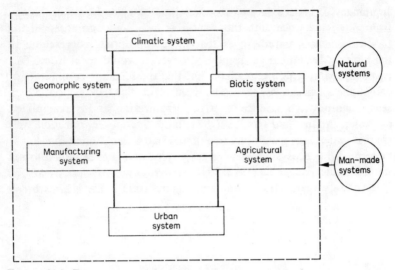

FIGURE 10.2. Ecosystem model of geography (man-made and natural systems).

the newer view of geography. From the point of view of geographical education, the ecosystem paradigm is less difficult to accept by those teachers who have been wedded in the past to the regional or explanatory description of landscape paradigm.

Assuming for the moment that the ecosystem paradigm becomes dominant, what then are the curricular objectives of geography in relation to primary and secondary education? At the primary stage it would seem to me that geography can help the developing child to make sense of his immediate environment, that is the environment of his home and school, particularly in helping him to develop a mental map of this environment. Geography within the primary curriculum is in a coherent way helping the child to unfold those concepts and that conceptualization of space which would develop in a haphazard way through the child's own personal experience. Perhaps geography also begins to hint at those man-land relationships and spatial regularities which will be elaborated in the secondary school. It is in the secondary school that attempts will be made to illustrate the geographer's problems and some of his ways of tackling them. I see geography as attempting to explain the spatial patterns which exist at the local, regional, national and world scale in terms of processes operating at those scales. Thus at some scales physical environment processes and their interaction with human organizations will feature strongly in the explanations, for example in the pattern of world trade in fuels. At others the spatial regularities will require explanations in which economic and social processes will be dominant, as in the explanations of urban hierarchies in general. Of course, as soon as one becomes concerned with unique cases, that is the application of geographical principles to particular areas, then there is a need to take in the peculiarities of that instance, as when one attempts to explain the distribution of population in Quebec province in Canada.

One may then ask why should the explanation of spatial patterns be a feature of secondary education? It is possible to give the answer given by White and argue that these are part and parcel of practical understandings without which it is difficult to obtain cognitive perspective. Indeed, we live in an environment in which such spatial patterns can be made very evident and cry out for explanation. The patterns formed by differences in incomes from one area to another, the patterns formed by different methods of exploiting agricultural land, the patterns formed by differential industrial development, the patterns formed by communications networks, trade link patterns, administrative area patterns, and so on. The teacher's job is twofold: to make the students aware of these patterns and to help them towards an explanation of them. But if we agree that geography is a value-laden subject, then part of the explanation must be an exposure of the value systems which have made such patterns develop. Further, this implies a judgement being made about those values and commitments to existing or new values. The forward-looking or predictive aspect of the subject revolves around the acceptance of new values or the application of a principle not yet applied, as in the case of the use of the city region principle in the development of new administrative areas, or the acceptance of the value that society would be better if neighbourhoods were mixed socially and injecting this value into town planning (De Wofle 1971).

It is important to reiterate, however, that if the examples chosen are those which appear relevant to the students being educated, the point of geographical education is to develop a series of ideas and skills which are not context-dependent but transferable to other situations. Thus in my thinking I am perhaps nearer to the position put forward by King and Brownell (1966) (see Chapter 4) that geography can be accepted as a discipline of knowledge and, therefore, one that should feature on the curriculum.

Such statements about the function of geography in the curriculum imply little about the exact organization of the courses, of time-tabling and of teaching arrangements. It is necessary to bring in here the issue of whether geography should continue to be taught as a separate subject or in association with other subjects to form schemes of integrated studies or of environmental studies or of any other combination such as European studies. As I see the problem, it is possible to argue that in the primary stages of education most children are not able to distinguish clearly between the various ways in which man has structured reality intellectually. To those children labels such as history, geography, mathematics, etc. have rather imprecise meanings relating to certain educational activities. Thus the teacher uses the resources of the school and the local environment to cause the child to develop certain elementary concepts, skills and principles in a way which is not necessarily structured along subject lines. A recent survey (Department of Education and Science 1974) has shown that geography as a separate subject in the primary schools of England and Wales has all but disappeared. A sample survey made in the London area has confirmed this (Cracknell 1974). The problem is to get over the elementary ideas of spatial location, spatial associations and spatial interactions in the less structured context of the 'integrated day'.

It is also possible to argue that at some later stage in education, probably in the late secondary stage and after, students must come to realize that any real-life problem needs to be tackled in a multidisciplinary manner. Whether the problem be building a bridge across the St Lawrence River, digging a tunnel beneath the Channel or planning a new town, there will be a need to use approaches developed in the visual arts, in mathematics, in physics and chemistry, in geography and geology, in economics, and so on. Thus some combined approach to a series of problems of this nature is desirable at some stage. But it will be clear that for this approach to be successful, there must be a prior stage at which the students have become aware of what the contributions of the various disciplines are. Consequently it seems clear that sometime during the secondary stage of education the students must come to know what it is to ask a mathematical question, what it is to ask a geographical question, what it is to ask an economic question, and so on. Teachers may be able to develop courses of 'integrated studies' in which the essential ideas of the various disciplines are well articulated, but it is an immensely complex task. I do not believe that in the present state of curriculum development in England and Wales we are in a position to produce 'integrated courses' which assure the teaching of appropriate geographical ideas and skills. This is not to say that geography must always be taught as a separate subject for two periods a week from year one to year five in the secondary school. If time is to be saved on the time-table in order to develop other social sciences, then it would seem more practical to incorporate geography in a broader curriculum context by, for example, teaching the geographical content as a continuous course lasting for one or two terms out of three in each year. This would make time available for other work but ensure that some sequence occurred in the teaching of each component.

Lastly, if adopting values means commitment to these values and action manifesting this commitment, then teachers of geography need also to express commitment to geography in action. The period of the late 1960s and early 1970s in Britain has proved a difficult one for teachers of geography, largely because one paradigm of geography was under attack and it was not clear what was to take its place. There was much uncertainty and for some doubt about the value of continuing with the 'explanatory description of landscape' view of geography. Now I believe that in the 'ecosystem' paradigm we have a conceptual framework which enables us to marry the old with the new and forge forward. There is already much evidence of this in new texts and learning materials now being published.

References

Abler, P., Adams, J. S. and Gould, P. (1970). *Spatial Organisation: a Geographer's View of the World*, Prentice Hall.

Aikin, W. M. (1942). *The Story of the Eight Year Study*, vol. 1 of *Adventure in American Education*, Harper and Row.

Allévy (1851). *Géographie de France Allévysée*, published by the author.

Annales de Géographie (1905). *Annales de Géographie*, no. 75, 15th May 1905.

Archer, R. L., Lewis, W. J. and Chapman, A. E. (1910). *The Teaching of Geography in Elementary Schools*, A. and C. Black.

Australian Geography Teachers' Association (1973). 'Geography in Education', *Geographical Education*, **2**, 1.

Baker, J. N. L. (1948). 'Mary Somerville and geography in England', *Geographical Journal*, **III**, pp. 207-22.

Baker, J. N. L. (1955). 'The geography of Bernhard Varenius', *Transactions and Papers of the Institute of British Geographers*, **21**.

Balchin, W. (1970). 'Graphicacy', in Balchin, W. (Ed.), *Geography: a Guide for the Intending Student*, Routledge and Kegan Paul.

Barnard, H. C. (1933). *Principles and Practice of Geography Teaching*, University Tutorial Press.

Bartz, B. S. (1970). 'Maps in the classroom', *J. Geography*, **69**, January 1970.

Bayliss, D. G. and Renwick, T. M. (1966). 'Photograph study in a junior school', *Geography*, **51**.

Beard, R. (1969). *An Outline of Piaget's Developmental Psychology*, Routledge and Kegan Paul.

Beauchamp, G. A. (1961). *Curriculum Theory*, Kagg Press, Wilmette, Illinois.

Bell, J., Dybeck, M. W. and Rushby, J. G. (1967). *Study Geography*, Stages 1-4, Longman.

Bennetts, T. (1973). 'The nature of geographical objectives', in Walford, R. (Ed.), *New Directions in Geography Teaching*, Longman.

Bernstein, B. B. (1971). 'On the classification and framing of educational knowledge', in Young, M. F. D. (Ed.), *Knowledge and Control*, Collier Macmillan.

Berry, B. J. L. (1973). 'A paradigm for modern geography', in Chorley, R. J. (Ed.), *Directions in Geography*, Methuen.

Biddle, D. S. (1974). *An Investigation into the Use of Curriculum Theory in the Formulation of a Systems Model for the Construction and Evaluation of Secondary School Geography Curricula in England and Wales,* unpublished Ph.D. thesis, University of London.

Biddle, D. S. (Ed.) (1968). *Readings in Geographical Education,* see Chapters 22-24, Whitcombe and Tombs.

Biddle, D. S. and Deer, C. E. (Eds.) (1973). *Readings in Geographical Education,* vol. 2, see Chapters 35-41, Whitcombe and Tombs.

Biddle, D. S. and Shortle, D. (Eds.) (1969). *Programme Planning in Geography—Principles and Practice in New South Wales Schools,* Martindale Press.

Bisset, J. (1805). *Geographical Guide: a Poetical, Nautical Trip round the Island of Great Britain,* J. Harris, London.

Blachford, K. (1973). 'Myths in geographical education', *Geographical Education,* **2**, 1.

Blaut, J. M. and Stea, D. (1971). 'Studies in geographic learning', *Ann. Association of American Geographers,* **61**.

Bloom, B. S. (Ed.) (1956). *Taxonomy of Educational Objectives,* Handbook 1: Cognitive Domain, Longman.

Bloom, B. S. *et al.* (1971). *Handbook on Formative and Summative Evaluation of Student Learning,* McGraw Hill.

Blyth, W. A. L. *et al.* (1972). *History, Geography and Social Science 8-13: an Interim Statement,* Schools Council.

Blyth, W. A. L. *et al.* (1976). *Curriculum Planning in History, Geography and Social Science,* Collins/ESL Bristol.

Boden, P. (1976). *Developments in Geography Teaching,* Open Books.

Braithwaite, R. B. (1960). *Scientific Explanation,* Harper Torchbooks.

Briault, E. W. H. and Shave, D. W. (1952). *Geography in Secondary Schools with Special Reference to the Secondary Modern School,* Geographical Association.

Brown, R. (1963). *Explanation in Social Science,* Routledge and Kegan Paul.

Bruhns, K. (1873). *Life of Alexander von Humboldt,* Longman.

Bruner, J. S. (1960). *The Process of Education,* Vintage Books.

Bruner, J. S. (1967). *Towards a Theory of Instruction,* Belknap Press.

Bryant, P. E. (1974). *Perception and Understanding in Young Children,* Methuen.

Buros, O. K. (Ed.) (1965). *The Sixth Mental Measurement Year Book,* Gryphon Press.

Burston, W. H. (1962). *Social Studies and the History Teacher,* Teaching of History Leaflet no. 15, Historical Association.

Burston, W. H. (1963). *Principles of History Teaching,* Methuen.

Burton, I. (1963). 'The quantitative revolution and theoretical geography', The Canadian Geographer, **7**, 4.

Calland, A. R. (1973). *An Investigation of the Images Held by a Small Sample of Primary School Children of their Local Environment,* unpublished M. A. dissertation, University of London.

Cannon, C. (1964). 'Social studies in secondary schools', *Education Review*, **17**, 1, November 1964.

Cantor, L. (1960). *Mackinder: his Contribution to Geography and Education*, unpublished M.A. thesis, University of London.

Carnie, J. (1972). 'Children's attitudes to other nationalities', in Graves, N. (Ed.), *New Movements in the Study and Teaching of Geography*, Temple Smith.

Carswell, R. J. B. (1970). 'Evaluation of affective learning in geographic education', in Kurfman, D. G. (Ed.), *Evaluation in Geographic Education*, Fearson.

Chandler, T. J. (1965). *The Climate of London*, Hutchinson.

Chisholm, G. G. (1889). *Commercial Geography*, Longman

Chorley, R. J. and Haggett, P. (1965). *Frontiers in Geographical Teaching*, Methuen, revised ed. 1970.

Chorley, R. J. and Haggett, P. (1967). *Models in Geography*, Methuen.

Chorley, R. J. and Kennedy, B. A. (1971). *Physical Geography—A Systems Approach*, Prentice Hall.

Claval, P. (1969). *Essai sur l'Evolution de la Géographie Humaine,* Cahiers de Géographie de Besançon, no. 12, 2nd ed.

Clegg, A. (1970). 'Developing and using behavioural objectives in geography', in Bacon, P., *Focus on Geography*, 40th Yearbook, National Council for the Social Studies.

Congrès des Science Géographiques, Cosmographiques et Commerciales (1871). *Reports and Proceedings*, Antwerp.

Cortambert, E. (1849). *Eléments de Géographie Physique*, Hachette.

Cowie, P. M. (1974). *Value Teaching and Geographical Education*, unpublished M.A. dissertation, University of London.

Cox, B. (1966). 'Test items in geography for a taxonomy of educational objectives', *Monthly Bulletin*, no. 44, Geographical Society of New South Wales.

Cox, B. (1975). *Substantive Disciplinary Structure in Geography*, unpublished Ph.D. thesis, University of Queensland.

Cracknell, R. (1974). *A Study of the Changing Place and Nature of Geography and Methods of Teaching the Subject in Elementary and Primary Schools of England and Wales from 1870 to 1974, with Particular Reference to the 7-11 Year Age Group*, unpublished M.A. dissertation, University of London.

Crone, G. R. (1964). *Background to Geography*, Museum Press.

Dale, P. F. (1971). 'Children's reactions to maps and aerial photographs', *Area,* **3**, 3.

Davis, W. M. (1902). *The Progress of Geography in the Schools*, reprinted from the First Year Book, National Society for the Scientific Study of Education, 1902, Dover Publications, 1954.

Deale, R. N. (1975). *Assessment and testing in the Secondary School. Schools Council Examinations Bulletin 32*, Evans/Methuen.

De Martonne, E. (1933). *The Geographical Regions of France*, Heinemann.

De Wofle, I. (1971). *Civilia—the End of Suburban Man.* Architectural Press.

Department of Education and Science (1974). *Geography in a Changing Curriculum*, H.M.S.O .

Dickinson, R. E. (1969). *The Makers of Modern Geography*, Routledge and Kegan Paul.

Dickinson, R. E. and Howarth, O. J. R. (1933). *The Making of Geography*, Oxford University Press.

Dupont de Ferrier, G. (1922). *Du Collège de Clermont au Lycée Louis le Grand*, Tome 2, E. de Boccard.

Dury, G. H. (1966). 'The concept of grade', in Dury, G. H. (Ed.), *Essays in Geomorphology*, Heinemann Educational Books.

Earth Science Curriculum Project (1967). *Investigating the Earth*, Houghton Mifflin.

East, W. G. (1935). *An Historical Geography of Europe*, Methuen.

Education Committee of the Royal Geographical Society (1950). 'Geography and social studies in schools', Royal Geographical Society.

Eisner, E. W. (1969). 'Instructional and expressive educational objectives: their formulation and use in curriculum', in *Curriculum Evaluation*, A.E.R.A. Monograph no. 3, Rand McNally.

Eliot Hurst, M. E. (1972). *Geography of Economic Behavior*, Duxbury Press.

Fairgrieve, J. (1926). *Geography in School*, University of London Press.

Febvre, L. (1922). *La Terre et l'Evolution Humaine—Bibliotheque de Synthèse Historique: l'Evolution de l'Humanité*, La Renaissance du Livre.

Feldman, D. H. (1971). 'Map understanding as a possible crystallizer of cognitive structures', *American Educational Research Journal*, III, 3.

Fenton, E. (1966). *Teaching the New Social Studies in Secondary Schools*, Holt, Rinehart and Winston.

Fisher, C. A. (1970). 'Whither regional geography?', *Geography*, 55.

Freeman, T. W. (1961). *A Hundred Years of Geography*, Methuen.

Gagné, R. M. (1965, 1970 2nd ed.). *The Conditions of Learning*, Holt, Rinehart, Winston.

Gagné, R. M. (1966). 'The learning of principles', in Klausmeier, H. J. and Harris, C. W. (Eds.), *Analysis of Concept Learning*, Academic Press.

Geikie, A. (1887). *The Teaching of Geography*, Macmillan.

Gilbert, E. W. (1965). 'Andrew John Herbertson 1865-1915. An appreciation of his life and works', *Geography*, 50, 229.

Gilbert, E. W. (1972). *British Pioneers in Geography*, David and Charles.

Goodey, B. (1972). *A Checklist of Sources on Environmental Perception*, Research Memorandum no. 11, University of Birmingham Centre for Urban and Regional Studies.

Gould, P. and White, R. (1974). *Mental Maps*, Penguin.

Graves, N. J. (1968a). 'An investigation into the teaching of Asia in English and Welsh secondary schools', I.G.U., *Abstract of Papers*, edited by S. Das Gupta and T. Romanowska-Lakshmanan, Calcutta.

Graves, N. J. (1968b). 'The High School Geography Project of the Association of American Geographers', *Geography*, 53, 238.

Graves, N. J. (1971). 'Objectives in teaching particular subjects with special reference to the teaching of geography', Bulletin of the University of London Institute of Education, N.S. no. 23.

Graves, N. J. (1972a). 'The problem of hierarchy in the objectives of geography teaching at the pre-university level', in Adams, W. P. and Helleiner, F. M. (Eds.), International Geography 1972, University of Toronto Press.

Graves, N. J. (1972b). 'School examinations', in Graves, N. J. (Ed.), New Movements in the Study and Teaching of Geography, Temple Smith.

Graves, N. J. and Moore, T. (1972). 'The nature of geographical knowledge', in Graves, N. J. (Ed.), New Movements in the Study and Teaching of Geography, Temple Smith.

Green, J. R. and Alice, S. (1879). A Short Geography of the British Isles, Macmillan.

Gunn, A. M. (Ed.) (1972). High School Geography Project—Legacy for the Seventies, Centre Educatif et Culturel, Montreal.

Guyot, A. (1873). Physical Geography, Scribner, Armstrong and Co.

Haggett, P. (1966). Locational Analysis in Human Geography, Arnold.

Haggett, P. (1972). Geography: a Modern Synthesis, Harper Row.

Hall, D. (1976). Geography and the Geography Teachers, George Allan and Unwin.

Hargreaves, D. (1967). Social Relations in a Secondary School, Routledge and Kegan Paul.

Harrow, A. J. (1972). A Taxonomy for the Psychomotor Domain, McKay Co. Inc.

Hart, P. J. (1957). The Teaching of Geography in 19th-Century Britain, unpublished M.A. dissertation, University of London.

Hart, P. J. (1975). 'Developing International Understanding, Interdependence' in, Graves N. J. (Ed) Teaching materials on population, international understanding and environmental education, UNESCO.

Hartshorne, R. (1939). The Nature of Geography, A.A.G., Chicago.

Hartshorne, R. (1959). Perspective on the Nature of Geography, A.A.G. and John Murray.

Harvey, D. W. (1969). Explanation in Geography, Arnold.

Harvey, D. (1973). Social Justice and the City, Arnold.

Heamon, A. J. (1973). 'The maturation of spatial ability in geography', Educational Research, 16, 1.

Helburn, N. (1968). 'The educational objectives of high school geography', Journal of Geography, 67, May 1968.

Henderson, H. C. K. (1968). 'Geography's balance sheet', Trans. Geographic Journal, 25. Institute of British Geographers, no. 45.

Herbertson, A. J. (1905). 'The major natural regions', Geographic Journal, 25.

Herbertson, A. J. (1915). 'Regional environment, heredity and consciousness', Geographical Teacher, 8.

Heywood, C. L. (1938). An Investigation of the Factors Involved in the Geographical Work of Boys and Girls, unpublished M.A. thesis, University of London.

Hickman, G., Reynolds, J. and Tolley, H. (1973). *A New Professionalism for a Changing Geography*, Schools Council.

Hirst, P. (1966). 'Education Theory', in Tibble, J. W. (Ed.), *The Study of Education*, Routledge and Kegan Paul.

Hirst, P. H. (1965). 'Liberal Education and the nature of knowledge', in Archambault, R. D. (Ed.), *Philosophical Analysis and Education*, Routledge and Kegan Paul.

Hirst, P. H. and Peters, R. S. (1970). *The Logic of Education*, Routledge and Kegan Paul.

Hogan, M. M. (1962). *The Evolution of the Regional Concept and its Influence on the Teaching of Geography in School*, unpublished M.A. thesis, University of London.

Honeybone, R. C. (1950). *An Investigation into the Attitudes of Adolescent Pupils towards Methods of Teaching Geography*, unpublished M.A. thesis, University of London.

Huntington, E. (1907). *The Pulse of Asia*, Houghton Mifflin.

Huntington, E. (1915). *Civilization and Climate*, Yale University Press.

Huntingdon, E. (1930). *World Power and Evolution*, Yale University Press.

Incorporated Association of Assistant Masters in Secondary Schools (1939). *Memorandum on the Teaching of Geography*, George Philip.

Ilsley, G. V. (1969). *An Investigation into the Problems of Testing the Reading of Medium Scale Ordnance Survey Maps as Evidenced by the Performance of a Sample of Candidates of the Certificate of Secondary Education Ability Range*, unpublished M.A dissertation, University of London.

Jahoda, G. (1963). 'The development of children's ideas about country and nationality', *B. J. Educational Psychology*, 33.

James, C. (1968). *Young Lives at Stake*, Collins.

James, P. E. (1969). 'The significance of geography in American education', *J. Geography*, **68**, Nov. 1969.

Johnson, M. (1969). 'The translation of curriculum into instruction', *J. Curriculum Studies*, **1**.

Jones, G. W. (1974). 'Children's choice of geography', *Geography*, **59**.

Jones, S. and Reynolds, J. (1973). 'The development of a new O level syllabus', *Geography*, **58**, 259.

Kellner, L. (1963). *Alexander von Humboldt*, Oxford University Press.

Keltie, J. S. (1886). *Geographical Education—Report to the Council of the Royal Geographical Society*, Supplementary Papers, Royal Geographical Society, vol. I, pt. 4.

Kerr, J. K. (1968). *Changing the Curriculum*, University of London Press.

King, C. A. (1966). *Techniques in Geomorphology*, Arnold.

King, A. R. and Brownell, J. A. (1966). *The Curriculum and the Disciplines of Knowledge*, Wiley.

Kirk, W. (1963). 'Problems of geography', *Geography*, **48**, 221.

Kohn, C. F. (Ed.) (1964). *Selected Classroom Experiences: High School Geography Project*, Geographic Education Series no. 3, National Council for Geographic Education.

Kramer, F. L. (1959). 'A note on Karl Ritter, 1779-1851', *Geographical Review*, pp. 406-409.

Krathwohl, D. R., Bloom, B. S. and Masia, B. B. (1964). *Taxonomy of Educational Objectives*, Handbook II: Affective Domain, Longman.

Kuhn, T. (1962). *The Structure of Scientific Revolutions*, University of Chicago Press.

Kurfman, D. G. (Ed.) (1970). *Evaluation in Geographic Education*, Fearon.

Kurfman, D. G. (1972). 'The functions of evaluation', in Gunn, A. M. (Ed.) (1972). *Op. Cit.*

Kurfman, D. G. and Richburg, R. W. (1970). 'The role of evaluation', in Patton, D. J. (Ed.), *From Geographic Discipline to Inquiring Student*, Association of American Geographers.

Lawton, D. (1973). *Social Change, Education Theory and Curriculum Planning*, University of London Press.

Lawton, D., Campbell, J. and Burkitt, V. (1971). *Social Studies 8-13*, Evans/Methuen Educational.

Letellier, Ch. C. (1812). *Géographie des Commençants, par Demandes et par Résponses; à l'Usage des Pensions*, Le Prieure, 6th ed.

Levasseur, E. (1872). *L'Etude et l'Enseignment de l'Histoire et de la Géographie*, Delagrave.

Levasseur, E. and Himly, A. (1871). *Rapport Général sur l'Enseignement de l'Histoire et de la Géographie*, Paul Dupont.

Long, I. L. M. (1953). 'Children's reactions to geographical pictures', *Geography*, **38**.

Long, I. L. M. (1961). 'Research in picture study', *Geography*, **46**.

Long, M. (1950). *An Investigation into the Relationship between Interest in and Knowledge of School Geography by Means of a Series of Attitude Tests*, unpublished M.A. thesis, University of London.

Long, M. (1971). 'The interests of children in school geography', *Geography*, **56**.

Luberman, F. (1961). 'The concept of location in classical geography', *Ann. Association of American Geographers*, **51**, pp. 194-210.

Lunnon, A. J. (1969). *The Understanding of Certain Geographical Concepts by Primary School Children*, unpublished M.Ed. thesis, University of Birmingham.

Lynch, K. (1960). *The Image of the City*, M.I.T. Press.

Macdonald, B. (1976). 'Evaluation and the control of education', in Tawney, *Curriculum Evaluation Today: Trends and Implications*, Macmillan.

Macfarlane-Smith, I. (1964). *Spatial Ability*, University of London Press.

Mackinder, H. J. (1887). 'The scope and methods of geography', *Proc. Royal Geographical Society*, **9**.

Marchant, E. C. (1964). 'Geography in education in England and Wales', *Geography*, **49**, 224.

Marchant, E. C. (Ed.) (1971). *The Teaching of Geography at School Level*, Council of Europe, Harrap.

Marsh, J. F. (1966). *An Investigation into the Differences between Rural and Urban Children in the Formation of Concepts of Town and*

Country, unpublished M.Ed. thesis, University of Aberdeen.

Marsden, W. (1976). *Evaluating the Geography Curriculum*, Oliver and Boyd.

Martin, A. F. (1951). 'The necessity for determinism', *Trans. Institute of British Geographers*, **17**.

May, J. A. (1970). 'Kant's concept of geography and its relation to recent geographical thought', University of Toronto Department of Geography Research Publications.

Mayo, W. L. (1965). *The Development and Status of Secondary School Geography in the United States and Canada*, University Publishers, Ann Arbor, Michigan.

Milburn, D. (1972). 'Children's vocabulary', in Graves, N. (Ed.), *New Movements in the Study and Teaching of Geography*, Temple Smith.

Ministère de l'Instruction Publique (1865). 'Instruction du 24 Mars 1865', in *Plan d'Etudes et Programmes de l'Enseignement Secondaire Classique*, Jules Delalain, 1866.

Ministère de l'Instruction Publique (1890). *Instructions—Enseignement Secondaire*, Imprimerie Nationale, Paris.

Mitchell, J. (1962). *Great Britain: Geographical Essays*, Cambridge University Press.

Monk, J. J. (1971). 'Preparing tests to measure course objectives', *J. Geography*, **70**.

Moore, T. W. (1974). *Education Theory: An Introduction*, R.K.P.

Morrill, R. L. (1970). *The Spatial Organisation of Society*, Duxbury Press.

Morse, J. (1789). *Geography*, Thomas Andrews.

Mundy-Castle, A. C. (1966). 'Pictorial depth perception in Ghanaian children', in Price-Williams, D. R. (Ed.), *Cross Cultural Studies*, Penguin.

Naish, M. C. (1972). 'Geography in the integrated curriculum', in Graves, N. (Ed.), *New Movements in the Study and Teaching of Geography*, Temple Smith.

Naish, M. C. (1974). 'Current trends in geography teaching', in Long, M. (Ed.), *Handbook for Geography Teachers*, Methuen.

Nash, R. (1973). *Classrooms Observed*, Routledge and Kegan Paul.

Oakeshott, M. (1933). *Experience and its Modes*, Cambridge University Press.

Ormsby, H. (1931). *France: a Regional and Economic Geography*, Methuen.

Pattison, W. D. (1964). 'The four traditions of geography', *J. Geography*, **63**.

Pattison, W. D. (1970). 'The educational purposes of geography', in Kurfman, D. G. (Ed.), *Evaluation in Geographic Education*, Fearon, Belmont, California.

Peters, R. S. (1963). *Education as Initiation*, Evans.

Peters, R. S. (1966). *Ethics and Education*, George Allen and Unwin.

Peters, R. S. (1973). 'Farewell to aims', *London Educational Review*, **2**, 3.

Phenix, P. H. (1964). *Realms of Meaning*, McGraw Hill.

Piaget, J. (1961). 'The genetic approach to the psychology of thought', *J. Educational Psychology*, **52**.

Piaget, J. and Inhelder, B. (1956). *The Child's Conception of Space*, Routledge and Kegan Paul.

Piaget, J., Inhelder, B. and Szeminska, A. (1960). *The Child's Conception of Geometry*, Routledge and Kegan Paul.

Pinchemel, P. (1965). 'The Nature and Spirit of Geography teaching', in *Source Book for Geography Teaching*, Longmans/UNESCO.

Postman, N. and Weingartner, C. (1971). *Teaching as a Subversive Activity*, Penguin.

Pring, R. (1973). 'Objectives and innovations: the irrelevance of theory', *London Educational Review*, **2**, 3.

Prior, F. M. (1959). *The Place of Maps in the Junior School*, unpublished dissertation for the Diploma in the Psychology of Childhood, University of Birmingham.

Renner, J. and Slater, F. A. (1974). 'Geography in an urban age: trials of High School Geography Project materials in New Zealand Schools', *Geographical Education*, **2**, 2.

Reynolds, J. (1971). 'Schools Council curriculum development project: Geography 14-18 Years', *Geography*, **56**, 250.

Reynolds, J. (1972). 'Curriculum change and the Schools Council Geography 14-18 Project', *Area*, **4**, 2.

Rhys, W. T. (1966). *The Development of Logical Thought in the Adolescent with reference to the teaching of Geography in the Secondary School*, unpublished M.Ed. thesis, University of Birmingham.

Rhys, W. T. (1972). 'The development of logical thinking', in Graves, N. (Ed.), *New Movements in the Study and Teaching of Geography*, Temple Smith.

Richards, P. (1974). 'Kant's geography and mental maps', *Trans. Inst. British Geographers*, **61**.

Robeson, B. S. and Long, I. L. M. (1956). 'Sample Studies the development of a method', *Geography 41*.

Robinson, H. (1951). 'Geography in the dissenting academies', *Geography*, **36**, 173.

Robson, B. (1969). *Urban Analysis*, Cambridge University Press.

Rogers, V. (1968). *The Social Studies in English Education*, Heinemann Educational Books.

Rokeach, M. (1972). *Beliefs, Attitudes and Values*, Jossey Bass

Rolfe, J. (1971). 'The completion of the American High School Geography Project', *Geography*, **56**, 252.

Rosen, S. (1957). 'A short history of high school geography to 1936', *J. Geography*, vol. LVI.

Rushdoony, H. A. (1968). 'A child's ability to read maps', *J. Geography*, **67**.

Saarinen, T. F. (1970). 'Environmental perception' in Bacon, P. (Ed.), *Focus on Geography*, 40th Yearbook of the National Council for the Social Studies.

Salmon (1785). *Salmon's Geographical and Astronomical Grammar*, 13th ed.

Salmon, R. and Masterton, T. (1974). *The Principles of Objective Testing in Geography*, Heinemann Educational Books.

Sandford, H. A. (1967). *An Experimental Investigation into Children's Perception of a School Atlas Map*, unpublished M.Phil. thesis, University of London.

Sandford, H. A. (1970). *A Study of the Concepts Involved in the Reading and Interpretation of Atlases by Secondary School Children*, unpublished Ph.D. thesis, University of London.

Sandford, H. A. (1972). 'Perceptual problems', in Graves, N. J. (Ed.), *New Movements in the Study and Teaching of Geography*, Temple Smith.

Satterly, D. (1964). 'Skills and concepts involved in map drawing and map interpretation', *New Era*, **45**.

Scarfe, N. V. (1950). 'Geography and social studies in the U.S.A.', *Geography*, **35**, 168.

Schaefer, F. K. (1953). 'Exceptionalism in geography: a methodological examination', *Ann. Association of American Geographers*, **43**.

Schools Council (1968). *Young School Leavers Enquiry*, H.M.S.O

Schools Council (1969). *The Middle Years of Schooling from 8-13*, Working Paper 22.

Schools Council (1971). *A Common System of Examining at 16+*, Evans/Methuen.

Schools Council (1972a). *Geography 14-18*, unpublished report.

Schools Council (1972b). *Geography and the Young School Leaver: the Project in Schools*, unpublished report.

Schools Council (1975). *Working Paper 53, The Whole Curriculum 13-16*, Evans/Methuen.

Scriven, M. (1967). 'The methodology of evaluation', in Stake, R. (Ed.), *Perspectives of Curriculum Evaluation*, Rand McNally.

Semple, E. C. (1911). *Influences of Geographic Environment*, Constable.

Senathirajah, N. and Weiss, J. (1971). *Evaluation in Geography*, Ontario Institute for Studies in Education.

Sharaf, T. (1963). *A Short History of Geographical Discovery*, M. Zaki El Mahdy, Alexandria.

Shortle, D. A. (1974). *Geography and the Disciplines of Knowledge Approach to the Curriculum*, unpublished M. Ed. dissertation, University of Sidney.

Simons, M. (1969). 'What are geographers doing?', *Universities Quarterly*, **24**, 1.

Sinnhuber, K. A. (1959). 'Carl Ritter', *Scottish Geographical Magazine*, **75**.

Slater, F. A. (1970). 'The relationship between levels of learning in geography, Piaget's theory of intellectual development and Bruner's teaching hypothesis', *Geographical Education*, **1**, 2.

Snow, C. P. (1959). *Two Cultures and the Scientific Revolution*, Cambridge University Press.

Sockett, H. (1973). 'Behavioural objectives', *London Educational Review*, **2**, 3.

Spencer, D. and Lloyd, J. (1974). 'A child's eye view of Small Heath, Birmingham', Research Memorandum 34, University of Birmingham Centre for Urban and Regional Studies.

Stamp, L. D. (1957). 'Major natural regions: Herbertson after fifty years', *Geography*, **42**, 198.

Stoddart, D. R. (1966). 'Darwin's impact on geography', *Ann. Association of American Geographers*, **50**.

Stoltman, J. (1972). 'Territorial decentration and geographic learning', *International Geography*, University of Toronto Press.

Stoltman, J. (Ed. 1976). *International Research in Geographic Education*, Western Michigan University.

Stufflebeam, D. *et al.* (1971). *Educational Evaluation and Decision Making*, Peacock, Itasca, Illinois.

Styles, E. (1972). 'Affective educational objectives and a technique for their measurement in secondary school geography', *Geographical Education*, **1**, 4.

Taba, H. (1962). *Curriculum Development: Theory and Practice*, Harcourt, Brace.

Tatham, G. (1951). 'Geography in the nineteenth century', in Taylor, G. (Ed.), *Geography in the Twentieth Century*, Methuen.

Tawney, D. (Ed. 1976). *Curriculum Evaluation Today: Trends and Implications*, Macmillan.

Taylor, C. C. (1960). *A Study of the Nature of Spatial Ability and its Relationship to Attainment in Geography*, unpublished M.Ed. thesis, University of Durham.

Taylor, L. C. (1971). *Resources for Learning*, Penguin.

Taylor, P. (1970). *How Teachers Plan their Courses*, N.F.E.R.

Temp, G. (1970). 'The evaluation of geographic programs and materials', in Kurfman, D. G. (Ed.), *Evaluation in Geographic Education*, Fearon.

Thurstone, L. L. (1944). *A Factorial Study of Perception*, University of Chicago Press.

Tomkins, G. S. (1968). Personal communication.

Towers, J. D. (1974). 'The development of geographical and spatial concepts and the concepts of country and nationality among 9-year old Scottish children', *Scottish Education Studies*, **6**, 1.

Trow, M. A. (1970). 'Methodological problems in the evaluation of innovation', in Whitrock, M. C. and Wiley, D. E. (Eds.), *The Evaluation of Instruction*, Holt, Rinehart and Winston.

Tyler, R. W. (1949). *Basic Principles of Curriculum and Instruction*, University of Chicago Press.

Ubarov, E. B., Chapman, D. R. and Isaacs, A. (1966). *A Dictionary of Science*, Penguin.

Underwood, B. L. (1971). *Aims in Geographical Teaching and Education 1870-71*, unpublished M.A. dissertation, University of Sussex.

Vass, E. J. (1960). *An Investigation into the Development of a Concept of Physical Geography*, unpublished dissertation for the Diploma in Child Psychology, University of Birmingham.

Vernon, M. D. (1962). *The Psychology of Perception*, Pelican.

Vernon, M. D. (1969). *Human Motivation*, Cambridge University Press.

Vidal de la Blache, P. (1913). 'Des caractères distinctifs de la géographie', *Annales de Géographie*, XXIIe année.

Wanklyn, H. (1961). *Friedrich Ratzel: a Biographical Memoir and Bibliography*, Cambridge University Press.

Ward, E. H. (1972). *Conceptual Thinking in Geography—an Enquiry into the Development of Understanding of Climatic Concepts*, unpublished M. Phil. thesis, University of Nottingham.

Watson, F. (1909). *The Beginning of the Teaching of Modern Subjects in England*, Pitman.

Weill, G. (1921). *Histoire de l'Enseignement Secondaire en France*, Payot.

Wesley, E. B. (1942). *Teaching the Social Studies*, 2nd ed., Heath.

Wheeler, D. K. (1967). *Curriculum Process*, University of London Press.

White, J. P. (1973). *Towards a Compulsory Curriculum*, Routledge and Kegan Paul.

Williams, H. T. (1963). *The Teaching of Social Studies in the Secondary Schools of England and Wales*, unpublished M.A. thesis, University of Reading.

Wood, L. J. (1970). 'Perception studies in geography', *Trans. Institute of British Geographers*, **50**.

Wood, S. (1970). 'An evaluation of achievement tests in geography', in Kurfman, D. G. (Ed.), *Evaluation in Geographic Education*, Fearon.

Wooldridge, S. W. (1949). 'On taking the Ge out of geography', *Geography*, **34**, 163.

Wooldridge, S. W. and East, G. (1951). *The Spirit and Purpose of Geography*, Hutchinson.

Wreford-Watson, J. (1963). *North America*, Longman.

Wrigley, E. A. (1970). 'Changes in the philosophy of geography', in Chorley, R. J. and Haggett, P. (Eds.), *Frontiers in Geographical Teaching*, 2nd ed., Methuen.

Yi-Fu Tuan (1974). *Topophilia: a study of environmental perception, attitudes and values*, Prentice Hall.

Young, M. F. B. (1971). *Knowledge and Control*, Collier/Macmillan.

Index